PRAISE FOR *A Rage*

One of the Best Books of
One of 20 Notable Reads from 2016, *Mother Jones*
One of the Best Nonfiction Books of 2016, *Publishers Weekly*
Winner of the Lionel Gelber Prize

"Subtly insightful." —**GERARD RUSSELL**, *The New York Review of Books*

"A masterful account of humiliation and despair." —*Tablet Magazine*

"Extraordinary . . . Worth is a wonderful writer . . . [He] brings [a sense of] tenderness—tinged with melancholy and regret—to his entire narrative, which seems intent upon resisting despair even when it is reflected back to him over and over again . . . [A] spectacular work of literary journalism." —**ELAINE MARGOLIN**, *The Jerusalem Post*

"This is the book you have to read on the Middle East—not just to understand the Arab revolutions but to feel them as human drama and tragedy. Robert F. Worth is a master who writes journalism as literature and history." —**GEORGE PACKER**, author of *The Assassins' Gate* and *The Unwinding*

"It would be hard to find a more astute and eloquent guide to this explosive corner of the earth than Robert F. Worth. He somehow managed to be on hand for a score of crucial moments in the Arab world's great convulsions, from the vast demonstrations of Tahrir Square to a just-liberated Libyan prison to the crushing of great hopes in the years that followed. Whatever lies ahead, I suspect that, as with John Reed's reporting on the Russian Revolution, people will be reading this vivid eyewitness account for years to come."

—**ADAM HOCHSCHILD**, author of *To End All Wars*

"Riveting, vivid, lucid, and wise, Robert F. Worth's *A Rage for Order* is reportage of the highest order: it illuminates current Middle Eastern crises through the daily experiences of ordinary, and extraordinary, men and women. I've read no finer or more nuanced account."

—CLAIRE MESSUD, author of *The Woman Upstairs*

"*A Rage for Order* brings the broad disappointments of the Arab Spring to the human level . . . , showing how events unfolded at the scale of individual lives. This is an important service, since when we talk about the Middle East, we tend to use large religious and ideological abstractions—Sunnis and Shiites, secularists and Islamists. Worth brings those words back to their roots in the lives of real people, showing how people who never dreamed of making war or revolution ended up being unmade by them."

—ADAM KIRSCH, *Tablet Magazine*

"As the Beirut bureau chief for *The New York Times*, Worth has seen a lot, and he writes compellingly about the dashed hopes and personal tragedies that followed the 2011 uprisings in Egypt, Libya, Syria, and Yemen."

—JOHN WATERBURY, *Foreign Affairs*

"Striking . . . Worth isn't so much writing a recent political history of an incredibly tumultuous time as he is telling the intimate stories of a dozen or so mostly ordinary people who were picked up, dragged along, and battered by events as if by bad weather, desperate for some traction to determine their own fate . . . Worth holds to his skepticism, but he leaves his readers with a glimmer of chance and change."

—KAELEN WILSON-GOLDIE, *Bookforum*

"Worth . . . draws on his intimate knowledge of the Middle East to offer a penetrating, unsettling analysis . . . Informing the vivid narrative are many revealing interviews as well as the author's own eyewitness accounts of events. A crucial portrait of a deeply troubled region."

—*Kirkus Reviews* (starred review)

"Veteran correspondent Worth traces the 'Arab Spring' through five countries, from the heady idealism of 2011 to the largely grim aftermath. Significantly, he does so through the stories of individuals rather than groups or sects, challenging simplistic, monolithic conceptions of rival factions . . . Worth provides no easy path forward. Instead, he skillfully presents the competing perspectives in play to explain the daunting impediments to stable states in the present-day Middle East." —*Publishers Weekly* (starred review)

"Worth utilizes his long experience in the Middle East to provide a riveting survey of the origins, course of events, and causes of the dashing of so many of the dreams fueling the uprisings. He concentrates on Egypt, Libya, Syria, Yemen, and Tunisia, and he effectively combines his personal observations with the experience of participants. The result is an informative, if often heartrending, account of events whose consequences are still unfolding." —JAY FREEMAN, *Booklist*

"The Arab world is in the midst of an unprecedented crisis. In his gripping account, Robert F. Worth narrates the reversal in its fortunes. Firsthand accounts, brimming with detail, unveil why the region rose up against dictatorship and then why it was not able to sustain democracy. Well written and informative, *A Rage for Order* is an eye-opening read for anyone interested in understanding the raging crisis in the Middle East." —VALI NASR, author of *The Dispensable Nation* and *The Shia Revival*

"Robert F. Worth's beautifully written book describes the tragedies and aspirations of the Arabs struggling under the yoke of authoritarian oppression and corrosive venality. Drawing on a deep understanding of language, culture, and history, Worth provides a series of finely delineated portraits, bringing to life the struggles of individual men and women in Tunisia, Libya, Egypt, Syria, and Yemen. There is simply no better account of the recent events that have convulsed the countries of North Africa and the Middle East." —BERNARD A. HAYKEL, professor of Near Eastern studies and director of the Institute for the Transregional Study of the Contemporary Middle East, North Africa, and Central Asia at Princeton University

"*A Rage for Order* is an outstanding book that captures the high hopes and deep despair of average Arabs who lived through the revolutions of 2011 in Egypt, Libya, Syria, and Yemen—and their tragic aftermath. This is a brilliant contemporary history by one of the United States' most distinguished Mideast correspondents, and a compellingly readable account." —EUGENE ROGAN, author of

The Arabs and *The Fall of the Ottomans*

ROBERT F. WORTH

A Rage for Order

Robert F. Worth spent fourteen years as a correspondent for *The New York Times* and was the paper's Beirut bureau chief from 2007 until 2011. He is a frequent contributor to *The New York Times Magazine* and *The New York Review of Books*. He has twice been a finalist for a National Magazine Award. Born and raised in Manhattan, he now lives in Washington, D.C.

A
RAGE
FOR
ORDER

A
RAGE
FOR
ORDER

The Middle East
in Turmoil,
from Tahrir Square
to ISIS

ROBERT F. WORTH

Farrar, Straus and Giroux | New York

In memory of Muhammad Abdelmalik al Mutawakel (1942–2014),
whose bravery and wisdom inspired many

Farrar, Straus and Giroux
18 West 18th Street, New York 10011

Copyright © 2016 by Robert F. Worth
All rights reserved
Printed in the United States of America
Published in 2016 by Farrar, Straus and Giroux
First paperback edition, 2017

The Library of Congress has cataloged the hardcover edition as follows:
Names: Worth, Robert Forsyth, 1965–, author.
Title: A rage for order : the Middle East in turmoil, from Tahrir Square to ISIS /
    Robert F. Worth.
Description: New York : Farrar, Straus and Giroux, 2016. | Includes index.
Identifiers: LCCN 2015041559 | ISBN 9780374252946 (hardback) |
    ISBN 9780374710712 (e-book)
Subjects: LCSH: Arab Spring, 2010– | Arab countries—Politics and
    government—21st century.
Classification: LCC JQ1850.A91 W67 2016 | DDC 909/.097492708312—dc23
LC record available at http://lccn.loc.gov/2015041559

Paperback ISBN: 978-0-374-53679-4

Designed by Abby Kagan

Our books may be purchased in bulk for promotional, educational, or business use.
Please contact your local bookseller or the Macmillan Corporate and
Premium Sales Department at 1-800-221-7945, extension 5442, or by e-mail at
MacmillanSpecialMarkets@macmillan.com.

www.fsgbooks.com
www.twitter.com/fsgbooks • www.facebook.com/fsgbooks

1   3   5   7   9   10   8   6   4   2

— Contents —

A
RAGE
FOR
ORDER

— Introduction —

On a gray winter evening in late February 2011, I threw my bags into the back of a beat-up minivan in Cairo and climbed inside. I was joining a caravan of reporters and aid workers and ride-along Egyptians headed for Libya's open border. We drove all night under a moonless sky, pulled along like driftwood on the great wave of revolutionary feeling that was crashing on the Arab world in those days.

I had just spent the most thrilling and bewildering weeks of my life in Tahrir Square. To say I had not expected them is ludicrously mild: I would have told you revolution in Egypt was impossible. I had been living in the Middle East on and off for more than seven years, and Cairo was a place that made me almost physically sick with its atmosphere of fatalism and decay. I had gone home to America that Christmas with no plans to return to the region: my tenure as *The New York Times*'s Beirut bureau chief was over. I'd seen too many suicide bombings in Iraq, too many assassinations in Lebanon, too many young men and women who lived sad, closeted lives. I thought I knew the Arab world too well to be surprised.

Seven weeks later, all this knowingness was gone. Cairo had proved me wrong again and again. As we drove westward across the Egyptian desert, I had a feeling in my chest I hadn't known since childhood: a sense that the world was being remade before my eyes. Crossing the Libyan border at dawn, I saw graffiti spray-painted in black across the abandoned guard posts: MAY SAFETY BE WITH YOU, SONS OF THE JANUARY 25 REVOLUTION. A long-haired Libyan rebel waved us on, grinning ecstatically. Benghazi, on the road ahead, was in rebel hands. Everyone assumed that Tripoli could not last long. And after that? Yemen, Syria, Saudi Arabia? The dominoes were falling, and the tyrants would soon be gone. What would come afterward was less clear. In that moment, to be cold and reasonable felt almost like treason.

It was impossible to imagine that some of the young Egyptians who were with me on that ride would by year's end be fighting each other in Tahrir Square, the revolution's symbolic heart. They would divide into warring camps and ideologies, accusing each other of betraying the revolt that brought them together. Some would end up with ISIS in Syria, sawing the heads off rival soldiers in the name of God. Others would make common cause with the same military leaders they had fought in 2011 and applaud the massacre of more than a thousand Islamists in Cairo in 2013. The Libyans I'd met in those early days, so full of hope and laughter, would fragment into hundreds of militias, their country shattered by civil war. The same and worse was in store for many of the young rebels I met in Yemen, Syria, and Tunisia.

Five years after the outbreak of the Arab Spring, its original message appears to have been wholly reversed. The demands for dignity and civic rights have given way to conflicts that loosened the very building blocks of social and political belonging. The protesters who chanted for freedom and democracy in 2011 had found nothing solid beneath their feet, no common agreement on what those words meant. In some countries, the state collapsed, while in others it survived as a kind of parodic self-exaggeration, its popular base frayed and defensive. Each country fell apart in its own way. In Libya, the rebellion empowered local militias—whether tribal, ethnic, or regional—that saw no reason to relinquish their fiefdoms. In Syria, sect became the dividing line. In Yemen, it was often clan or tribe affiliation. Sectarian gangs cannibalized the state, echoing the rivalry of their Saudi and Iranian paymasters. More and more, it felt irrelevant to speak the language of sovereign nations, with so many people in the former Ottoman world living outside the control of any recognized government. The Kurds of Syria and Iraq were independent in all but name. Parts of southern and northern Yemen had cut all ties to their nominal rulers. Most notoriously, some ten million people were living at the mercy of the self-declared Islamic state. The bedrock of modern Arab societies—borders, governments, systems of law—was more vulnerable than anyone had guessed, or so it seemed.

Why did we not see it coming? Looking back, I think it was partly a willed refusal. It was the dictators and their agents who were constantly warning that the revolts would end in civil war and Islamist bloodlust. They'd been saying so for years—even before the uprisings— and all the while doing everything they could to make those predictions come true. Faced with such cynicism, it was natural to insist on believing in an alternative, no matter how unlikely. The protesters could rise above their own divisions only by believing it was possible.

This leap of faith was itself an achievement for a people who'd grown resigned to the cliché of Arab fatalism. You couldn't help rooting for them. After living in the region for years, I too was sick of people invoking history as the Middle East's great burden and scapegoat. When I told a Syrian friend in 2013 that I was preparing to write this book by reading more about the history of her country, she pleaded, "Please, just don't make it seem as if we are always doomed to repeat the past."

I promised I would not. But the past has a way of creeping back in at exactly those moments when you try to disavow it. I remember seeing maps in the hands of Libyan exiles who were on their way back home to claim property in 2011 and 2012. The maps were usually yellowed and creased, having been kept in a desk or file cabinet for decades, like buried treasure. Each seemed to describe a different country: Libya, it seemed, was a matter of perspective. Some of them were more than a century old, in Ottoman Turkish. Some were in Italian or English, from the colonial period. Some were more recent, in Arabic. The claims often overlapped, because the owners had left or been expelled from the country at different times, and the authorities who had created the maps—a city, a region, a colonial power—had succeeded each other with no sense of common identity. Some families were laying claims to huge areas where government buildings and courthouses now stood. Most were smaller, a house or a farm that had been stolen, a piece of family heritage that had never been forgotten. The owners saw no reason why they shouldn't get them back. They didn't seem to understand that their maps were a civil war in miniature, a palimpsest of clashing aspirations. There was no one to adjudicate any of their claims. So they began taking the law into their own hands, buying guns and evicting the people living in their villas.

Weak national bonds were part of the problem, as were tribes, but these things could not fully explain what made the revolts of 2011 slide into something so much darker. In a way, that larger question was the one people had been asking for centuries about Arab crises and defeats, and the answers themselves have become a vast literature full of its own factionalism and gall. You could begin the story more than a thousand years ago in the battlefields of Iraq. You could begin it in 1839, when the Ottoman sultan first began the reforms that would dissolve his empire and unmoor the Arabs. You could start in 1919, with the failed liberal revolution in Cairo. You could even go outside the Middle East—many people did—and say the Arabs were having their version of the Thirty Years' War, or of the European revolutions of 1848. These analogies often said more about who was speaking than anything else. The combatants in the Arab civil wars have their own dates and starting points, and some of them have been contagious. In June 2014, shortly after declaring their new caliphate, the jihadi fighters of ISIS tweeted pictures of themselves using a bulldozer to crash through the earthen berm that forms the frontier between Syria and Iraq. They announced that they were destroying the "borders of Sykes-Picot," the popular term for the map imposed on the Middle East by European colonialists a century ago.

For most Arabs, the most important context was more immediate. They had grown up with dictators whose birthright, as it were, came from the struggle for independence after the Second World War. The great standard-bearer then was Egypt's Gamal Abdel Nasser, whose willingness to defy the West during the Suez Crisis of 1956 made him more popular, in all likelihood, than any other Arab leader since the Prophet Muhammad. But Nasser's legacy was toxic: beneath his emotive speeches and egalitarian posturing, he built a brutal police state. And the confidence he had inspired in Arabs evaporated even before his death in 1970. Nizar Kabbani, perhaps the most celebrated Arab poet of the twentieth century, saw it early, writing in the wake of the disastrous 1967 war with Israel:

> *Friends, the ancient word is dead; the ancient books are dead; our speech with holes like worn-out shoes is dead . . . Our poems have gone sour; women's hair and nights, curtains and sofas, have gone sour; everything has gone sour. My grieved nation, in a flash, you turned me from a poet writing for love and tenderness to a poet writing with a knife . . . Our shouting is louder than our actions; our swords are taller than us . . . Friends, smash the doors; wash your brains . . . Grow words, pomegranates and grapes; sail to countries of fog and snow . . . Write poems and proverbs; and pray to God for victory.*

Nasser's Arab heirs found themselves sitting in his chair but robbed of the popular legitimacy that had made him a beloved figure. It is no accident that the Arabic word for legitimacy, *shar'eeya*, is related to *sharia*, Islamic law. The nimbus of spiritual authority that had briefly clung to Nasser did not extend to the men who came after him. They knew they could stay in place only through fear, and they set about reinforcing the machinery of surveillance and repression that Nasser had started building. "No ruler in this region sees himself as legitimate," I was told by Muhammad al Mutawakel, a wise old Yemeni political figure and friend. "So they all constantly look over their shoulders, scheming against their rivals, because they see no reason why their rivals should not be in their place." Mutawakel was born when Yemen was ruled by a xenophobic thousand-year-old religious dynasty. He lived through its republican revolution and the subsequent descent into kleptocracy, only to be murdered by fanatics, like so many of the Arab world's most tolerant and thoughtful people, outside his home in late 2014.

It has since occurred to me that Mutawakel's observation about paranoid Arab tyrants was directed not just at Nasser and his imitators. In a sense, the Arab world has never built a peaceful model for political succession, and some say this is the key to its repeated agonies. The Prophet Muhammad tried to create such a model after he established the Arab world's first real state. His seventh-century heirs were designated *khalifa*, meaning deputy or successor, and at first, the glow of association with the Prophet allowed these caliphs, known as God's shadow on earth, to lead the community by popular acclaim. But eventually tribal and religious rivalry divided and weakened the Arab peoples. They became the subjects of Turkish and Mongol and Persian converts to the religion they themselves had founded. These usurpers struggled with the same demons: Ottoman sultans conscripted Christian slaves to help run their empire and had their own brothers ritually strangled with a silk cord on reaching the throne, all to forestall the risk of rival lineages. All these safeguards failed eventually. Even republican democracy, the great rallying cry of the postcolonial years, was finally unmasked as a pretext. One of the signal grievances that led to the uprisings of 2011 was the accusation of *tawreeth*, hereditary succession. The dictators of Egypt, Libya, and Yemen, who held themselves up as democrats to the world, were in fact forging dynasties, grooming their sons to follow them. The former dictator of Syria, Hafez al Assad, had already done so.

The protesters of 2011 believed they had a solution to the succession problem: genuine democracy. But even so, few of them plotted against their regimes in a serious way. Apart from a small group of activists in Egypt who had studied the work of Gene Sharp, an American theorist of nonviolent resistance to tyranny, they were spectacularly unprepared for upheaval. The Islamists had an underground movement, but it was a divisive one, and far from preaching revolution, many urged

Technology?!

accommodation with the regime. They had no blueprint for translating their religious slogans into reality.

In fact, what happened in 2011 was not so much a beginning as an end. It was the final disintegration of something that had been rotting for decades: the Arab republican states, which finally collapsed of their own weight. By 2010, the Arab world's police states were no longer meeting their own standards. Strongmen who had spent decades mastering the arts of divide and rule, of "balancing" local conflicts against each other, found themselves unable to cope with deepening economic crises, unemployment, rising food and commodity prices, the effects of drought, and corruption that had grown beyond their control. Demography intensified all these problems: by 2010, the vast majority of the Arab world's people were under thirty. Most of them had slim chances of getting a decent job, despite the fact that they were more literate and better educated than their parents. In 1980, about half of Arabs could read and write. By the year 2000, that number had risen to 61.5 percent, and among people age fifteen to twenty-four, it was about 80 percent. These numbers translated into higher expectations. But in economies dominated by sluggish bureaucracies and patronage, the young saw no reward for initiative, and humiliation everywhere. Tentative efforts to liberalize the economy in Egypt and Syria in the early 2000s only increased the wealth gap between those with *waasta*—connections to the ruling elite—and those without. Young Arab men with no income could not marry or move out of their parents' homes. They were tantalized by visions of a Western world of freedom and affluence. Starting in the 1990s, they had been hearing new voices, on al Jazeera and other satellite TV stations, that exposed the state-run propaganda of their childhood and mocked the pretenses of their rulers. The Internet amplified this new awareness while granting people a much greater ability to communicate with each other. All these things helped pave the way for what began in 2010: a slow groundswell of outrage. In country after country, martyrs were being held up, dead or maimed or humiliated men and women whose fates seemed to crystallize the indignity visited on an entire people.

In Egypt, the first hints of change came in early June 2010, with a pair of photographs. One of them showed a smiling, clean-shaven youth, with his name written at the bottom: Khaled Saeed. The second photograph showed the same face, now hideously mangled: teeth smashed out, jaw askew, blood spattered on the cheeks, dead eyes staring upward. Many Egyptians had been tortured and killed by the police before. But Khaled was not a typical victim; he lived on a nice middle-class street, not a slum or Islamist ghetto. His death quickly inspired a Facebook page, conceived and edited in distant Dubai by a young Egyptian Google employee named Wael Ghoneim. "We are all Khaled Saeed" spread beyond Facebook to become almost a movement, gaining hundreds of thousands of followers and generating protest rallies in a matter of weeks. The story of Khaled's murder expanded and stretched, its contours shifting, like some vast air balloon. It exerted an irresistible attraction, drawing the attention of anyone who had viscerally felt the injustice and stifling pressures of Mubarak's Egypt. The regime's critics seized on it. In late June, Mohamed ElBaradei, the former head of the International Atomic Energy Agency, visited Khaled's family and led a rally in Alexandria against police brutality.

Similar stories, sometimes embellished into myth, were rising in every Arab country, all of them driven by the same kinds of frustrations. Al Jazeera broadcast them relentlessly, using its red scrolls and banners and frantic crosscuts to insinuate a narrative of rising regional crisis. That autumn, I drove through drought-cracked fields in northeastern Syria and found peasants seething with anger. Some believed the government had deliberately withheld water supplies from them. It was the fourth year of drought, but people I met up north seemed less inclined to blame nature or God than the Syrian regime, which had quietly dropped its old Socialist commitments to the peasantry and poor, and did nothing for them.

In the suburbs of Damascus, tens of thousands of displaced farmers and their families were living in tent cities, surviving on handouts from foreign charities. Even in the country's capital, with its array of boutique hotels and restaurants, its Benetton shops and its *jeunesse dorée* in Jaguars, the smell of fear was growing stronger in 2010. You heard telltale phrases, uttered in different variations: *All it needs is a match to ignite. Just a spark and it will explode.* The Syrian philosopher Sadik al-Azm, who was living in Damascus at the time, later wrote: "Beneath Damascus' shiny surface a malignancy of hatred and oppression was growing and mutating into a winding mass of violent energies ready to spring. Practically every Damascene had one prayer on the tip of his tongue: 'Please, oh Lord, inspire him to do something before it is too late.'" No one needed to be told that the man he referred to was Bashar al Assad.

In late November 2010, I was back in Egypt for the parliamentary election. Voting in Egypt always elicited cynicism and rage, but this time the fraud was especially flagrant. At one polling station inside a school, government-hired thugs burst in, fired guns into the air, and then roared off in a minibus. The police, who had watched the whole thing passively, closed the polling station, leaving hundreds of would-be opposition voters cursing on the sidewalk. The thugs had shot an old man in the leg, but one of the police officers was smirking at the whole charade. I spent the rest of the day going from station to station, and everywhere I found ordinary people screaming that they hadn't been let inside, their votes were being stolen. At the same time, those who trumpeted their loyalty with Mubarak stickers on their shirts were often ushered graciously into the polls. Even by Egyptian standards, it was outrageous. Demonstrations began breaking out, small but telling. In Shobra al Khaima, a working-class district, I watched young men bravely risk arrest by climbing the iron gates of a shuttered polling station, banging on the metal with trash can lids and shouting, "Down with Mubarak!"

What happened next seemed, at first, like yet another futile gesture. On December 17, 2010, a twenty-six-year-old Tunisian vendor named Mohamed Bouazizi doused himself with gasoline at a dusty intersection in the southern farming town of Sidi Bouzid. Arabs had burned themselves to death in outrage before, but this time something was different. "How do you expect me to make a living?" Bouazizi shouted from the middle of a traffic jam, less than an hour after a local bureaucrat had confiscated his vegetable cart and scales. Then he flicked a lighter and set himself on fire. The protests began almost at once, before Bouazizi faded into a coma and died, and before the success of the Tunisian revolution transformed him from an obscure destitute fruit and vegetable vendor into the man who set off the Arab Spring. It took less than a month for the protests to evict Tunisia's dictator, Zine El Abidine Ben Ali, on January 14. The Egyptian protests kicked off on January 25, and in eighteen days Hosni Mubarak was gone. The torch passed quickly to Libya, Yemen, and Bahrain, where the protests were more chaotic and less successful. In Syria, the first demonstrations began on March 15; they devolved in less than a month into a brutal campaign of repression.

This book is not a comprehensive history of the Arab uprisings that began in December 2010. Instead, it is a much more selective effort to make sense of their fallout: the collapse of political authority across much of the Arab world, whether through war or sheer disintegration, culminating in the establishment of the Islamic state in Syria and Iraq. The story is told through people whose lives intersected with the uprisings and their aftermath in five countries: Egypt, Libya, Syria, Yemen, and Tunisia. I touch on Iraq only in passing, because the American invasion of 2003 imposed on it a somewhat different trajectory. I have avoided Bahrain entirely, despite its much-publicized popular uprising in the spring of 2011, because it does not share the same republican history, and because the revolt there was cut off so quickly and so decisively. I have little to say about the role of the United States and other Western powers, because I believe it was mostly secondary. There are certain clear exceptions to this rule, including the NATO bombing campaign in Libya. Much has been said about how American reluctance to engage in Syria changed the outcome there, but this remains largely hypothetical. The Arab political landscape was certainly changed by the American invasions of Iraq, but the forces that propelled the uprisings of 2011 were, in my view, indigenous.

The book originated with my own zigzagging efforts to follow the course of the uprisings and their aftermath between 2011 and 2013. Parts of it are adapted from my articles in *The New York Times Magazine*, where I was a staff writer at the time, and the daily editions of *The New York Times*, where I spent years as a correspondent based in Baghdad and Beirut.

The book is divided into two parts. The first deals with the outbreak of the revolts and their quick descent into war in three countries. The second is about the various efforts to build a new order, of one kind or another, on the ruins of the old regimes. It is an episodic story, encompassing many borders and characters, and there have been moments in the past five years when little seemed to unite the diverse outcomes in Tunis and Damascus and Sanaa beyond the presumed thread of a single regional insurrection. But time has bolstered the sense of a shared narrative, along with the shared contagion of ISIS. More benign infections may travel across the same borders: the success or failure of the democratic experiment in Tunisia will alter all views of what is possible in Syria, in Iraq, in Yemen. It, too, will affect our understanding of what happened across the Arab world in 2011.

The uprisings spread in that year not just because of social media and a common language, but also because so many of the political dilemmas—and the tools people used to address them—were the same. In a sense, the thousands of young men and women flocking to the Islamic state were acting on the same impulse that drove the protesters of Tahrir Square: the need for a homeland where they are treated like citizens. It may sound perverse to invoke that word for both a utopian urban space and a violent theocracy where slavery is held sacred. But many young Egyptians traveled from one to the other, and one of their stories is in this book. Those journeys were fueled by a hunger for something they'd always been denied: order, harmony, a sense of belonging. They wanted a place where the cross-strands of their ethnicity and faith and tribe would not be cynically exploited against them—as so many divide-and-rule strongmen had done over the years, from the Turks to the British to Mubarak—but embraced and reconciled. When nonviolence failed to achieve those things, some of them sought the same goal through an orgy of killing.

— PART I —
Revolts

Oh my people, please! There are no heroes. The heroes are the
ones on the streets. The heroes are each and every one of us.
The time when one hero would ride his horse to lead the masses
is long gone.

—WAEL GHONEIM, February 7, 2011

And thus, on every side beset with foes,
The goaded land waxed mad; the crimes of few
Spread into madness of the many; blasts
From hell came sanctified like airs from heaven.

—WILLIAM WORDSWORTH, "The Prelude"

1

— One People (Egypt) —

The kids called it "the house of revolution." It was a huge place with a balcony right on Tahrir Square, more like a decaying antiques shop than an apartment. There were at least a dozen rooms full of dusty old furniture and gilt-framed paintings, encyclopedias in several languages, dead plants, and chipped tile tables covered with laptops and ashtrays and newspapers and plates of half-eaten food. Its owner was a forty-nine-year-old slacker and bohemian named Pierre Sioufi, who'd thrown it open as soon as the demonstrations began, giving refuge to protesters not out of any political conviction but because he was afraid there would be a massacre and he wanted to protect the kids. The house became an essential annex for the revolt against Hosni Mubarak, a pit stop and plug-in zone with a perfect ninth-floor view of the square.

Within days after the first protests started, on January 25, 2011, an eclectic crowd had colonized the place. There were Cairene artists and intellectuals, scores of college-age protesters, journalists and human rights workers, even a few Islamists, all resting and plotting and sharing information throughout the day and night. They would cook a huge pot of lentils every evening and carry it downstairs to distribute to those sleeping in the square. People came and went constantly, stepping over sleeping bodies, glowing laptops, and Pierre's cat and two terriers. No one was in charge, and yet somehow someone fixed the toilet and washed the dishes and stocked the kitchen with bread and beans and fruit. A bookseller had set up a stand by the door downstairs, selling banned books. (Most were opposition pamphlets and anti-Mubarak polemics, but also, oddly, some books about Hitler and Stalin.) Al Jazeera set up a live feed on the roof, just above Pierre's vast wraparound balcony, and because everybody was watching al Jazeera—not just across the Arab world but even inside the square—you had a peculiar feeling of being behind the scenes in a vast and mirrored opera house.

Pierre presided over it all like a benevolent Arab version of Allen Ginsberg. He must have weighed three hundred pounds, a pear-shaped figure with a beard and shoulder-length gray hair that soared in every direction. He sat at a cluttered oak desk by the door, welcoming visitors, giggling, and chain-smoking Marlboros. When I first arrived he wore a faintly Dada T-shirt bearing the Kentucky Fried Chicken logo of Colonel Sanders, and below it the words, in Arabic, MAY YOUR GRANDFATHER REST IN PEACE. I introduced myself, and he glanced up and pushed back the thick plastic glasses that were always falling off his nose. "I'm just like everyone else here," he said. "No one knows anything." He came from a wealthy Coptic family and had dabbled in art and acting, but for the most part, he said, "I don't do much. I'm a revolutionary, but I'm a salon revolutionary." The kids adored him. He seemed to embody the refusal of all authority: the only kind of father figure their movement would accept.

On that first day at Pierre's place I met a Muslim Brotherhood member who described how the police had tortured him in 2002, using electrical wires on his genitals. He had been arrested and jailed dozens of times since then. Now he had brought his wife and children to the square and would not leave until Mubarak stepped down, he said. Also listening to this grim monologue, on a mattress next to me, was Khaled Abol Naga, a famous Egyptian actor and heartthrob. A few feet away was Khalid Abdulla, the boyishly handsome British Egyptian star of *The Kite Runner* and *United 93*. Before the revolution, these two men would have drawn squeals of adoration from the twentysomethings around us. Now no one seemed to notice them; the revolution had eclipsed their fame. Both men had camcorders and treated the young protesters as if *they* were the celebrities. "The best thing Mubarak did was to push people so hard they all melded together," Abol Naga told me, as we sat on broken chairs in Pierre's TV room. "The poor, the wealthy, the secular people, the Muslim Brothers—we all came together, and it spread to every city in Egypt."

One afternoon I found myself on Pierre's balcony next to a tall, elegant man in a three-piece pin-striped suit and a pharaonic-motif tie. He said he was the honorary consul of Italy in Egypt, and he handed me a business card that identified him as Cavagliere Ladislav Skakal. Below us, Tahrir was an unbroken mass of people, swaying in some places, calmer in others, like the surface of some vast turbid lake. Green-and-white banners rippled in the breeze above it, and by the black stage, the sound of a tinny hectoring voice on speakers merged with the crowd's osmotic roar. "You see that green pole? That's where the Zamalek bourgeoisie are," Skakal said with an amused smile, pointing to one side of the sunlit square. (Zamalek is a bastion of old-money Cairenes and foreigners on an island in the Nile.) "On that side are the Islamists; there it's more rural; and there are the warriors, the tough guys who fought with the Mubarak supporters."

He was right, more or less. But the square was much more than the sum of its camps. There was an emotion in the air that encompassed all of us, made us feel we'd shed our old skins and the past was irrelevant. It wasn't just the slogans and chants, *the people want the dictator to fall*, the shared poetry of revolution and dignity. It wasn't just the heart-lifting feeling that was conjured everywhere with the same phrase: the barrier of fear is broken. Larger than all this was a sudden but vast shift in perspective, as if Earth had tilted on its axis, allowing you to miraculously see truths that had been hidden from you all along. The tyrant, once vast and august, was now revealed as a laughable old fool. Your own countrymen, your own city, so degraded by soot and misery and fear, were delivered back to you and became beautiful. So many people spoke the same words: it was like falling in love. These feelings utterly transformed the dingy, cracked sidewalks, the high-rises where snipers lurked, the slurry of plastic trash underfoot, and the stink of sweat and urine. Most of all, there was the passionate insistence that the revolution would triumph, that justice would replace injustice, that the country's problems—its sectarian hatreds, its corruption, its terrorist gangs—were all artificial, trumped up, the cynical props of the old regime. All of it would fade away now that the people were empowered.

Looking back, I ask myself why these shouted words moved me and so many other cynical outsiders to tears. It was not because we believed them. We had seen too much of the Arab world's fault lines for that. At this distance, after so much blood, it would be easy to laugh or wince at how wrong the protesters were. But I remember the faces that spoke those words, and what they seemed to express was not just naïveté or willed ignorance, but this: *I know these things are not true. But perhaps, if we will them with enough conviction, they will come true someday.*

Tunisia's revolution was the first—Ben Ali was gone barely two days after the protests reached the capital—but Egypt was the model. Tahrir was a place where the drama could play out in public, where the consequences were understood by all. Egypt mattered, because of its history and its sheer mass: eighty-two million people, a fifth of the entire Arab population. Egyptians had lost many things over the years, but not their genius for street theater, for jokes and protest songs and slogans that could be adopted wholesale by crowds from Morocco to the Gulf.

And yet, in the first days after Ben Ali fell on January 14, most people doubted that Egypt would move. The country was weighed down, they said, by its size and ancient inertia, and held in check by its sprawling "deep state" of plainclothes policemen and hired thugs. You sensed that inertia when you walked around downtown Cairo: the dilapidated old cafés and squares, always evoking past glory and current decay; the old *bawabs*, caretakers, standing in doorways, sweeping away dust that would settle right back again; the ever-present atmosphere of nostalgia for a lost greatness. Egyptians were like hippos, a friend of mine put it: they lifted their heads to glance around now and then, but invariably sank back into the Nile mud. Only a few voices seemed genuinely confident. One of them was a small, round-faced young Egyptian woman named Asmaa Mahfouz, who posted a video of herself on Facebook urging people to come out and demonstrate in Tahrir Square exactly one week later. In the video, posted on January 18, she speaks intently into the camera, her head covered with a hijab, her pale face contorted with defiance. "Never say there is no hope," she said. "As long as you say there is no hope, hope will be lost. As long as you come out and take a stand, hope endures. So come out with us and there will be hope. Never fear the government, fear God. God says: 'Indeed Allah will never change the condition of a people until they change what is in themselves.'" That video, ricocheting across the Internet, inspired others and helped build a furtive sense of optimism among the country's middle-class youth. The first protest was scheduled for January 25, 2011, to coincide with National Police Day, a holiday commemorating the killing of fifty officers by British colonial forces in 1952.

On the night before the demonstration, one of the protest's main architects, a thirty-two-year-old lawyer named Ziyad al Elaimy, was at home on the couch, preparing himself by leafing through a book called *Mechanisms of Resistance Behind Bars*. It is a dry but useful Palestinian primer on how to maintain your sanity in prison. He felt he needed some tips, because he expected the following day's protest to last "about ten minutes" before the police put a stop to it and threw him in jail. Elaimy is a big man with a jowly face and deep-set eyes that give him an air of calm sobriety. Of all the self-proclaimed revolutionaries I met in Egypt, he was perhaps the least burdened by narcissism, and among the bravest. Rebellion was almost a vocation with him. His mother had spent six months in jail for her role in antigovernment protests in 1977, and his parents had been taking him along with them to protests since he was five years old. "He was so young he couldn't even pronounce the slogans right," his mother told me. "But he knew that lawyers got people out of jail, so he decided to become a lawyer." He had been in jail four times, starting at sixteen years old, and he had residual injuries on his knee and arm from police beatings. But if his insurgent spirit was inherited, his politics and methods were not. He and his friends had abandoned the communism they grew up on in the 1990s, because they felt it was just as paternalistic as the Mubarak regime. They were sick of the old Egyptian deference to a Big Man whose authority could not be questioned. They had been building their own grassroots organizations for years, mostly unconnected to Egypt's weak and corrupted opposition parties. Gandhian nonviolence had become a guiding principle for many of them, and they had been teaching workshops on it since 2009.

In mid-January 2011, Elaimy had helped form a steering committee of thirteen people representing a number of activist groups, from the Revolutionary Socialists to the youth wing of the Muslim Brotherhood. They had made an elaborate plan for the protests of January 25 in the cluttered living room of Elaimy's mother's house. On a coffee table, they'd laid out a star-shaped map of marching routes starting in outer areas of Cairo and converging on several hubs in the center; from there each group would continue on to Tahrir Square. Scouts were assigned to the head of each march to make sure it remained nonviolent. Other groups would join the earlier marchers at designated points along the way. They had walked all the routes a week or so beforehand, timing themselves so that they could arrive in the center simultaneously. They had deliberately publicized false routes to people they did not trust, so as to fool the police. They knew they were being monitored.

Just after noon on January 25, Elaimy met a group of two dozen friends at the El Hayiss Sweet Shop, a café in a ratty working-class neighborhood of western Cairo. On a prearranged signal, they began marching down the street together. They chanted slogans: "The people demand an end to corruption!" and "Egyptians, unite!" Elaimy girded himself, expecting the police at any moment. Instead, as they entered a neighborhood called Nahia, he began to notice that people were joining them. A few dozen at first, then a hundred. By the time a clutch of policemen appeared, it was too late; the march could not be contained and the cops melted back to the sidewalk. At that point, Elaimy re-members thinking: this will not be a short detention, it will be a *long* one. But the march kept going, and kept getting larger. People were pour-ing out of apartment towers and office buildings to join them. Others shouted their approval from upper-story windows. Elaimy's cell phone began buzzing with ecstatic texts from friends. He felt as if something was blooming simultaneously in his chest and on the streets, a music you could see as well as hear: it was a happiness sweeter than anything he had known for years. This was no longer the little scheme he and his friends had cooked up on his mother's couch. He had no idea where it would lead. But he allowed it to carry him along.

Tahrir Square resembles a vast teardrop-shaped traffic circle at the heart of Cairo, with a grubby green patch at its center. On most days it is thick with honking cars and exhaust from dawn to dusk. But in essence, it is a theater, and it was designed that way. Ever since 1919, when British troops gunned down twenty-three Egyptians there, it has been a symbolic center for patriotism. It is ringed by monuments and towers that seem to peer downward like giants onto the green: the Arab League headquarters; the fortresslike government building known as the Mogamma; the Omar Makram mosque; and just beyond, the salmon-colored colossus of the Egyptian Museum. On Tahrir's eastern side is the nostalgic grandeur of downtown, with its 1920s beaux arts apartment buildings.

By the time Elaimy got to Tahrir, it was no longer a traffic circle; thousands of people were surging into it from all the major boule-vards, chanting for an end to corruption, police abuse, and to Egypt's decades-old Emergency Law, the legal fig leaf for state repression. There was a simultaneous demonstration at the Egyptian High Court, not far away, and that, too, was much larger than expected. Thousands of people broke through the security cordon near the courthouse and made their way to Tahrir, chanting ecstatically as they went. The police made several halfhearted efforts to disperse them, but the crowds were not daunted. By nightfall, the square was in chaos, but thousands of pro-testers remained. In the darkness, Elaimy and his friends gathered to trade reports, still giddy with their victory. Slowly, the goal began to shift: some people were already dispensing with calls for reform and chanting, "The people want the fall of the regime."

Not far away, at the downtown office of the Muslim Brotherhood, a man named Muhammad Beltagy arrived, hoping to find out what the organization's leaders were thinking. Beltagy was one of the Brotherhood's rising stars, a beloved forty-seven-year-old doctor in the Cairo slum of Shobra al Khaima who had served in Parliament from 2005 until 2010. He had spent much of the day at the High Court demonstration and was now excited about the continuing protest in Tahrir. He wanted to join it and urgently wanted the Brotherhood to give its official blessing. But the group's leaders had issued no statement; they were cautious, elderly men who preferred to wait and see how things played out. Members were free to protest if they liked, but not as representatives of the movement. A dozen younger members, men in their twenties who admired Beltagy for his energy and independent views, were also in the building. Beltagy gathered them and the group left, headed for the square.

They got there at about midnight and made their way through a jostling, ecstatic crowd now totaling tens of thousands, some of them seated on the green and preparing themselves to spend the night. On the eastern side of the square, some of Ziyad Elaimy's youth movement friends were setting up a stage, with a microphone and speakers. One of the first people to take the mike was a big, thickset man in a suit, with a bullish face and almost no neck. "What we are witnessing here is a revolution," he said in a booming voice. "The Egyptian security state is our Bastille, and we will not stop until we secure our rights." The crowd roared. This was Alaa Aswany, Egypt's most popular novelist and a longtime critic of Mubarak. A few more speakers, activists and intellectuals, followed. Eventually, Muhammad Beltagy, the Brotherhood leader, went to the back of the stage and began asking if he could speak. He was eager to flout the Brotherhood's caution and to declare his support for a democratic revolution. The man in charge, a young leftist poet, refused to give him the mike. He did not want an Islamist—

even a relatively liberal one like Beltagy—to claim any ownership of this movement.

The moment of triumph lasted less than an hour. A column of riot police stormed the square, firing tear gas and concussion grenades. Young men fought back, hurling chunks of pavement, but most of the protesters left the square, and by dawn it was almost empty. For the next two days, the square was a sporadic battleground, as smaller crowds of protesters and police ebbed and flowed. The rest of the country was erupting in violent protest, but Ziyad Elaimy and other young protest leaders were busy getting the word out for the next big push. They called it the Friday of Anger, January 28, 2011.

The day began quietly, as Fridays always do in the Arab world, with families preparing for the weekly mosque prayers. At noon, people filed out of mosques across Egypt. In Cairo, rivers of people formed and marched down boulevards, with police lines warily shadowing them. Their confidence grew as they saw the police falling back. "Egyptians, come out!" they chanted. "Raise your voice—whoever chants will not die!" The crowds were now vast, and far more diverse: rich matrons with designer handbags, old peasants in smocklike galabiyas, girls in tight jeans, bearded religious sheikhs. The Muslim Brotherhood had finally abandoned its caution the night before and formally urged its followers to take part. By midafternoon, street battles had broken out in cities across the country. In Cairo, a thousand-man column of helmeted riot police blocked the Qasr al Nil bridge leading to Tahrir, firing tear gas and water cannons into the advancing crowd. Young men picked up the gas canisters and threw them back, and others tore up pavement to throw. The battle lasted all afternoon, and finally, after dusk, the crowd broke through in triumph. Elsewhere, mobs formed, breaking into police stations and setting them on fire. They gutted the four-story headquarters of Mubarak's National Democratic Party, near Tahrir Square, and thick smoke was soon pouring from the building's blackened windows.

By nightfall, the police had withdrawn from the entire downtown area. Tahrir was packed with thousands of ecstatic people, and for the first time, they seemed confident that it was theirs. From January 28 until February 11—more than two weeks—Tahrir Square would be effectively cut off from the rest of Egypt. The police did not enter, and the army maintained a cordon outside. On the inside, a new alchemy was under way. There were still plenty of middle-class youth around, the kind of people who had kicked it all off with their Facebook campaigns. But there were Brotherhood members too. There were even Salafis, with their distinctive scraggly beards and short tunics, wandering the crowd in wonder. This was a surprise: Salafis were not supposed to be political. They were modern-day puritans, whose name comes from their rigid emulation of Islam's early heroes: al salaf al salih, the righteous ancestors. The Salafis mostly disdained the Brotherhood's mingling of religion and politics. But everything was changing now, or so it seemed. The crowd mixed social classes too. There were poor vendors from Cairo slums like Imbaba, and lots of Ultras, the hard-core soccer club fans who had been at the forefront of the street battles on Friday. These were people who did not ordinarily spend time together, or even inhabit the same worlds. Late that night, a slight, timid young man named Amr Magdy who worked part time as a stringer for al Jazeera struck up a conversation with a young Salafi and a Muslim Brother. The three of them sat down on a blanket on the green and talked for three hours about the revolution and where it would take Egypt. When I met him, two days later, Magdy told me the other two men had started off that night insisting that Islamic government was the only kind they could accept. By 5:00 a.m., when they grew too tired to continue, the two Islamists had conceded that the Egyptian people should be trusted to make the choice.

Similar conversations were happening all across the square and continued in the coming days. On the stage, Alaa Aswany, the novelist, began performing routinely after midnight. He was the revolution's self-proclaimed mascot, half prophet and half clown. "The revolution is a new birth, not just for Egypt but on an individual level," he told the crowd one night. "It's like falling in love: you become a better person." He had written the words "the people" thousands of times, Aswany said, but only now did he understand what they meant. "I think there is a kind of mood in this revolution, where if you are inside of it, you are willing to face anything."

Strolling through the crowded square, you could almost mistake it for one of Egypt's ancient Mawlid ceremonies, the lively, open-air rituals commemorating the birth of the Prophet Muhammad. There were vendors selling roasted corn and fruit juice, processions of people in clerical robes, all kinds of chanting, music, even puppet performances. But the square was also becoming something radically new and unfamiliar: an ideal community in miniature, an embattled Paris Commune on the banks of the Nile. Even uneducated people seemed to grasp intuitively that this was not just a protest but an attempt to build a small-scale alternative to Mubarak's Egypt. Christians began standing guard while Muslims prostrated themselves in prayer, and the Muslims returned the favor. People clutched brooms and swept the sidewalk as if it were holy ground. Young men and women formed security cordons that guarded every entrance to the square, and patted down anyone coming in with an amazing combination of thoroughness and politeness. Usually, they apologized. Soon, they began chanting a welcome for those arriving—"Oh heroes!" or "These are the Egyptian people!" and another as you left, sometimes "Don't forget—come back tomorrow!" This was done with a simple-hearted enthusiasm and joy that more than once brought me to the verge of tears. Not one of those men, you felt, would hesitate to give his life in defense of the square, and none of them was armed—unlike the soldiers outside.

The square was something else, too: a theater. The inventiveness of the slogans and signs and songs was amazing, and every day brought dozens of new variations. One man had covered his body entirely with paper on which was handwritten a long disquisition about the People and its spontaneous emergence as a self-governing entity. Protest songs from the '60s were repurposed, with new lyrics to suit Mubarak and his froglike head. So were children's songs like "Night Has Gone and the Day Has Come" by Muhammad Fawzi. Many of the slogans translate poorly into English, dependent as they are on Arabic rhymes and references. One man carried a banner demanding an end to "*istihmar*," a coinage that rhymes with the word for "colonialism" and means "turning into a donkey." (Many Egyptians feel that this is what has been done to them over the past thirty years.) Everyone in the square seemed to feel not only that they had to act in accordance with a new and more elevated creed but also that they had to broadcast this new conviction to the world, through the countless eyes and cameras that were trained on Tahrir Square throughout the night and day. It wasn't just al Jazeera and the other Arab satellite channels. There were dozens of reporters and documentarians around, not to mention the Egyptians using their cell phones to record everything they saw.

Almost everyone you met had a story that seemed to crystallize his or her outrage. Each story added meaning to the vast pot of emotion stirring inside the square. One afternoon I met a skinny man in a cardigan sweater who told me about the theft of a $55 million Van Gogh from the Cairo art museum where he worked as a security guard. (He had an advanced degree in art history, but he didn't have the connections to get a better job.) "The theft could easily have been prevented, but they didn't want to spend ten Egyptian pounds to fix the broken cables on the security cameras, or install an alarm system," he said. "Meanwhile they're skimming millions from the budget. It is the same corruption, from Mubarak on down. This is what we have come to."

Standing in the square, you would sometimes see an opening form in the dense crowd, as people pulled backward and applauded: this usually heralded the arrival of some political dissident, whose critiques of the regime and years in jail had made him or her a kind of honorary citizen of Tahrir. One rainy afternoon, a white-haired old man in a fuzzy gray sweater went gliding slowly by, the crowd parting to let him through like the sea before Moses. On his arm was a lovely younger woman, presumably his daughter. It was Sherif Hetata, an eighty-eight-year-old author and doctor, the husband of the pioneering feminist Nawal el Sadaawi, another Tahrir luminary. I stopped him and asked for his impressions. "This is something we've never lived before," he told me in a mild, gentle voice. "I've seen Egyptian history since the time of King Farouk. I saw demonstrations in 1946, 1951, 1952, 1977, 1986, and now 2011. For a person like myself who's lived all these years, it's a lesson. These are the forces that can build the country in the future, if they get the chance to do that."

The square was officially leaderless throughout its eighteen days. This, older protesters often told you, was a startling departure from the demonstrations of earlier decades, which suffered from both poor organization and the egoism of the mostly left-wing protest leaders, easily targeted by the state. "In the seventies, we had no good way to communicate with each other," one former Communist told me. "Social media and cell phones were a huge advance. In our time, it was harder to get people to come out and harder to control the message, so things could sometimes turn into a riot."

But leaderless insurrection could also shade into chaos, and so by early February a governing structure of sorts was emerging in the square. Ziyad Elaimy and his friends, recognized as leaders of the "revolutionary youth," had their own gathering place, near the Omar Makram mosque. They met regularly there to discuss the latest events and coordinate their plans with other protest groups, in Cairo and around the country. Their role as catalysts of the revolt, refracted in dozens of newspaper and television reports, had given them a near mythic status. A second leadership group consisted of established political figures, all longtime foes of the Mubarak regime, known as the People's Parliament. It had first been conceived in the wake of the parliamentary elections two months earlier, and many of its members were candidates who probably would have won seats if not for the flagrant fraud of that vote.

One of the leading figures in this group was Muhammad Beltagy, from the Brotherhood. He had an added importance because he was widely trusted by the revolutionary youth as well, and he spent much of his time shuttling back and forth between the two camps, negotiating their efforts to form a united council. The government was fully aware of all this, and the Mubarak regime made several efforts to strike a deal with the Tahrir group. One night Beltagy was sitting in the square with a group of younger Brotherhood members when a uniformed military intelligence officer walked up and introduced himself. He spent the next two hours trying to persuade Beltagy to lead his people out of the square, promising their demands would be met. Mubarak had delivered a televised speech earlier that evening in which he promised not to run again when his term ended in September, an apparent effort to defuse the protests. Now the regime seemed to be following up with direct outreach to the square's leading figures. Beltagy refused. In the end, the officer warned that things could turn violent, and very soon. He urged Beltagy to reconsider, and then got up and left.

The next day, just after noon, I was standing near the edge of the square when a man came running toward me, screaming, "They're attacking us! With *camels*!" Minutes later, a clutch of protesters came past, carrying a man with blood streaming down his forehead. Then another, and another. As I moved toward the square, crowds of people were running the other way, their faces wild. The air was full of shouting. When I got close enough, I heard what sounded like gunshots and saw objects flying through the air. The Battle of the Camel had started, the square's greatest trial. Thousands of Mubarak supporters had been hired to attack the square and clear it, some of them on horse and camel. The protesters responded by forming brigades: some dug up paving stones for ammunition, and others moved closer, to hurl rocks and stones at the thugs. By this time, *baltagiyya*, Egyptian slang for "thugs," had already entered the lexicon of the entire Arab world. The front lines were dominated by young men from the Brotherhood and the Ultras, the soccer fans. The battle went on all afternoon. The square's improvisatory genius was amazing to watch: the kids used masking tape to wrap newspapers or cardboard packaging around their forearms for protection. Garbage can lids became shields. I saw young men wearing kitchen bowls and colanders on their heads, like helmets. Some had the words THE GOVERNMENT OF THE REVOLUTION scrawled on them. That evening, from the balcony of a nearby hotel, I looked down at the square, still a war zone. Smoke was rising from burning cars and trash fires. Gunshots rang out occasionally. Another sound, an ominous metallic clanging, came from the far side of the square. Only later did I find out it was protesters beating their improvised sheet-metal shields.

By the next day the protesters had won, but at a terrible cost: at least eleven dead and some six hundred injured. If President Mubarak's speech had created doubts among some in the square, the brutality of the attack erased them and reinforced the sense of collective resolve. The fighting also expanded the square's villagelike autonomy. Doctors began streaming in from all over the country to bulwark the makeshift clinic at the square's edge. Next to it was a well-stocked pharmacy, where young women handed out almost any kind of medicine for free.

On Friday, February 11, with the protest in its eighteenth day, I was standing on the balcony at Pierre's bohemian hangout on the edge of the square. Night was falling after a tense day, full of rumors of violence. Mubarak had been expected to announce his departure the day before, but he had held on, delivering a defiant speech. Now the crowd was as large and as angry as ever. No one knew what to expect, and some were predicting that the protest could go on for weeks, or months. A burst of wild cheers emerged suddenly from a point near the center of the crowd. It spread south and west, like ripples on a pond, swelling into a roar of wild joy that soon encompassed the whole dark turbulent sea of bodies gathered there. Mubarak was gone. I looked at my watch: it was 6:06. Behind me, over the din, I could hear Egyptian state television blasting a scratchy recording of the Egyptian national anthem. The screen showed images of pyramids and cityscapes and coastlines, like postcards. People were hugging each other, running wildly back and forth to the balcony, their eyes glowing with tears and disbelief. Pierre loped past me to the TV room, his arms waving wildly. I was amazed a man so big and ungainly could move that fast. I followed and saw Pierre jumping up and down in front of the screen, the floorboards shaking with his mass. On the TV was Omar Sulaiman, the intelligence chief whom Mubarak had appointed as vice president the week before. Sulaiman's face looked ghastly, liver-spotted, almost a death mask, as he announced that the president had ceded his powers to the military. A severe-looking man in uniform stood just behind him.

I ran down the darkened stairwell, taking the steps four at a time. In the street, a man running past almost knocked me down, screaming at the top of his lungs, "Our freedom! Our freedom!" A few yards away another man, dressed in laborer's clothes, arrived at the edge of the square on Talaat Harb Street and dropped to his hands and knees, kissing the filthy asphalt. A young girl in a head scarf leapt onto a car and began shaking her hips in an ecstatic dance. The crowds in the square were surging around wildly, as if drunk; I felt my body being tossed violently as I struggled in vain to get through. Finally I turned back around. A tank was parked at the corner of Talaat Harb Street, and people began to crowd all around it in a wild throng, chanting, "The army, the people, are one hand!" The three soldiers on top of the tank looked down nervously, clutching their rifles, as if waiting for orders. I ran back to Pierre's place and bolted up the stairs again. Magdy Ashour, a Muslim Brotherhood man, was standing near the balcony in an army surplus jacket, smiling. "We came out of the grave at last," he said. "It's a beautiful step. But it's just the start." Khalid Abol Naga, the actor, walked up, his handsome face beaming, and hugged Ashour. Next to them, a group of people were dancing in a circle, their arms linked, chanting, "The people, at last, have defeated the regime!"

A few feet away, in Pierre's living room, I found the mother of Khaled Saeed, the young man murdered by the police in Alexandria. Leyla Saeed had become a kind of grande dame of the revolution, and now that it had succeeded, people were paying homage to her. She stood by the television, a rosy-cheeked sixty-seven-year-old woman in a black head scarf and purple shawl, clutching a furry white pillow with an image of her dead son on it. Her face was wet with tears. A young man kneeled down and kissed her hand. Someone else rushed up and handed her a cell phone. It was Wael Ghoneim on the line, the young Google executive who had set up the "We are all Khaled Saeed" website. She clutched the phone to her ear, walked slowly out the French door to the balcony, and broke into sobs again as she spoke to Ghoneim. Night had fallen, and fireworks were shooting up from Tahrir Square, exploding in bright pink and green showers and illuminating the tall minaret of the Omar Makram mosque. I sat down with a group of blissed-out protesters at the feet of Leyla Saeed and her brother, Ali Muhammad al Saeed. Leyla said she wished her son could be there. Her brother looked at the young people around him and said, "The older generation have done nothing for you. We're dwarves by comparison.

We're here to celebrate your revolution and kiss the ground beneath your feet."

On that night, as protesters stumbled giddily homeward through a morass of honking horns and waving Egyptian flags, silent detonations were taking place in the consciousness of Arabs everywhere. Tahrir had already been filtering into their minds for weeks, but success made it a thousand times more potent. The square was now a vanguard in a movement with no borders.

On the morning after Mubarak fell, people wandered through the rubble of Tahrir Square with dazed smiles, as if they still couldn't quite believe it. The day was hazy and calm, to suit the dreamlike mood. There were Egyptian flags everywhere, and troops of families with children paraded through, gazing at the disheveled tents and trash-strewn pavement in wonder. A few protesters had begun sweeping the streets and picking up broken paving stones, an effort that was as much camera-ready symbol as reality. Dust clouds rose from brooms into the still air, forming illusory mountains before settling earthward again. Someone had put up a phony road construction sign: PLEASE EXCUSE THE DISTURBANCE, WE ARE BUILDING EGYPT. The whole country went on holiday. It had been the same in Tunis after Ben Ali fled. There was a period of collective disbelief. Slim Amamou, a dissident Tunisian blogger, found he'd been named a cabinet minister just days after being released from prison. He continued tweeting from inside cabinet meetings. One of his posts was about a yogurt he had just bought. Its expiration date was longer than the four weeks it took to carry out the revolution. "The most rapid revolution in history," he wrote. "Because we are connected. Synchronized."

Even months later, the Tahrir moment could still extend rays of warm feeling into the darkness, rekindling the sense of unity among once and future enemies. In late April, I spent an afternoon talking about the revolution at an outdoor café by the Nile with six leading members of the Gamaa Islamiya, the radical Islamist group whose members waged a brutal insurgency during the 1990s that left almost a thousand people dead. One of them had been the group's military commander. Another was a son of the "Blind Sheikh," Omar Abdel Rahman, who is now serving a life sentence in North Carolina for a plot to blow up New York landmarks. These men, in long beards and galabiyas, had renounced violence, but they were all Salafi Muslims. So I was a little surprised that along with them was a younger, beardless man with a tattoo. I asked him when he had joined the Gamaa. He looked back at me incredulously. "Me? Join the Gamaa Islamiya?" he said. "I'm a liberal. I'm very liberal. I am corrupt! *I'm a DJ!*"

Everyone broke up laughing at that, even the old guys, their beards jiggling with mirth over their potbellies. For a moment I felt sure they were going to pull off their beards and wigs and reveal the whole setup as a Monty Python–style sketch. But no, this young clubgoing hipster was good friends with the holy warriors. It turned out they'd fought the cops together in Tahrir. When I asked about their time in the square, the Gamaa guys looked at me earnestly. "What we witnessed those days, it was more like a holy scene than a human scene." Another one piped up: "What we witnessed there confirmed our rejection of violence, and our belief that the voice of the revolution is higher than the voice of bullets." The DJ nodded sagely. He said he'd been with the Gamaa men during the Battle of the Camel, the square's most violent moment. "I'll be honest, I never thought I'd even talk to people from the Gamaa Islamiya," he said. "I thought they're terrorists, and that's it. But we spent that whole day together, protecting each other, protecting the square, and I got to know Hassan here. When he told me he was with the Gamaa, I said, 'What? Are they all like you?' And I met with the rest of them. That was when I realized, we're not so different at all." The Gamaa men grinned, and one of them slapped hands with the DJ.

But those moments were increasingly rare. The feelings of trust were giving way to something else, something undefinable at first. The changes had begun only a few days after the square's great victory. It was the liberal bourgeoisie who felt it first: a shiver of anxiety, a foreboding. These were the people who had trumpeted so proudly the apparent secularism of this revolt, its unifying language of civic rights and decency. Again and again, they'd pointed to the absence of Islamist slogans during the protests. They took it for proof of Alaa Aswany's proclamations at his weekly salon: the Muslim Brotherhood, he said, was "nothing but a scarecrow fabricated by the regime." Surely it would fade away now that its oppressor was gone. Surely democracy, like a scouring burst of sun, would cleanse those backward religious loyalties and leave only citizens standing in the light, with nothing left to divide them. Surely the liberals were Egypt's true majority.

They knew in their guts it wasn't true. The Islamists were there, all right. They were the ones who'd made the uprising succeed, with their numbers, their discipline, their bravery under attack. It was true they hadn't chanted their own slogans in Tahrir. They had linked hands with the liberals, they had hushed the zealots in their ranks and declared the uprising a national cause. But that wasn't because they'd transformed into secularists overnight. It was a matter of calculated self-restraint. They didn't want to give the regime an excuse to strike them (no one would complain if you just threw some Islamists in jail). They were hiding in plain sight, using the liberals as cover. And now, for the first time in sixty years, they had no more reason to hide. The Muslim Brotherhood's followers were just beginning to wake up to the extent of their power. Its leaders were emerging from prison. Within a few weeks, almost all of them would be out, these bearded, devout men blinking at the unfamiliar sun and reckoning with a depth of freedom they had never really expected. It would not be long before they began translating that freedom into Islamist victories at the ballot box and leading Egypt into an era of confrontation that would test the legacy of Tahrir Square.

2

— Revenge (Libya) —

One night, months after the revolution had declared victory and the Leader was dead, Jalal Ragai drove me over to his house with a group of his men. It was dim and cluttered, a den of dusty black couches and tables littered with cups and ashtrays. I sat on the floor with half a dozen members of Jalal's brigade. Jalal set his laptop on the edge of the couch and turned off all the lights. The screen glowed blue, and suddenly we were looking at a small, empty room with a brown leather desk and a chair. You couldn't tell if it was day or night. This was the interrogation room in Yarmouk prison, where Jalal and his men—some of them now sitting next to me in the darkness—had been held a year earlier. Their jailers had recorded everything. This, Jalal had told me, was irrefutable evidence of the regime's crimes. A prisoner in a white blindfold appeared on-screen, arms tied behind his back, and was shoved into the chair. A voice behind the camera began interrogating him: "Who gave you the money? What were their names?" A Nokia cell phone ring could be heard in the background. The prisoner was taken off-camera, and then a horrifying electronic buzzing sound could be heard, accompanied by moans and screams of pain. The torture prod.

"They almost killed us in that room," Jalal said.

The video continued. A slim, dark-skinned guard entered the torture room, carrying a tray of coffee. He had a look of bored arrogance on his face. He sipped his coffee casually as the electric torture prod buzzed and the prisoner screamed. Occasionally the guard—his name was Jumaa—joined in to kick the prisoner hard in the ribs or call him a dog. His presence there seemed extraneous; he came and went, apparently joining in the beatings for the sheer pleasure of it. Jalal clicked onto another video segment. In this one, Jumaa and two other guards were kicking and beating a blindfolded prisoner with extraordinary ferocity. "Kill me, Ibrahim, kill me!" the prisoner screamed again and again. "I don't want to live anymore, kill me!" The man he was talking to was Ibrahim Lousha, whom I already knew by reputation as the most notorious torturer at the Yarmouk prison, a man who had killed dozens of prisoners and forced the living to drink his own urine. Ibrahim's voice could be heard, saying, "Do you love the Leader?" The prisoner replied frantically, "Yes, yes!"

Yet another video showed a handcuffed man whose body looked twisted and broken, speaking in a shaky voice. Jalal then showed a still photo of the same man—after the revolution—lying dead on the ground, facedown, his hands bound. Another still shot, this one of a blackened corpse. "This man was covered with oil, we think, and then burned," Jalal said.

So it went, a series of appalling scenes of torture, interrupted by comments: "That guy survived and is living in Zleetin" or "That guy died in the hangar." But Jalal and his friends, including those who had been in the prison with him, were so used to this kind of horror that they spent half the time laughing. At one point, Jalal pointed to the wall behind the blindfolded prisoner's head, where a rack of keys could be seen. "Hey, look, on the end, those are the keys to my car!" he said. "I'm serious!" He and his friends cracked up and could not stop, the helpless peals of laughter filling the room. Later, Jumaa appeared on the screen grinning raucously and doing a little mock-sensual dance behind the terrified prisoner. To me, Jumaa's dance was sickening, but Jalal and his friends found it so funny that they replayed it again and again, clapping their hands and doubling over with laughter. Driving home that night, a friend offered me an old expression: *Ash sharr al baliyya ma yadhak*, which means, more or less, "It's the depth of the affliction that makes you laugh."

This was early 2012, a year after the uprisings started. Some of the torturers on that videotape were now themselves prisoners and were being kept in the basement of Jalal's new command headquarters, a former military training facility on the edge of Tripoli, Libya's capital. They were now at the daily mercy of the same men they had tortured. The process of interrogation was being reversed. But there were no working courts yet to hear the evidence, no laws to hold them to account. Jalal and his men were a kind of living experiment: Was it possible to overthrow an Arab dictator without falling into the same destructive cycle of brutality and revenge?

The same could be said about all the Arab uprisings, from Tunisia to Yemen. Clan solidarity and the tradition of blood feuds posed real challenges to any kind of transition. But the problem took its rawest form in Libya. Qaddafi left his countrymen with a void: no army, no police, no unions, nothing to bring them together. Rebels like Jalal and his men started out in 2011 as liberators who hoped to restore law and order, but soon they became a law unto themselves. It was up to them to decide whether their country became something more than an archipelago of feuding warlords.

The Libyan protests started on February 15, 2011, four days after Mubarak's fall. As in Egypt and Tunisia, the plans for peaceful demonstrations had spread via Facebook. In Benghazi, the largest city in eastern Libya, people gathered to demand the release of a detained lawyer. But Qaddafi had been watching al Jazeera with everyone else, and he knew where this was headed. The protesters were met with truncheons, and then with bullets; they picked up weapons almost at once. Within three days, the rebels had driven Qaddafi's forces out and laid claim to almost half the country. Reporters and aid workers and exiled Libyans began pouring across the open border with Egypt, where there was no one to greet you but long-haired young men waving the rebel flag.

When I arrived in Benghazi on the afternoon of February 23, the city was still drunk on victory. Crowds of people were chanting slogans outside the city's main courthouse, a stack of gray cinder-block buildings on the seafront corniche. The wind whipped a cold sea spray off the Mediterranean into our faces, but no one seemed to notice. This was ground zero of the revolt, the headquarters of the new provisional rebel government. Young men in red military berets strode around with tags on their chests, their faces glowing with zeal. "By God, Libyans were afraid to say Qaddafi's name before, and now they are fighting him," one of the rebels told me. "This is a good thing." Ad hoc municipal committees were meeting in rooms once used for trials and interrogations; paper signs hung on the doors stating their new purpose. The walls were covered with fresh graffiti lampooning Qaddafi. Passing cars were honking their horns in celebration. It had been raining for days—the rebels called it a sign of divine approval—and now vast puddles in the muddy streets reflected an operatic evening sky, with storm clouds rolling away to reveal bright stars over the sea. Libya is mostly desert, but in the east you can stumble on landscapes of unexpected lushness and beauty: forests of juniper and pine, and red-earth hills strewn with Roman ruins overlooking the Mediterranean.

I walked a few blocks from the courthouse and was amazed by the damage. There were burned and bullet-riddled buildings everywhere, the marks of a brief but total war. The center of the fighting had been the city's main military base, a castlelike building with high walls. Everyone called it the Katiba, brigade. The wall had been toppled into rubble in two places, and men and boys were wandering through the grounds, staring in wonder at burned-out military trucks and abandoned cars. Some told me they were there to search for relatives who had disappeared years before in the maze of Qaddafi's prisons. One old man grabbed my arm and shouted, "Before, to see this place was to die. Now it is ours."

Everywhere I went in Benghazi, people seemed to be stumbling around in a state of awe, as if they were only now discovering the true face of the country where they had lived their entire lives. The collapse of Qaddafi's regime had exposed an unknown world of walled military compounds, torture rooms, palaces, and farms belonging to the Leader and his gang. Protesters had burned and destroyed almost all of them, every police station, every jail, every security branch—and there were so many: external security, internal security, national security, intelligence. On my second day in the city I met a gap-toothed twenty-eight-year-old man named Osama al Fitory. He was an unemployed accountant, and had been among the first Facebook protesters on February 15, when the revolt started. He had a clownish, affectionate smile, and he spoke in a rapid-fire stream of anecdotes and jokes that was impossible to keep up with; it was as if a decade of dammed-up words had just been unleashed.

Osama came from a family that—like many in Benghazi—had hated Qaddafi passionately for generations. His grandfather had been a wealthy businessman whose fortune had been destroyed by the Leader's quasi-Marxist economic policies. "One day in 1984, my grandfather had a big shipment coming into the port in Benghazi," Osama told me. "The revolutionary committee confiscated all of it and started selling it in government markets. My grandfather heard about it, and he died later that day." The family had once also owned several shops and apartment buildings. But starting in the 1970s, Qaddafi introduced a principle from his revolutionary *Green Book* known as *al bayt li sakinihi*, the house to its resident. Anyone renting or using a property instantly became its owner. Squatters took over the al Fitory family properties, and the revolutionary committees took their shops. One Benghazi businessman I met described, weeping, how he had been jailed and tortured for months while Qaddafi's auditors checked his books for signs of theft or self-dealing. They found none. "After that we kept a very low profile," the businessman told me.

The ostensible goal of Qaddafi's *Green Book* was to create an egalitarian society where the ills of capitalism would vanish and the people would govern themselves, free of the fallacy of Western-style representative democracy. In practice, all the privileges were transferred to members of the revolutionary committees, who become an unacknowledged ruling class in Qaddafi's delusional Jamahiriya, or Republic of the Masses. Everyone in Libya knew who these revolutionary committee leaders were and where they lived. Vigilante mobs had formed quickly, though most of their big targets had already fled to join the Leader in Tripoli. Driving through downtown Benghazi, I noticed a burned building in a residential district. I asked if it was another police station. "No," said Osama, "that is Huda's house." Huda bin Amer, he explained, was the leader of the Revolutionary Committee in Benghazi and one of Qaddafi's most feared lieutenants. She had come to prominence in 1984, at a public hanging of several men accused of plotting to kill Qaddafi. As one of the dying men jiggled on the end of his rope, Huda—everyone knows her by her first name—rushed up and pulled on his legs, to dispatch him more quickly. No one could document that this story took place, but it is told universally and has become part of her public persona. She is famous for having coined the phrase, "We don't want talk, we want hangings in the public square."

On the road again, we passed Benghazi's main theater; someone had written on it in big letters, QADDAFI: THE THEATRICS ARE OVER. Osama chuckled as he reeled off the new revolutionary calendar Qaddafi had invented to go with his brave new world. January became Ayannar (Where's the fire?), May became Ma' (Water), August became Hannibal (as in the Carthaginian general). Osama recited all twelve months. Even ordinary words like "shop" and "embassy" were replaced by the Leader's populist neologisms: madina, for instance, the word for city, became shaabiya. (These do not seem to have caught on with ordinary Libyans.) Osama grew more and more animated as he cataloged Qaddafi's eccentricities, as if he were only now discovering the outrageousness of it all. "We are all asking ourselves, how could this happen? Who is this man?" he said. "You listen to him talk, and you can't believe he's sane. Sometimes he talks like a heretic. Me, I think he's crazy or took too much drugs. You watch TV, and he talks for seventy-five minutes nonstop, shouting at the top of his lungs. He covers every subject—magic, health, religion, politics—and not a single sentence makes sense!" Later, when I pressed him with more questions about Qaddafi, Osama looked over at me with a weary smile and said, "Stop trying to make sense of us. We don't even understand ourselves."

Other Libyans I met expressed the same sense of dawning outrage, as if the collapse of Qaddafi's authority had tilted their perspective on everything. The fear of surveillance and spies—a constant of Libyan life—had lifted, and now people seemed to be allowing themselves to feel things they had long kept sheltered inside. One businessman described a video shown on state television a few years earlier, in which Qaddafi is seen waiting in a long line at a bank to apply for a housing loan. When the Leader reaches the teller, he is turned down. "How does he have the audacity to show this?" the businessman said, his eyes suddenly wild with anger. "Does he really expect people to believe this dictator waits in lines at banks?"

Symbols of Qaddafi and his family provoked the greatest fury. Near the airport on the edge of town, soldiers took Osama and me to see one of the Leader's palaces. It looked as if a tornado had blown through it. Shattered glass lay everywhere, upturned plants and broken chairs and bloodstains littered the pale marble floors. Qaddafi's men had abandoned the place just before Benghazi fell to the rebels, escaping on a plane. Now it lay empty and silent, with the warm afternoon light falling in through cathedral-high ceilings: a cryptic remnant of the Leader's madness. "This is where he kept his whores," one of the soldiers said. He led us through to a bedroom where knotted piles of brightly colored women's clothes lay on the carpet, with prescription-drug bottles and playing cards and perfume and cigarettes. Farther on was a bedroom with a vast bed frame, its headboard decorated in Louis Farouk–style gold tracery and plump silk cushions.

On the following morning, Osama and I drove west to follow the rebel fighters heading for the front, in a trash-strewn desert landscape that looked like a scene from *Road Warrior*. Men of all ages were riding battered pickup trucks and taxis, howling and firing their pistols and rifles at the sky. Some had heavy antiaircraft guns that shook the ground. At a staging point near the town of Ajdabiya, I found teenagers making Molotov cocktails and civilian mechanics repairing machine guns as they prepared to ride into battle. Others kneeled on the ground with belts of ammunition draped over their chests, Rambo style, and prostrated themselves in prayer. One of the curious things about the Libyan uprising was the lack of any visible political or religious affiliation among the rebels. Qaddafi had suppressed political life so thoroughly that it had yet to reemerge. There were Islamists, of course, but few of them advertised their loyalties in the revolt's early days.

When I first got to Brega that morning, Qaddafi's air force had just bombed the area. I got out of the car and ran forward to get a look at the damage. There was a huge crater in the red sand next to the highway. A group of young rebels was squinting up at the sky for signs of a returning bomber. They seemed daunted, for the first time. Most of them barely knew which end of a gun the bullet came from. Now, they seemed to realize, they were up against a modern army. A few days later, the whole wild-haired rebel juggernaut reversed itself, the pickup trucks and motorcycles roaring back along that same road, the triumphant shouting transformed into terror. By March 19, Qaddafi's men had pushed the rebels all the way back to Benghazi and were on the verge of retaking the city when the first French fighter jets appeared in the sky.

That was the war's turning point. For the first time since the Arab uprisings began, the West had stepped in with force instead of just words. NATO's military intervention was meant to be about no-fly zones and the prevention of war crimes, a "responsibility to protect," as the UN diplomats put it. It was more than that, and everyone knew it. The governments of France and the United States had signed Qaddafi's death warrant. The Arab League had given the operation its blessing, perhaps because Qaddafi had earned so many enemies over the years. The spokesmen of the Libyan rebel coalition had persuaded Nicolas Sarkozy and Hillary Clinton that they bore the responsibility of preventing a genocide. Mustafa Abdel Jalil, the meek-faced chairman of the Libyan National Transitional Council, was the kind of man who made you believe in the Libyan cause.

The rebels in Benghazi went wild all over again when news of the NATO intervention came through. People began flying French and

American flags. The air strikes crippled Qaddafi's air force and prevented him from bombing the rebels into submission. They also pushed Qaddafi's forces back into the desert. But NATO could not destroy Qaddafi's regime from the air, and the rebel army—weaker and more disorganized than anyone had realized—was incapable of finishing the job. So the civil war ground on for months. The most brutal fighting was in Misrata, on the coast east of Tripoli, where Qaddafi's columns surrounded the city with tanks and pounded it with mortars for weeks in March and April. The local people were reduced to using hand-tooled weapons, in street-to-street fighting that left parts of the city reduced to rubble. Tripoli, where the rebels had been crushed early on, was a weird island of calm, with Qaddafi organizing rallies of flag-waving loyalists and promising—as he had from the start of the rebellion—to destroy the "rats" who had dared to challenge him. By early summer, people had begun to use the word "quagmire." Even with daily rounds of NATO air strikes, the rebellion lagged.

The problem was partly the same one that had dogged Libya for a century: it was not a country. The three Ottoman provinces of Cyrenaica, Tripolitania, and Fezzan had never been yoked together until the Italians invaded in 1911 with the goal of building a colony. Three decades of intermittent war followed, as the Italians inflicted the world's first aerial bombings. It left a third of the Libyan population dead. Even King Idris, who was drafted by Britain to govern Libya after World War II, seemed to view the country as an implausible mash-up and rarely visited Tripoli. Qaddafi overthrew him in 1969, and in a sense, he both created modern Libya and destroyed it. The people who rose up against him in 2011 fought city by city, militia by militia, neighborhood by neighborhood. There was no collective effort. By the time the rebels began massing for their assault on Tripoli in August of that year, the experience of war had helped to create new bonds among Libyans. But that solidarity was an entirely local matter.

When I first met Jalal Ragai, the Tripoli militia leader, he had been out of jail only a few days. It was August 2011, and the battle for Tripoli was still on. He had formed his own militia, and he and his men were already searching for the Qaddafi loyalists who had tortured them and murdered many of their friends and relatives during their months in the Yarmouk prison. I asked him what he would do when he caught them. "We will detain them," he said. "We will interrogate them." Then his face lurched into a big, undisciplined smile. "We will treat them better than they treated us, God willing."

We were standing on the second floor of the reclaimed military-training building, which was in Tajoura, an eastern suburb of Tripoli. Jalal was short and powerfully built, dressed in ill-fitting fatigues, with a thick, bushy beard and a machine gun strapped across his back. He had about seventy men under his command, and the way they treated him made clear that they held him in high esteem. But he didn't exude the air of a commander. His hair was a mess, and his eyes seemed to lurch around the room as if he were drunk. He apologized for his appearance, saying he had scarcely slept in days. At one point, he took out a passport-size photo and passed it to me. "This is me when I was a normal person," he said. It was almost unrecognizable: a smiling, well-groomed man in a button-down shirt.

Jalal had decided to join the rebels in March 2011, shortly after the initial protests in Tripoli had been brutally put down. He was a manufacturer of uniforms for Qaddafi's army. His work involved spending lots of time hanging around with die-hard loyalists, but it didn't really bother him. He thought the battle against Qaddafi was one for his children to fight. He saw no hope that anything could change in his own lifetime. Then, after the uprising started, he watched videos of people dying in the streets in Benghazi and began to feel guilty. He started small, with Facebook campaigns and spray-painting. Eventually he began importing pistols and rifles from Tunisia. At the same time, he kept on socializing with military commanders, telling them fervently how much he hated the rebels, praising the *Green Book*, and quietly pressing them for information about battle plans and weapons depots. He wasn't sure how much the information was worth, but he forwarded it to members of the rebel government in Benghazi. He told me he provided information to al Jazeera and other satellite channels, and that he deliberately exaggerated regime losses and rebel gains; he was lying to everyone. He laughed when he told me this. "I was copying Qaddafi's own personality, his acts," he told me. "It was crazy."

They caught him in June, as he was on his way to meet a contact for a weapons deal: two men sidled up and poked their gun barrels into his ribs. The beatings started the moment they shoved him into their car. They got worse once the officers took him to Yarmouk, the makeshift detention center just outside of Tripoli. The guards were often drunk or stoned, and seemed to enjoy the torture. Not just beatings but also mind games: telling a prisoner he was to be freed, and then at the last minute throwing him back into the shed. Much of the beating was carried out by women, a special humiliation for Arab men. One of them was a big Chadian woman with a shaved head who beat the men on their genitals. Jalal quickly gained a reputation in that hell for bravery and generosity. "The guards used to throw water bottles at a group of prisoners, and they'd grab and fight over them," another prisoner told me. "Jalal would catch the bottles and share them with other prisoners." Jalal was lucky in the end. He was transferred out of the overcrowded shed to a smaller annex a quarter of a mile away, on the grounds of a construction company. He was there when the battle for Tripoli began, and the guards—abandoned by their commanders—shot and killed six of the prisoners before giving up and fleeing. Jalal had talked his way out of his cell that morning and then freed the remaining men, who climbed over the gate and began walking back toward Tripoli. Jalal borrowed a car from a man he met near the jail, and within hours he had started forming his brigade.

When I met Jalal, he and his men were on their way back to Yarmouk. There was still fighting going on in pockets of the city, and there was a strange atmosphere of fear and elation; young men roared down the boulevards in pickup trucks firing their AK-47s, and you weren't always sure whose side they were on. We drove through areas that had been regime controlled until a day or two earlier, and reached a huge military base that had been the headquarters of the 32nd brigade, commanded by Qaddafi's youngest son, Khamis. A gigantic "32" loomed over the castlelike front gate of the gray concrete building. It was late morning, already fiercely hot, and as we got out of the car and walked to a smaller gate on the opposite side of the road, there was a peculiar smell.

We walked into a courtyard, and instantly the smell rose into a gag-inducing stench. This was the Yarmouk prison block. Several bodies lay on the dusty ground, already slightly bloated, the blood pooled around them now dark and dry. They wore uniforms, and one of them had his hands bound behind his back. I heard a commotion from the far side of the compound, ten yards away, and one of the men with me said, "The prison we were held in was over there." It was hardly a prison. It looked more like a tin shack for chickens. The metal was dark with rust or burn, and as I approached the open door I saw a thin trail of whitish smoke rising from the inside. I peered into the darkness, and as my eyes focused I realized I was staring at skulls. There were dozens of them, some shattered, with jaws piled on top of ribs and femurs and the snakelike curl of spines. The bowl-shaped bones of a pelvis lay here and there, a hand or finger or foot, all of them bleached white and piled over a carpet of ash and a few black objects that appeared to be burned-out tires.

There had been 150 men crowded into that shed; only about 15 had survived. Some of them were standing around me, sobbing and doubling over in anguish. One of them told me about the dead: a group of teenagers, a pair of brothers, an imam who'd led them all in prayer. He told me how the guards had thrown grenades into the shed through an open window and then raked the men repeatedly with machine guns. The prisoners were so tightly packed that when the grenades struck, falling bodies formed a kind of blanket and saved some men from death. The guards took a break to reload, and the survivors dug themselves out, their clothes soaked with blood. One of the guards had left a door open, and he told them to run. They did, leaping over a low wall at the edge of the compound and then sprinting between houses and farms as bullets sliced into the soft soil around them.

The survivors of that massacre, and their relatives, formed the nucleus of Jalal's militia. Like the other armed groups in Libya, they preferred to call it a *katiba*, a brigade. In the months that followed, they focused on one mission: hunting down and capturing the men who had imprisoned them. They did not bother to join the hunt for Qaddafi, which went on for two more months. They did not stop after the Leader was found hiding in a drainpipe on October 20, shorn of the loyalists who had protected him until the end. Qaddafi's last moments—captured, like so much else, on video—seemed to bring the rest of the world up short. There was no way to disguise this as "transitional justice." The clips showed a young rebel ramming a knife up Qaddafi's ass. Later, he was shoved onto the hood of a car, his face and body covered with blood. He stumbled forward, seeming to beg for mercy, as the men around him shouted "Allahu Akbar" again and again. In the next clip, his lifeless body was dragged through the yellow dust. This was revenge in its rawest form, and it did not bode well for Libya.

By the spring of 2012, Libya still had no government. It had no army. These things existed on paper, but in practice, the country had not begun to recover from Qaddafi's rule. Rebels had spray-painted CHANGE THE COLOR on all the walls painted Qaddafi's signature green, as if that alone could somehow jump-start the creation of a new state. As one Libyan wag put it to me, Qaddafi's crackpot dream of radical democracy had finally been achieved: Libyans were governing themselves. Police were almost nonexistent. Streetlights in Tripoli blinked red and green, and were universally ignored. Sewage treatment plants sat abandoned; the muck flowed straight into the Mediterranean. Residents carted their own garbage to Qaddafi's ruined stronghold, Bab al-Aziziya, and dumped it there: the piles had grown mountainous and the stench overpowering. What Libya did have was militias, more than sixty of them. Each exercised unfettered authority over its turf, with "revolutionary legitimacy" as the only warrant.

The first thing you saw as you approached Jalal's militia base was a bullet-scarred bus—almost a holy relic—that was used as a shield by rebels during the first protests in Tripoli in 2011. Across a patch of waste ground was an ugly run-down building made mostly of cinder blocks. On its second floor was a long hallway, the walls of which were covered with pictures of those who died at the Yarmouk prison during the fall of Tripoli. One of them appeared twice: a man with a youthful, sensitive face, framed by rimless glasses and pale gray hair. This was Omar Salhoba, a forty-two-year-old doctor who was shot and killed on August 24, more than two days after Tripoli fell. He was revered at Yarmouk for his insistence on treating injured fellow prisoners and his brave, failed efforts to break the men free. Omar's older brother Nasser was now the brigade's chief interrogator. He was lean and wiry, with a taut face and dark eyes that seemed fixed in a wistful expression. When I met him, he was sitting in his office, a spare room with peeling paint and a battered desk with files stacked on it. He wore jeans and a blue-and-white button-down shirt, and he nervously chain-smoked. "I never left this place for the first three and a half months after we started," he told me just after we met. "It's only recently that I started sleeping at my apartment again."

It was not the first time Nasser had lost a brother to Qaddafi. In 1996, he was in training to be a police investigator, his boyhood dream, when his brother Adel was gunned down in a Tripoli soccer stadium. The fans had dared to boo Saadi el-Qaddafi, the dictator's son and the sponsor of a local team, and Saadi's guards opened fire, killing at least twenty people. When the Salhoba family was told they could not collect Adel's body unless they signed a form stating that he was a *mushaghib*, a hooligan, Nasser went straight to the Interior Ministry headquarters and confronted officials there, an unthinkable act of defiance. "I was furious," he told me. "I started waving my gun around and shouting." Guards quickly subdued him, and though they allowed him to go home that night, he soon got wind of his impending arrest. On his family's advice, Nasser fled to Malta, where he stayed for seven years, earning a meager living by smuggling cigarettes and falling into drinking and drugs. Even after he returned to Libya, his rampage at the Interior Ministry kept him blacklisted, and he could not find steady work. It was his little brother Omar, now a successful pediatrician with two young daughters, who kept him going, lending him money and urging him to clean up his act.

Then came the revolution. And while Nasser waited it out, cynical as ever, Omar—the family's frail idealist—risked his life by sending thousands of dollars' worth of medical supplies to the rebels. On June 7, Omar was operating on a sick child at his Tripoli clinic when two intelligence agents arrived and bundled him into a car. No one knew where he had been taken. More than two months later, on August 24, Nasser got a call telling him Omar had been shot in the Yarmouk prison. Gun battles were still raging in the streets, and Nasser searched for more than a day before a rebel showed him a picture of his brother's bloodied body. Muslim ritual requires bodies to be buried quickly, and Nasser drove to a military hospital, frantically holding up the picture, until a doctor told him that Omar's body had been sent to a local mosque to be buried. Nasser found the mosque and reached the grave-yard just minutes after the body had been sealed into a cement tomb. He reached out his hand and touched the tomb: the mortar was still wet. "I feel so bad I wasn't able to save him," Nasser told me more than once. "My brother was the special one in the family. I could never be compared to him."

The three men responsible for Omar's death were all now living in the basement of the militia base. The executioner was a twenty-eight-year-old named Marwan Gdoura. It was Marwan who insisted on speaking to the Yarmouk commander that morning, even though most of Tripoli had fallen to the rebels. It was Marwan who shot Omar and the other five victims first; the other two guards fired only after he had emptied two clips from his AK-47. I learned all this over the course of my conversations with them in the brigade jail. They were perfectly open about their roles at Yarmouk, though they spoke in soft, penitent tones, saying they had tortured and killed only on orders.

When I asked Nasser about his own interrogations of Marwan, he stepped wordlessly out the door of his office. Scarcely a minute later, he reappeared with Marwan, a slim young man in a gray tracksuit. Mar-wan sat down on a chair, leaning forward, his hands clasped in front of him. He had small, narrow-set eyes, a thin beard, and monkish dark hair cut close to the head. His gaze was direct but meek, and I could see nothing vicious in his face or manner. The rebels had already told me that Marwan was very devout and spent most of his time praying or reading the Koran. I asked about his background and then moved to the events of August 24, when Nasser's brother and the other five men were executed. Marwan spoke softly but without hesitation. "One thing is very clear," he said. "You're a soldier, you must obey orders. At that moment, if you say no, you will be considered a traitor and added to the victims. And if you don't do the execution, others will." Nasser smoked quietly as Marwan spoke, glancing at him now and then with a look of professional detachment.

Marwan explained that the Yarmouk commander, a man named Hamza Hirazi, had ordered him by phone to execute six prisoners, including Omar and several officers who had been arrested for helping the rebels. "We brought them from the hangar and put them in a small room," he said when I pressed him for details. "The killing happened with a light weapon. We closed the door and left." Marwan did not tell me what others had: that in the last moments before the bullets ripped into his body, Omar turned and made a final plea: "Marwan, remember God."

Marwan then narrated his final month as a Qaddafi loyalist: hours after the execution, he had fled with about two hundred soldiers under Khamis Qaddafi. The convoy had run into rebels, and Khamis had been killed in a gun battle. The loyalists fled to the city of Bani Waleed, where Saif al Islam Qaddafi was receiving condolences for his brother's death in a military barracks. "I won't lie to you, I shook his hand and kissed him," Marwan told me. After camping out in an olive grove for a few days, a dwindling band of loyalists drove south to the city of Sabha. Men were deserting and driving home every day, Marwan said. But he stayed until there were only five or six loyalists left, in a farmhouse outside Sabha. It was only when a truck full of well-armed rebels attacked the farmhouse that he fled into the desert. He hid out until dark and then made his way to a nearby town, where he caught a minibus northward, dressed in civilian clothes. A day later, he arrived back at his hometown of Sirman, not far from Tripoli. I asked him why he had stayed with Qaddafi's forces for so long. "I wanted to go home all along, but I had no car," he said.

This seemed hard to believe. I was reminded of what some of

Marwan's fellow prisoners had told me: that he was the true Qaddafi loyalist among the guards. All the others had gone home on the day of the massacre. Marwan was the one who insisted on standing firm and on carrying out the orders to kill the six prisoners. Some of the other prisoners said they resented him and blamed him for their fate. Naji, another guard, had even told me he now wished he had killed Marwan, to prevent him from carrying out the executions.

Nasser was now staring at Marwan, his eyes narrowed, through a cloud of cigarette smoke.

"During all that month after Tripoli fell, did you think about the six people you executed?" he said.

"I did think about them, and also about the prisoners who were killed and burned in the hangar," Marwan replied.

"But this was different, you executed these six people yourself," Nasser said. "Did you talk about it with the other soldiers?"

"No," Marwan replied quietly. There was a long pause. Nasser looked away, as if he felt he ought to stop, and then turned back toward Marwan.

"You say you followed orders. Suppose I get an order to do the same thing to you. Should I do it?"

Marwan stared down at the coffee table in front of him, a chastened look on his face.

Later, after Marwan had gone back downstairs, Nasser explained that he still found him an enigma. "I've asked him repeatedly why and how," he said. "I've talked to him alone and in groups. Marwan told me one can't truly understand it unless one goes through the same experience." I asked Nasser if he believed Marwan truly felt remorse, as he said he did. Nasser grimaced and shook his head slowly. Not long ago, he said, Marwan had gone out of his way to avoid stepping on a portrait of Qaddafi that had been placed in a doorway (the rebels all relish stomping on it). He apparently thought no one was watching. "I was furious, I beat him with the *falga*," Nasser said. "It was the only time I've ever done that. To think that he still feels that way after all this time, that he would kill all of us here if he could."

Nasser went on. "What's the definition of revenge? To make the family of the person who did it feel like my family. I could have killed Marwan at any time, nobody would have known. But I don't want to betray the blood of our martyrs. We want a country of laws."

One evening at the brigade headquarters, Nasser and Jalal allowed me to sit with them during one of their investigation meetings. The two men sat on a couch smoking, looking through a packet of documents sent by someone who wanted them to arrest a Qaddafi-era figure. These kinds of letters still arrived at the rate of two or three a week. Jalal explained, "When there's something substantial on the person, we go and get him." They sifted through the papers, and at one point Jalal handed me a photocopied clipping, written in French, from a Burkina Faso newspaper. "Does it say anything bad about him?" Jalal asked. The story was about a former ambassador named Abdel Nasser Saleh Younes. I translated the main points. As I did so, I had the uneasy feeling that my answer could decide whether they would go out into the night and grab this man from his home or put him into indefinite detention in the basement. "Nah," said Jalal finally. "I think this is just another person looking for revenge."

Nasser and Jalal said they were eager to hand over their prisoners as soon as there was a reliable government to take them. But they—and others—were keen to let me know that in a few cases, notorious killers have been turned over and then promptly released. Jalal, who was starting to develop political ambitions, seemed especially anxious to prove that he had solid reasons to hold on to his twelve prisoners. He had evidence that no one else had seen: the torture videotapes made by Qaddafi's jailers. He had taken them from the ransacked offices of Hamza Hirazi, the commander at Yarmouk.

By the time I watched those videotapes at Jalal's house, I had already met some of the men who appeared on the screen. It was strange to see the transformation: the men I talked to in the basement were all meek, apologetic, full of remorse. In the videotape, they had looks of bored arrogance on their faces. They did not recoil from the prisoners' pain at all. This jump in attitudes from past to present was hard for me to accept, but Jalal and his men mostly found it amusing. I once spent an hour listening to a group of rebels chat companionably with one of their own former guards at Yarmouk about the cruel beatings he'd given them with an industrial pipe. After his capture, the same pipe was used on him. Naji, a former guard, complained that one man had beaten him so hard the pipe broke. One of the rebels replied that the man in question had a ruptured disc from Naji's own prison beatings, so it was only fair. After a few more minutes of this surreal banter, the militia's deputy commander strolled into the room and gave Naji's palm a friendly slap. "Hey, Sheikh Naji," he said, "you got a letter." He opened it and began to read. "It's from your brother," he went on, and his face lit up in a derisive smile. "It says, 'Naji is being held by an illegal entity, being tortured on a daily basis, starved, and forced to sign false statements.' Oh, and look at this: the letter is copied to the army and the Higher Security Committee!" This last detail elicited a collective burst of laughter. Even Naji seemed to find it funny. "We always tell the relatives the same thing," one of the men added for my benefit. "There is no legal entity for us to hand the prisoners over to."

A few days after watching the torture videos, I went to see Ibrahim Lousha, the primary torturer who was visible on the videotape. He was being held by one of the brigades in Misrata, about two hours' drive from Tripoli, in a battered old government building. I was led to a big empty room and told to wait. I turned around, and suddenly there he was, looking like a mere child slumped in a chair. He wore gray sweatpants and a blue V-neck sweater and flip-flops. He had big eyes and a buzz cut, and a morose expression on his face, like a bored schoolboy. He sat with his hands together on his lap, his left leg bouncing restlessly. Misrata had become infamous for the torture of Qaddafi loyalists in recent months, but Ibrahim said he had been treated well. No one was monitoring us, aside from a bored-looking guard on the far side of the room.

He was twenty years old, he told me, the son of a Tripoli policeman. I asked him about the torture at Yarmouk, and he answered numbly: beatings, electricity, other methods. "We didn't give them water every day," he said. "We brought them piss." Whose piss? I asked. "Our piss.

In bottles. Also, we gave them a Muammar poster and made them pray on it." I asked him if he was ordered to do these things. He said no, that he and the fellow guards came up with these ideas while drinking liquor and smoking hashish. Wasn't that an insult to Islam, to make people pray to Qaddafi? I asked. "We didn't think about it," he said. He told me that on the day of the massacre, a commander named Muhammad Mansour arrived late in the afternoon and ordered the guards to kill all the prisoners in the hangar. Then he left, without saying anything about why they were to be killed or where the order originated. "We looked at each other, and then I got the grenades," Ibrahim said. He was answering in monosyllables, and I had to press him constantly for more details. "The other guards had the grenades. I told them, give the grenades to me." He threw two grenades into the hangar, one after the other, and the door blew open. He could hear the screams of the dying prisoners. I asked him what he had thought about after he went home to his parents and siblings. He had made no effort to escape. "I was thinking about everything that happened," he said, his face as expressionless as ever. "The whole disaster, the killing. I was thinking between me and God."

It was hard to imagine any future for this man other than the firing squad. Like Marwan, he was a killer whose regrets were unconvincing. But Ibrahim was in Misrata, and that meant he was not going to be handed over to the transitional government anytime soon. Nasser and Jalal resented this and seemed keen to prove that they, by contrast, were trying to cooperate with the authorities. One afternoon, Nasser proudly announced to me that his brigade was, in fact, part of the government. It was true: the next day I found hundreds of *thuwar*, rebels, lined up outside an old Tripoli police academy building waiting to be paid. The new transitional prime minister, worried about Libya's masses of armed and unemployed men, had decided to pay them on the pretext that they had freed the country from Qaddafi and deserved compensation. He thought he was buying time for the transition. But in effect, he was officially recognizing the militias as Libya's most powerful entity. And because the payments were ongoing, he was giving the *katiba* members every reason to stay together and flout the government's authority. Their first handout was about $1,900 per rebel, $3,100 if you were married with a family. Anyone could sign up, and so eighty thousand men registered as *thuwar* in Tripoli alone. On the morning I was there, eleven hundred men were scheduled to be paid. Inside the building, officers sat at battered desks, counting out thick wads of Libyan currency. The men waited their turn, many of them laughing and singing. One of them told me, "If we'd really had this many people fighting Qaddafi, the war would have lasted a week, not eight months."

One morning in early April 2012, Nasser Salhoba told me that his frustration with the man who killed his brother had reached a boiling point. He had spent months talking to Marwan, asking him why he did it, demanding more details about his brother's final days, lecturing him. He was angry, but more than that, he was baffled. "I see Marwan as such a cold person," Nasser told me. "He was the head of the snake. Of all the guards, he insisted on following orders. The others didn't want to kill. He was so emotionless, and still is. I wanted to see, is he the same person when he sees his family?"

So Nasser called Marwan's father and invited him to come see his son and bring two family members. The family had stayed away, apparently fearing that the *thuwar* would take revenge on them all. On the following Friday, eight of them showed up at the brigade in Tajoura. Nasser greeted them at the door and led them downstairs. "It was a very emotional moment," Nasser told me. "You can imagine how I felt when I saw my brother's killer embracing his brother." The two brothers kept hugging each other for a long time, sobbing, and finally Nasser, unable to bear it, pushed them apart. Later, he took one of the cousins aside and asked him if he knew why Marwan was being held. The man said no. "I told him, 'Your cousin killed six very qualified people whom Libya will need, two doctors and four officers. One of them was my brother.'" The cousin listened, and then he hugged Nasser before the family left.

For Nasser, the family meeting was a revelation. "He was very emotional," he said of Marwan. "His sister loves him, his brother loves him.

You see him with them, and it's such a contrast with this cold killer." He seemed comforted by this, less burdened, though he could not say exactly why. He told me that now he felt that he understood Marwan a little better, even if his crime remained a mystery.

On the following Friday, Marwan's father returned, this time with two relatives. Nasser helped them carry two crates of food—yogurt, fruit, home-baked biscuits—downstairs to Marwan's cell. When Nasser came back upstairs, Marwan's father was standing by the door. He went straight up to Nasser, looking him sorrowfully in the eye. "He embraced me and kissed me on the forehead," Nasser said. "So he must know."

Nasser's anger had not subsided. But the long months of interrogations had given him an unexpected solace: a chance to get to know his brother better and to sift through his own failings. "I keep asking the prisoners small details, like how many times he was beaten, what he talked about, how he seemed," Nasser told me. "He used to get into fights, demanding proper medical attention for the other inmates. Whenever they were tortured, they would be brought to his cell so he could treat them." Nasser had been impressed and moved by what he heard about his brother's bravery. Once, Omar had paid a guard to take a prescription to a pharmacy. He had written a plea for help on the note, in English. But the woman at the pharmacy had simply translated the note for the guard, who went straight back to Yarmouk and beat Omar severely. Omar kept on trying, sending notes to colleagues who either could not, or would not, help.

One thing in particular was haunting Nasser. According to the prisoners, Omar had talked a lot about Nasser in jail, saying he was sure his brother would rescue him if he could. Now Nasser wondered why he hadn't tried harder. "I feel such remorse I wasn't able to help him," he said again and again. He told a long story about a well-connected soldier he'd known, who might have been able to do something if Nasser had pushed him hard enough. He hadn't seen Omar during the last ten days before the arrest, and now he chastised himself, imagining alternative endings. "I would've done anything, even gone to the front for Qaddafi's people, if that would have saved my brother," Nasser told me. "At the end of the day, it's what's inside you that counts." But he didn't sound convinced.

Nasser didn't stop with the recent past. He reviewed his whole life for me, trying to understand where he'd gone wrong. He had always been the family's bad angel, a prodigal son. Omar had been the conscientious one. He had returned to Libya after a decade abroad in 2009, telling friends that he was ashamed of Libya's backwardness and eager to help out. He had brought back books about Qaddafi written by dissidents, and a conviction that the country needed to change. At the time, Nasser thought his brother was being naïve. Now he understood he was right. It was as if Omar had become a screen on which Nasser's own failures were projected: the lies, the cowardly survival mechanisms that come with living under a dictatorship. I had the sense that Nasser was struggling to learn from his brother, and in an odd way, trying in turn to teach something to Marwan. After Marwan's family left, Nasser went downstairs and spoke to him. "I said, 'Look what I did, and look what you did,'" Nasser told me. "'You killed my brother, and I arranged for you to see your family.'"

Omar's life had cast a similar shadow onto other people. One of them was his closest colleague, a doctor named Mahfoud Ghaddour. Omar's fellow prisoners from Yarmouk told me he was always trying to contact Ghaddour, whom he saw as a possible savior. In fact, Ghaddour was aware that Omar was being held in Yarmouk—one of the frantic messages Omar sent from the prison got through to him—and yet he did nothing. Ghaddour told me so himself, during a long talk in his office at the hospital. "I started looking in that place, using contacts with people in the government," he said. "But it was somewhat difficult. They started changing their mobile phones. I had difficulty to get help."

Ghaddour said this with a wincing half smile. I found it impossible to believe. I knew other people who had gotten relatives out of Yarmouk. As a prominent doctor, Ghaddour had plenty of contacts he could have called on. And even if he'd failed, he could at least have contacted Omar's family, or his in-laws, who were desperate to know where he was being held. Ghaddour must have sensed my skepticism. He continued with a long, rambling narrative in which he tried to blame other people for not rescuing Omar from the prison, and talked at length about how dangerous it was in Tripoli at that time. But there was something pained and apologetic about his manner, as if he were groping toward a confession. He cared about Omar but did not want to make trouble for his own family. He had done what so many others had done in Qaddafi's Libya: kept his head down, letting others take the risks. These were the survivors in Libya, the ones who adapted well to a place where fear was the only law.

One afternoon, Nasser drove me to see his brother's widow in Souq al Jumaa, a middle-class neighborhood of Tripoli. Omar's daughter opened the door, a pretty ten-year-old with lots of orange and pink bracelets on her wrists. She greeted me in English and led us to a Western-style living room with a white shag carpet. Her name was Abrar. Her four-year-old sister, Ebaa, skipped across the room with us to the couch, where both girls sat beside me. After a minute their mother, Lubna, came downstairs and introduced herself, a round-faced woman in a blue head scarf. She launched right into a narrative about the family: their years living in Newcastle and Liverpool, their return to Libya, and her husband's disappearance. "We were so scared all during that time," she said. "Even now when I hear an airplane I am frightened." As she spoke, her daughter Ebaa toyed with my beard and stole my pen and notebook. Finally she cuddled up next to me, clutching my arm and pressing her head into my shoulder. "She has been like this ever since her father died," Lubna said. Abrar ran off to find a journal she had kept about her father's death. It was a remarkable document, an account written on lined paper in a child's straightforward prose. "Then we got a phone call saying my daddy died, and my mama banged her head against the wall and screamed, and I cried," she wrote of the day they found out. The essay was followed by a series of dreams she'd had about her father. In all of them, he reassured her that he was in paradise, and in two dreams he offered to introduce her to the Prophet Muhammad.

At one point Lubna mentioned that she had urged her husband to take them all to Tunisia, where it was safer. Abrar piped up, speaking in the same direct, poised tone as her essay: "We said, 'Take us out of Libya.' He said, 'Never, the hospital needs me. The kids need me. I will never leave. I will die in it.'" Throughout our visit, Nasser sat on the couch quietly, now and then offering toys to the younger girl. On our way out, the girls offered to show us their father's home office. It was a small room, sparsely decorated, with his British medical degrees framed on the wall, and two big drawers full of toys for the girls. "This is what kills me," Nasser said. "All men love their children, but with him, it was even more."

We walked through the gathering dusk to the car. I asked Nasser about his future. He wanted to become a police investigator, but for a real department, not just the brigade. This was his way of showing loyalty to his brother: to vindicate Omar's belief in making something better out of Libya, to keep faith with the idea of a democratic state and the rule of law. I was reminded of something Nasser had told me earlier: "I didn't always get along with my brother, but only because he wanted me to be better." We drove toward Martyrs' Square, the new name given to the plaza where Qaddafi once urged Libyans to fight to the last man. Nasser dropped me off near my hotel, and I looked back for a moment to see his long, earnest face as he waved goodbye.

3

— Sects (Syria) —

As the hopes of Tahrir receded, the visions of unity it inspired gave way to a terrifying undertow. People who had trusted each other for decades now saw barriers rising between them. The world was suddenly full of threats to all that was sacred: to the state, to your clan, to God. These were battles in which there could be no compromise. You had to take sides, and if your friend was beyond the barrier, so be it. The barriers varied from place to place. But beneath this surface variation, a common pattern was recognizable. In each country, the loosening of state authority seemed to unspool a related set of assumptions, as if all these strands were part of some larger Ottoman fabric that could no longer be rewoven.

How did it happen? How does an unspoken word between neighbors turn into the stuff of civil wars? I once asked that question of a Syrian schoolteacher. She was a woman of fifty, with a long face and wire-frame glasses that gave her a severe look. With her was her son, a genial, handsome man of thirty who ran an NGO providing medical and school aid to Syrians in the war zone. We were drinking tea in a streetside hotel café in southern Turkey, where they were living in exile. "You must understand, we were not like this," she said, looking urgently at me. "Most of my friends were Alawi. My colleagues at work were Alawi. Our neighbors, Alawi. We did not even think about this. We are Sunni, yes, but sometimes we did not even know if this or that person is Alawi. It was not important."

I had heard the same passionate speech from other Syrians, and I think she meant it. But I was startled by the way the teacher's tone changed when I asked her about a young Alawi woman who had been very close to her family before they left Syria. She paused before answering. She said, a little uncomfortable, that the young woman was "a nice girl." Then she added, "But the Alawis don't have a religion. They are a traitor sect. They collaborated with the crusaders, and during the French occupation they sided with the French." Her son, sitting next to her, agreed, saying the Syrian people had been deceived. "As for us, we will teach our children the real nature of these people," he said. "They will not be like us, unaware of the real nature of the Alawis."

It was jarring, this blithe shift from one voice to another, from an assertion of unity to an angry slur. It was tempting to smell hypocrisy, to accuse them of having hidden their sectarian feelings all along. But I think that would be unfair. They were not lying about their old relationships with people of other faiths. They were responding to something new: power had shifted, the old order was shaking, and they could no longer reconcile past and present. Their words were an effort to reach across that gulf, to seize the reassurance that came with an older identity. Something similar had happened a decade earlier in Iraq, when the American invasion exposed the tacit Sunni assumption of superiority. "You must understand, these people were shopkeepers," I was told by one Sunni politician in Baghdad, when I asked him about the new Shiite political parties that were suddenly running the country. You could hear the undertone: *People should know their place.* In Syria the assumptions were very different, and in some ways more poisonous, since the Sunnis and Alawis both felt certain kinds of entitlement. But the 2011 uprising provoked the same kind of emotional disarray.

This unraveling took place everywhere in Syria, not just in the bombed-out neighborhoods that became the civil war's signposts: Homs, Aleppo, the suburbs of Damascus. My own window was a mid-size city called Jableh on the Mediterranean coast. It was in some ways a model place to see the way the 2011 uprising ramified into the lives of ordinary Syrians. Unlike the big cities, where the news outlets focused their coverage, Jableh was out of the limelight in the regime heartland of the northwest, and it remained peaceful for the whole first month of the protests. Its people had more time to observe, and sometimes resist, the sectarian narrative that was overtaking Syria. It has a fairy-tale remoteness, with a faded port that dates back to Phoenician times, cliffside cafés gazing out at the Mediterranean, a Roman amphitheater, and a population that reflected fairly well Syria's mix of religious sects. The center of town is mostly Sunni, surrounded by hills full of Alawi and Christian villages.

One of the first people I met there was a young woman named Aliaa Ali. She was the daughter of a retired Alawi military officer, and she was twenty-five years old when the uprising began, a devoted supporter of the Assad regime. She had a broad, pretty face, with knitted brows that conveyed a mixture of petulance and determination. She was extremely intelligent and fully aware, thanks to a year spent in England, of the West's harsh view of her president. Unlike many loyalists, she was willing to acknowledge the brutalities of her own side, and at times she seemed embarrassed by the Syrian police state. "There is a lot that needs to change here, I know that," she told me when we first met. "But the fact is that it turned sectarian much sooner than people think." When I asked her how it happened, she began telling me about the loss of her closest friendship, with a Sunni woman named Noura Kanafani. I later got to know Noura, and their accounts of the friendship matched. One of the first moments each of them told me about was something that had taken place in 2010, a year before the uprisings began.

It was a spring morning, and the two women were lying next to each other on Aliaa's bed, as they often did. Noura had come over with strange and upsetting news. She'd received a marriage proposal, and her mother, an anxious, round-faced doctor with conservative ideas, wanted her to accept. She was already twenty-four, too old to still be without a husband. An earlier engagement to a conservative older man, her former college professor, had fallen through. But the new suitor was even more conservative, Noura told her friend. He said he wanted her to stop going to movies and wearing short dresses. He said he would not tolerate her having Alawi friends. His words still echoed in her mind: "How can you be friends with those people when you know what they did to us?"

The question had shocked Noura. She did not know what "those people" had done. The word Hama evoked only vague stories about something dark and unspeakable that happened in that city during the 1980s, before she was born. Her family stayed clear of politics. They were a large and well respected clan of doctors and teachers, solid middle-class folk with urban roots and not much interest in religion. They knew what everyone knew: that Sunni Muslims were the majority of Syria's population, perhaps 70 percent, and that some pious Sunnis considered Alawis to be heretics and resented being ruled by them. There was some social snobbery, too: old Sunni families saw President Assad's family—and the Alawis generally—as crude arrivistes from the mountains. But discussing any of this was a taboo in Syria. You heard about it only indirectly, like the day when Noura's mother had said dismissively that "people from the coast"—this was code for Alawis—sent their children to Russia to study, while "other people" (meaning Sunnis) sent them to London. Aliaa had been upset by that and said it wasn't true. She herself was studying English and planning to go to Britain. It hadn't come up again. But now the conservative suitor's comments had pushed the subject into the open. Lying on the bed together that morning, Noura giggled as Aliaa recounted the bizarre myths people spread about Alawis in Syria: that they had tails, that they practiced secret orgies. It was all so stupid.

Noura and Aliaa had become friends in high school and had been inseparable ever since. They seemed to complete each other, like a matched pair of good and evil angels on opposite panels of a Renaissance church ceiling. Aliaa was dark-haired and almost fierce looking, and Noura pale and blonde, with a heart-shaped face and a soft look in her eyes. Aliaa's house was two blocks away and Noura felt completely at home there, taking off her head scarf and leaving her hair uncovered no matter who was home. They still walked to the university arm in arm, and Noura had told Aliaa she would name her first child after her. She envied Aliaa's confidence and depended on her to make decisions; Aliaa, the strong-willed one, the eldest of her family, relished Noura's awe and affection. There had never really been a question, but after discussing the proposal for an hour or so, the two of them still lying on Aliaa's bed, Noura abruptly said, "I can't live with a man who thinks Alawis are forbidden." Marriage would have to wait.

Nine months later, in mid-January 2011, that conversation echoed in Noura's mind. It was right after the revolution in Tunis, and suddenly all the neighbors were asking her the same question. *Are you going to do that? Are you going to make protests here?* Her first thought was about the word "you." What did it mean? You the political opposition? You the Sunnis? You the enemy? Noura wasn't sure how to answer. She was excited about the images she saw on al Jazeera, especially after Tahrir Square. Her aunts and cousins were jumping up and down when Mubarak fell, they couldn't get enough. But the neighbors—the Kanafanis lived in a mostly Alawi district—seemed anxious, frightened, even. One of them quoted Qaddafi's madman speech about hunting the protesters down "house by house." He told one of Noura's aunts, "Bashar will do the same to you." Another one, after hearing the aunt say she supported the revolutions, told her half jokingly that he'd like to shoot her. It was troubling; these were people who had the keys to their apartment, who had helped raise Noura and her cousins since they were babies.

Then, in mid-March, just after the uprisings started in Syria, something happened that frightened them all. Noura was sitting on her aunt Maha's balcony with her mother and some of the cousins, breathing the spring air and the sounds and smells of a Thursday night: kebab and tobacco smoke and laughter. On the road below them, a line of cars began gathering, dozens of them, the men inside laughing and honking and waving flags from their open windows. It looked almost like a protest rally. But it didn't take long for the reality to dawn. Some of the cars were SUVs, with blacked-out windows and pictures of Bashar and Hafez al Assad on them. They had come down from the mountain, the Alawi heartland. These were the Assad regime's foot soldiers, and they had come to assert themselves, to show their teeth. They started chanting the slogans you always heard at regime rallies: "Long live the president!" and "God, Syria, and Bashar!" The Kanafani family watched them for a few minutes, a sense of unease settling over them. They'd seen this hundreds of times before. But with the protests rising all over the Middle East, it felt different. Al Jazeera had given them confidence. One of Noura's cousins, an impulsive twenty-four-year-old named Tareq, stood up with no warning and bellowed down to the street, "Hey! It's not 'Long live the president.' You should say 'God, Syria, and Freedom.'" The rebel slogan.

Instantly, the young men in the cars went silent. The horns stopped. One of Noura's other aunts, Amma, clutched Tareq's arm and told him firmly to sit down. For a long moment, the family found itself in a virtual spotlight, as dozens of hostile young Alawi men glared up at them. No one on the terrace said anything. Finally the cars began moving on. Amma spoke, her voice tight with fear: "You don't know these people. They are brutal. What we are doing might cost us our lives and the honor of our daughters."

This happened before the first protest chant was heard in Jableh. But already, another sound was in the air, a dark counterpoint to the Pied Piper song of revolution and Arab unity that al Jazeera had been playing for three months. A week before that evening encounter on the balcony in Jableh, Saudi Arabia had sent its tanks across the eight-lane causeway into the puppet kingdom of Bahrain, putting an end to the uprising there. Pearl Square, the Tahrir of Bahrain, was destroyed and repaved. Nobody needed subtitles: the region's great Sunni power was announcing that it would not tolerate a protest led by Shiites. You could almost hear the clink of shields being realigned around the region, from Yemen to Morocco. For years, the daily horrors of Iraq's sectarian civil war had been a perfect cautionary tale for dictators; all they had to do was point in the direction of Baghdad and the democracy talk would fade to silence. It worked, until 2011. And now, Iran and Saudi Arabia, the two poles of Shiite and Sunni Islam, were rounding on each other once again, like two great bulldogs. The Syrian protesters would have to sing awfully loud to drown out those barks.

It was around this time, in late March 2011, that a high-ranking Syrian general named Manaf Tlass was ushered into the presidential palace in Damascus for a one-on-one meeting with President Bashar al Assad. The two men embraced in the Syrian manner, arms clutching elbows and three quick kisses on the cheeks, before sitting down. They made an odd pairing. The president was tall and angular in his crisply pressed suit, with a birdlike watchfulness and an elongated neck and head that made him look as if he'd been painted by El Greco. Tlass was shorter and rounder, with shaggy hair and teen-idol good looks. His half-open shirt seemed to confirm the playboy reputation he'd had for years. They shared a dynastic bond: Tlass's father had been a right-hand man to Bashar's father, Hafez al Assad. But they were not close. Tlass had been best friends with Bashar's older brother, Basel, the heir apparent. Basel had died in a car crash in 1994, and Tlass's influence had waned since then.

The Syrian uprising was a week old at the time of their meeting. It had started down south in the city of Daraa, where teenagers had spray-painted a message to Assad on a wall: IT'S YOUR TURN, DOCTOR—an unmistakable reference to the fate of Ben Ali, Mubarak, and Qaddafi. Arab cartoonists had been making the same point for weeks, with images of a nervous Bashar in line for dismissal. The Syrian regime did not think it was funny. The regional security director, a cousin of Bashar's named Atef Najib, ordered the teenagers arrested and tortured. Their parents, according to the legend, were told, *Forget your children. Go home and make more children, and if you don't know how to make them, we will show you.* That was the spark. The protests started in Daraa and spread quickly to Damascus, Banias, Hasakeh, Deir al Zour. The Syrian police state had responded as all police states do when they are threatened: with bullets. The demonstrations had only grown larger. Syria seemed to be following the lead of Tunisia and Egypt and all the others. But everyone knew that Bashar al Assad presided over a much more brutal regime and would not go down easily.

After only a few minutes of conversation, Bashar put his question very bluntly: "What would *you* do?" Tlass was ready for it and had prepared his answer. He told the president it was not too late to calm things down, but it would take strong measures. *Go to Daraa yourself. Fire Atef Najib and, more than that, put him in jail. This will send a message. Force is not the way to win this.* Tlass volunteered to play a role by meeting with local councils in several cities and identifying concrete grievances that could be addressed: policing, corruption, water and electricity shortages. This would get people off the streets. After talking for fifteen minutes, Tlass paused. Bashar seemed interested. He encouraged Tlass to start right away. But the president was notorious for making every guest think his advice had been taken. As Tlass shook the president's hand and said goodbye, retracing his steps out of the palace, others were on their way in, with far more influence and very different advice. Before the year 2011 was out, Assad's army would be using tanks and fighter jets to pound whole neighborhoods into rubble. His Alawi militias, the *shabiha*, would be massacring Sunni civilians in their homes and leaving scrawled sectarian slogans on the doors. The few Alawis who dared to support the opposition in public would be isolated and shamed, and tortured if they persisted. Assad would release Sunni jihadis from his prisons en masse, in hopes of turning the opposition into the terrorist front he had labeled it from the start. He would do everything he could to transform a democratic uprising into something far more vicious, something the outside world would recoil from rather than embrace.

Aliaa told me she first confronted her friend while they were taking one of their drives along the coast in mid-March 2011. Noura was at the wheel. "What do you mean you're against the regime? Don't you think it's more complicated than that?" Aliaa said. "Of course there's a lot that is wrong here. But come on, you spend most of your time thinking about shoes and clothes. Since when did you decide to become a political activist?" Noura kept her eyes on the road and held her ground. They had discussed the revolutions in Tunis and Egypt plenty of times, but this was the first time Noura had taken a stand against Bashar.

"Okay, I know I'm not so educated about politics," Noura said, "but I don't want Bashar to be my president. It's as simple as that. I want my son to have a chance to be president. Can you dream that one day your son would be president?" Aliaa said nothing. Noura felt a twinge of guilt and wondered if she had gone too far. Not that Aliaa would mind, but her neighbors would surely be enraged by this kind of talk; it was a red line, and they were arriving at her house now, the window open. Aliaa opened the door, then leaned over to kiss her friend on the cheek. "See you tomorrow," she said, as if nothing had changed.

Noura had missed the first demonstration in Jableh, and that had made her all the more willing to speak up. It was on March 25, and that morning the message lit up on thousands of cell phones as people gathered for Friday prayers: *Gather outside the Abu Bakr mosque.* People started showing up around one o'clock, dozens at first, then hundreds, and finally thousands. The revolution had reached Jableh at last. "God, Syria, and Freedom," they chanted, and then marched past the old Roman amphitheater to a government building downtown. There was a small contingent of police officers watching, and probably plenty of others in plainclothes, but they just stood by and stared. Most of the Kanafani clan was there, including Noura's aunt Maha, the family firebrand, and her children. Noura was not. Her mother, Zahra, was anxious about what might happen and didn't want to risk her job as a gynecologist at the al Fayad Center. When Noura heard about the march afterward from her cousins, all of them glowing and exuberant, she was jealous. She made up her mind to join the next time. She started making protest signs at home, in Arabic and English. A week later, she joined her cousins and even spoke at the microphone onstage, ignoring her mother's cautions. Revolutions come only once in your life, she told herself.

It was during those early days that Aliaa and Noura's shared conception of the world began to split apart, like speakers of the same language who are suddenly marooned on different islands. Aliaa heard the same protest chants as her friend, but she found them menacing. One by one, her relatives and friends brought her stories about the protesters that hinted at bloody intentions and sectarian agendas. Ahmed, a fellow Alawi she'd gone to school with, had been beaten up at the very first protest by a crowd of angry Sunni men. His arm had been broken, and it could have been worse if some Sunni friends in the protest crowd had not run up and protected him and, later, driven him to the hospital. That night, back at home, the same friends came to his house to check on him. "They said something that was very shocking to me," Ahmed told me, two years later. "They told me, 'From now on we must be with you whenever you go to a Sunni neighborhood.' We didn't have this kind of language in Jableh before." Aliaa and her relatives were also troubled that the protests always came from mosques, and all the marchers—or almost all—were Sunni. Why? Within two weeks, hints of sectarian language crept into the protest slogans. One of them was "We don't want Iran, we don't want Hezbollah, we want someone who fears God." This was loaded language in Syria: a dog whistle to Sunnis to rally against their Shiite enemies, Alawis included.

In early April, Aliaa was driving on a road near the coast, twenty miles from home, when she heard loud explosions and gunfire that lasted several minutes. The drivers panicked; no one knew where it was coming from. Only after getting home to Jableh did she learn that nine Syrian soldiers had been ambushed and killed nearby. Three of them, it turned out, were from Jableh. The opposition media quickly put out a story that was picked up in European and American news channels: the dead men were would-be defectors who had been killed by their Syrian army superiors. The story fit neatly into a narrative of regime breakdown and defection that was being reinforced constantly on al Jazeera, a mouthpiece for the rebellion. But no evidence for the story ever emerged. And amateur video taken at the scene suggested that the killers were rebel gunmen. For Aliaa and her friends, it fit a different pattern: the protesters and their allies were spreading lies, refusing to recognize the violence on their own side. And that pattern blurred easily, in their minds, into a comforting corollary: surely the regime's mass arrests, its prison house torture, its wholesale massacres, all the unbearable gore being uploaded to YouTube—surely it was exaggerated, surely some of it was fake.

Aliaa repeated these stories to Noura, but she refused to believe them. The protests were peaceful, Noura said, and there had been no sectarian language. It was the government that was spreading these rumors. And the government, she said, her voice rising uncharacteristically into anger, was killing innocent people all over Syria. Aliaa asked what made her so sure. Everyone knew al Jazeera was biased, and why would President Assad do such a thing? It was "not logical" for a government to kill its own people, she insisted. Noura felt it *was* logical. Her aunt Maha had been telling her about the events of Hama, in 1982, when the regime brought in its tanks and crushed the Islamist insurgency there, killing some twenty thousand people; Maha said the real number was much higher and told her, "We paid the price last time, we won't pay it again." Maha had always been the most confrontational of her aunts, and she looked the part, with her mannish face and bold stare. Now Noura listened to her with a sense of awe and even a bit of self-reproach, as if she had spent her life hiding from a truth that was within her reach.

But with Aliaa, she sensed that she could not broach all this. It would be too much. So she backed down, returning to her old meek self. "Maybe we just heard different things," she said. And they left it there.

Jableh held out for a long time against the onrush of violence elsewhere in Syria. For an entire month after the first protest in late March, the police allowed the rallies to proceed. A group of leading citizens formed a committee to resist the sectarian rumors that kept spreading (they usually involved men driving around in jeeps and shooting up neighborhoods). The regime seemed to be testing the waters, making efforts to tamp down the protests without violence.

Twice, ranking regime officers invited members of the extended

Kanafani clan for discussions. They appear to have been counting on the support of the Kanafanis, perhaps because the family had so many Alawi friends. The first time, the contact was made through a family friend, a prominent Alawi engineer. He offered to host the meeting in his home in Jableh, where the Kanafanis would be far more comfortable. Meeting regime officials was always a frightening affair in Syria, especially in government buildings, where the basement torture room is never far away. This time Aunt Maha's husband and two of her sons arrived at the home of their friend, and waiting for them in the living room was a man in an expensive suit. They recognized him right away: it was Alaa Ibrahim, a very wealthy businessman with close ties to the regime. He shook their hands and made polite small talk. Then he asked about the protest movement, its demands, and why they had chosen to join it. Maha's older son, Mihyar, said he had no objections to Bashar remaining president, but he wanted to see reforms. They chatted for fifteen or twenty minutes. And then Mihyar's younger brother Tareq—the same one who just a week or so earlier had stood up and shouted at the regime supporters in cars—dropped a bomb. "Mr. Ibrahim," he said, "you are so thoughtful and decent—why can't we have you as president, for instance? Why does it have to be Bashar?"

Instantly, Ibrahim's body stiffened. The tone of the meeting changed. He warned them that targeting the president was a red line. Syria was not Egypt or Libya or Tunis, he said, and if they failed to understand that they would be sorry. The men got up. After handshakes and tight, dutiful smiles, they left the house.

The second meeting, a few days later, was less pleasant. This time the family received a call from Political Security, the Assad regime's nerve center in Jableh. The voice on the phone demanded that the men of the family come to the headquarters. This was a frequent ritual in Assad's police state, but terrifying nonetheless: plenty of people were arrested and jailed for months on the slimmest of pretexts. When they arrived, Maha's husband and sons were brought to the sparsely furnished office of an official named Samer Sweidan. They sat down. "What do you want?" Sweidan said. "You have a house, you have a job, with a salary of forty thousand Syrian pounds a month [about $850].

Isn't that enough for you?" Mihyar answered first. "It's not about hunger and poverty," he said. "We want dignity, we want law and civic institutions. We want to feel we are real partners." The discussion went on for a while. And then Tareq, once again, broke the rules. He'd been watching al Jazeera, and he felt the revolution was bound to prevail. He wanted to be a hero. "I don't want Bashar as president," he said. "Why shouldn't we vote? Why shouldn't we get to decide who is president?"

There was a pause, and Sweidan looked at him coldly. "Think carefully," he said. "I can throw you in prison right now." Tareq refused to be intimidated. "Fine, throw me in prison," he said. "At least I'll have my books, I can study there. But if I'm free, I'll go to the street and let my voice be heard like anyone else." Tareq's father and brother held their breath. But the officer let them all go home. The regime wasn't ready to play hardball in Jableh. Not yet.

By mid-April 2011, the protesters were still in the streets of Jableh. The brutal treatment of the protesters in Syria's bigger cities—broadcast every day on al Jazeera—fueled their anger, and their demands grew bolder. They now chanted, "The people want the fall of the regime," the slogan that had brought down Mubarak, and more ominously, "In the ground, we will put Bashar in the ground." On April 24, hours after a last meeting between the regional governor and a group of protesters, the regime finally lost its patience with Jableh.

Noura's mother, Zahra, was driving back home that afternoon from Latakia, a bigger city an hour up the coast, when she saw something lurch into her rearview mirror: a military jeep driving very fast, with men in camouflage clutching machine guns. She pulled over, terrified, and waited as a whole convoy of soldiers passed. Other civilian cars were stopped on the shoulder next to her. Some of the drivers had got out of their cars and were staring at the convoy in wonder. No one knew what was going on. Zahra got back on the road, and arriving in Jableh half an hour later, she found soldiers blocking the main entrance to the town. That was when a friend called to tell her that seventeen people had been shot dead during a protest. It was like a war, the friend said, there were soldiers everywhere.

Until that day, Zahra had refused, alone among her sisters, to join the protests. She disliked politics, she said. Like everyone else, she had seen TV footage of the dead protesters in Daraa and had found herself asking: Who gave them the right to end people's lives, as if they were killing birds? But the thought dropped, as it often had in the old days. She worried that street protests were the wrong way. Besides, she loved her job at the hospital and didn't want to risk losing it.

When Zahra finally got home that afternoon, her hands were shaking. She went to the kitchen and washed the apples she'd bought in Latakia, then put them in a bowl on the table. One of the neighbors' children, a sweet-faced thirteen-year-old named Hassan Eid, wandered in, took an apple, and began eating it. She looked at him. Hassan was Alawi. She'd known him all her life, considered him almost part of the family. But now, she told herself, this boy's father or uncle or brother might be shooting demonstrators, at this very minute. He might be killing her own sisters. Five minutes later, Hassan's parents sent a cousin over to bring him home. Zahra wondered if he would ever come back. The phone rang, and when she answered it an acquaintance spoke, his voice breathless and full of emotion: *Dr. Zahra, you're needed, someone is bleeding here, in the Old City, please come help us.* He hung up, and in the silence that followed, she wondered what to do. The Old City was almost impossible to reach, with all the checkpoints. Treating wounded protesters would surely be seen as a crime. But she was a doctor. She hesitated a moment longer, and then decided: she would go. She picked up her bag and turned toward the door. Then the phone rang again, and the same voice spoke, calmer this time. *It is okay, never mind, the man died.*

Zahra's attitude changed after that. The city itself changed; there were checkpoints now, and the demonstrations took place only at night, in the narrower streets of the Old City. One night Zahra got another call. A different voice this time but the same message: *Dr. Zahra, please, you must come, no one wants to help the injured.* She left the house and got in her car, her medical bag hidden under the seat, terrified that she'd be stopped at any moment by men with guns. The streets were silent and empty, except for military vehicles. At the first checkpoint, a soldier asked where she was going. She told him in a pleading voice that her old mother was unwell because of the noise and the smoke, she had to help her. The man let her pass. She reached the mosque where the protesters had told her to meet them, and as soon as she walked in, she saw three people lying on the carpet. Two of them were dead, their faces already gray, blood drying on their bodies. The third was bleeding, moaning, and in great pain; a bullet had entered his stomach and gone out through his back. Zahra had never treated someone with bullet wounds before, but she cleaned up the wounds and made stitches. In another room were three other wounded people. One of them was a sixty-year-old man who hadn't even been in the protests. After treating the others, she took him to a private hospital, then drove home. It was after 2:00 a.m. The next day she skipped work. She felt sure someone would find out. But the calls for help kept coming, and she kept going, always with an alibi, always at night. She started having the same nightmare. In the dream, she was alone on the street at night, and suddenly she heard the screech of brakes as a police car stopped short and men came running out, pointing guns at her head. When she woke up, she was still alone, looking out the window at the empty street. Her life had become an echo of the dream. Zahra was a widow; her husband had died of cancer two years before the revolution.

After she got the courage to go back to work, Zahra was chatting one day with a colleague, a man she'd known for years. He was Alawi, but he'd always made clear to her, in private, that he disliked Bashar. He had told Zahra a year or two earlier that his dream was to have his son vote in a free election in Syria. Zahra would never have broached that kind of subject before—it wasn't her way—but now she felt it was time. She reminded him of what he'd said about Bashar before the revolution. He looked at Zahra and glanced around, as if to make sure no one had heard. "Look, Zahra, I cannot talk about this now," he said. He walked away, and from then on, he avoided her.

The Kanafani family mostly stopped going to any protests after the crackdown. But it didn't matter; there was a black mark against their name now, and people treated them differently. One of Zahra's oldest friends, an Alawi woman named Maysaa whom she'd gone to medical school with, stopped calling her. A mutual friend called her and explained: "Maysaa asked me to say that she is sorry, but she is afraid to talk to you." Zahra cried afterward. But a month later, something hardened in her, maybe because of all the arrests, the killings taking place every day. Another old Alawi friend, a fellow gynecologist named Rafida who worked at a hospital in Saudi Arabia, called Zahra from Riyadh. When Zahra told her she wasn't sure she could stay in Syria, her friend started sobbing. "Zahra, is it possible I'll come back to Jableh and find you're not there, that we can't go for walks and picnics by the sea?" Rafida said. "Zahra, for me Jableh means you." Zahra felt obliged to master her emotions this time. She sternly told her friend that it was time for her to face up to the reality of the Syrian regime's cruelty.

Noura and Aliaa spent less time together, even though they were no longer attending classes at the university because of the crisis. In early summer, they went for a drive, and within minutes Noura declared, "Aliaa, the soldiers are killing protesters in Homs. It's like a massacre." Aliaa replied in her usual way: "Why would they do that? Maybe you should check on it." Noura shot back, "It's because the people want freedom, that's why." They were passing through an Alawi neighborhood, and a soldier flagged them down and offered Aliaa a friendly warning. "Be careful," he said, gesturing at Noura, because her family was known. The same thing had happened in reverse when they were in Sunni areas. They drove on, and after a minute, Noura said, "If Sunnis ever attacked you, I'd protect you. And I know you'd do the same for me." They said nothing for a moment, and then looked at each other. Both women burst out laughing. The idea still seemed strange, incomprehensible.

The hundreds of people killed in the regime's crackdown turned to thousands. Aliaa and her family had long since stopped trusting anything they heard on the satellite channels or on the BBC. They listened instead to Syrian news, or Lebanese channels allied with the regime. There the headlines were different: Sunni sheikhs were calling for religious war, and Saudi Arabia was promoting them. Aliaa saw the signs herself and resented the Western media for failing to pick up on it. A bizarre superstition spread, echoed on Internet religious forums and ridiculed outside of them: if you banged on metal after midnight during the holy month of Ramadan, Alawis would disappear. One night in July, a loud clanging sound awakened the family. Aliaa's father got out of bed and staggered to the balcony; in a building just opposite, a man was beating on a metal lid. "Shut up!" her father shouted. "We're not going to disappear." Later, they found an X mark outside the door of one of their neighbors, the brother of a high regime official. Was he targeted for assassination?

Aliaa's younger brother Abdulhameed, an amateur boxer, had his own shock not long afterward. He was in Egypt at the time, doing a maritime training course and living with five Syrian friends in a rented house in Alexandria. One night, a young man with an Iraqi accent knocked on the door and asked hesitantly if Syrians were living there. Abdulhameed said yes, and the Iraqi walked off. Late that night, a group of men tried to break down the door, shouting curses about Alawis and Bashar. Abdulhameed and his friends drove them off. But a few days later, a Facebook posting appeared, listing the address of the house. "These men are Syrians funded by Iran and Hezbollah to spread Shiism in Egypt and they must be killed," it said. Abdulhameed and two of his friends gave up their studies and went home.

In August, Zahra finally made the decision to leave the country, at least for a while. She'd been called in to talk to Political Security twice, in frightening interrogations. She'd denied treating injured protesters, but she felt the regime was closing in on her. She bought a ticket to Cairo, and Noura came with her to the airport. They waited hours on a line, and then, just as she was about to clear customs, two Mukhabaraat (Intelligence) agents walked up. We need to ask you some questions, they said. And they took her away.

Noura took a taxi home, wondering how long it would be until she saw her mother again. As the car arrived at the front door, she saw the Alawi couple who lived on the first floor of her building, the ones whose son was one of Bashar's private guards. She had never thought about it much before, but now, all the anxiety and fear of the past few months welled up inside her. The regime, she said to herself, is made of people like this, our neighbors, living right next to us, thinking Bashar is God and supporting everything he does. She was out of the car now. She looked directly at the couple and then, very deliberately, spat on the ground. It was the bravest thing she had ever done. The couple said nothing. She walked past them into the house.

That night, several of her mother's friends called to reassure her, telling her to stay calm, that the regime wouldn't hurt her mother. Noura called a couple of Alawi friends to see if there was anything they could do. They seemed frightened to be talking to her at all. *I'm sorry, if I ask questions about your mother this will be a black mark for me, you understand, I'm sorry*, one of them said. Sometimes Alawis seemed more frightened of the regime than anyone else. Maybe because they knew it better. Over the next few days, even members of Noura's own family seemed to withdraw, as if her mother's black mark had infected her, too. It was the loneliest time in her life. After a week, her mother called for the first time. She said she was all right. She used a code that she and Noura had agreed on beforehand, referring to her as Farah. "Tell Farah to go stay at her cousin's," her mother said. It felt silly. No one would fool the Mukhabaraat this way. But she went. Her aunts Maha and Wissam had been arrested too, during a trip to Aleppo. The whole family was under suspicion. She spent the next two weeks living at her cousin's place, rarely going outside. Finally, in mid-September, she got a call from her mother saying she was being released. She was thrilled and went home to wait for her there.

She was sitting in her bedroom, after dark, when she heard the explosion, very loud and very close. She ran to the window and looked down: a car was engulfed in flames. She looked harder and realized it was her mother's car. The flames were rising higher, and thick black smoke began to pour toward the house; she could smell it. A gunshot rang out, then another. She ran deeper into the house, screaming. This was it, she thought, they are coming for me, to arrest me, to kill me. She fumbled for her phone and called her mother. Zahra answered and Noura sobbed and shouted, telling her to come quickly. Zahra was at her brother's house, not far away. She told Noura to calm down, it might be an accident. *Wait for me.*

The car burned. That was all. No one was coming to kill them. But even

Zahra felt sure this was a message, though she wasn't sure it was from the regime. Their neighborhood was mostly Alawi, and many people there must be very unhappy to have a prominent Sunni doctor who cared for wounded protesters living among them, she thought. She felt she couldn't trust anyone anymore. Noura took days to recover. Even afterward, her nerves were so bad that Zahra began giving her a mild sedative every day.

Aliaa left in August for England, where she was doing a master's degree in English teaching at Warwick University. She and Noura didn't speak for almost two months. One night in October, Aliaa was half asleep when she heard a buzzing on her laptop: Noura was calling to video-chat. It was 4:00 a.m., but they spent an hour talking and laughing, as if nothing had changed. Politics came up briefly, but they dropped it and talked instead about their families, about England, about mutual friends. When they hung up, Aliaa burst into tears. She felt as if their friendship would survive despite everything. But Noura, in the predawn darkness of her bedroom, found herself thinking about something Aliaa had said: one of their mutual friends, a former class-mate named Hossam who supported the revolution, had unfriended Aliaa on Facebook. Now Noura began to feel guilty somehow. So many people were in jail, so many had been killed, and here she was talking with Aliaa, who was with the regime.

In December, Noura attended one last demonstration. The Arab League had sent a delegation of observers to Syria and the protesters grew bolder, thinking they were safe as long as the visitors were in Jableh. Noura joined a daytime rally with a group of people bringing CDs documenting regime abuses to the Arab League team. But the po-lice attacked, beating protesters with clubs and firing into the air; Noura ran headlong with a group of friends, terrified, with bullets cracking just overhead. Soon afterward, her mother got a call from Political Se-curity, telling her to come in for another talk. This time, she got lucky. The office called back and said the meeting was delayed a week.

The family made its decision right away. Within days, Noura, her mother, and two aunts were crowded into a car, their suitcases crammed into the trunk. They had taken only essentials, knowing the trip would be hard. But they knew they might be gone a long time. In Latakia they got a ride northward into the border country. Then they walked for eight hours along a cold, muddy trail, with smugglers helping them carry the bags. They had to ford a river near the border, walking across one by one on a fallen tree. It rained much of the trip, and at times Maha thought of her old house and wanted to turn around and go back. But once they got to Turkey, her son Tareq was waiting for them. He had already rented an apartment in Antakya, the nearest city. All three families piled into it, their belongings heaped on the floor. They were exiles.

When Aliaa heard that Noura and her family had left Syria, she looked at her old friend's Facebook page and discovered that Noura had unfriended her. But as she kept looking at Noura's page almost every day, she saw a slow transformation. Noura's public postings were passionately anti-Assad, and eventually they began to include more and more religious language, and some sectarian slurs against Alawis. Later that year, Noura married a Sunni man from Jableh whose Facebook page showed the black banner used by Al Qaeda. Noura's younger brother Kamal, whom Aliaa had carried around and fed crackers when he was a boy, had his own Facebook page too, with an image of him clutching a Kalashnikov. In early 2013, just after giving birth to her first child, Noura posted a long passage praising Saddam Hussein, followed by the sentence: "How many 'likes' for the conqueror of the Shia and other heathens?"

All through 2012, the Syrian rebellion was simultaneously decaying and gaining ghoulish new life, like a reanimated carcass. The first wave of rebels, the urban young men and women who spoke of democracy, were fleeing to Beirut or London or Dubai. They were replaced by legions of young zealots who slipped across the border with holy war and martyrdom on their minds. To the outside world, the conflict became a gory mosaic of images and video clips shot on jiggling handheld cell phone cameras. The corpse of a thirteen-year-old boy, his genitals severed, his body covered with burns. A man being buried alive, while a Syrian commando orders him to say that Bashar is God. (The man refuses and is buried.) The bodies of women and children in a rebel village, lifeless, in heaps. A rebel fighter eating the viscera of a

Syrian regime soldier. These images scattered like broken glass across the Internet, were mounted on posters, held aloft by chanting crowds, transformed into demands at the United Nations and the Arab League. A handful of these images, it turned out, were fake or, rather, old atrocities from Lebanon or Palestine, or even from car accidents, plane crashes, crime scenes. No one could say for sure where this fakery originated or how it spread, but its discovery came almost as a relief: both sides were eager for reasons to absolve their own crimes. "This is why we don't believe anything they say about the regime or the *shabiha*," Aliaa told me. "It's all fake." And so the war went on, a blizzard of horrors that anyone could ignore as if changing the channel on a TV remote.

The question no one could quite answer was how it had happened so quickly. Of course Bashar's men had spread sectarian rumors. They had threatened their own people to stay in line, they had even released hard-core jihadis from the regime's own prisons, all with the goal of opening up old wounds. But those wounds were real, and they were close to the surface. In less than a year, a regime crackdown had transformed into what looked like millennial religious hatred.

In November 1862, an American missionary named Henry Harris Jessup opened the door of his Beirut home and found himself confronting a stranger. The man before him was "short of stature, had a low forehead, projecting chin and Negroid lips, ruddy countenance, and altogether as repulsive a man as I have ever met in the East," Jessup later wrote. The visitor was an Alawi, and he called himself Soleyman of Adana.

Jessup was accustomed to greeting strangers. He was one of a small group of Protestant missionaries living in greater Syria who were mostly seen as benevolent outsiders. They taught Arabs about the Bible and provided a refuge for people fleeing from ethnic and sectarian feuds. Jessup, at age thirty, was tall and starkly handsome, with piercing eyes, a high forehead, and a long beard that spread, in patriarchal splendor, around his stiff white collar. He had been in Lebanon for only six years, but he already spoke Arabic so well that he preached in the language. Soleyman pulled out a letter, which Jessup unfolded and read. It said that Soleyman was a man of considerable learning and a convert to Christianity from the "mystic Nusairi faith," another word for the Alawi religion. The letter's writer, a well-known scholar living in Damascus, had helped free Soleyman from military service on the grounds that he was now a Christian, one of the groups exempted by the Ottomans.

This was a rare discovery for Jessup. The Alawis and their religion were at that time an almost total mystery to outsiders, and they were the subject of wild and lurid rumors. Soleyman, it turned out, was not only an Alawi but one of the *khass*, the elite few in that community to be initiated into the religion's secret tenets. Jessup invited him in and asked him to sit down. They began talking right away, and the conversation spread over many hours in the following days. Soleyman's initiation had begun at the age of seventeen, when an Alawi sheikh handed him a glass of wine and placed a sandal on his head. "Say thou, 'by the mystery of thy beneficence, O my uncle and lord, thou crown of my head, I am thy pupil, and let thy sandal lie upon my head,'" the man intoned. After a series of other rituals spread over nine months, a sheikh asked him to recite a vow of secrecy: "Wilt thou suffer the cutting off of thy head and hands and feet, and not disclose this august mystery?" Soleyman swore. He was inducted into the thousand-year-old mystical beliefs of the Alawis, including reincarnation and the deification of Ali, the cousin and son-in-law of the Prophet Muhammad. The Alawis venerated Christ and Muhammad, but also Plato, Socrates, and Aristotle. They used strange passwords to recognize each other, and had a practice of impersonating members of other faiths, though they privately reviled Muslims and Christians as wretched heretics, destined to be reborn as apes and pigs. At Jessup's urging, Soleyman wrote up everything he knew about the Alawi faith in book form over the space of a few weeks. Jessup got it printed, and it was the first—and for a long time the only—authentic source for outsiders about the religion.

Soleyman also talked about the misery of life among the Alawis. They were mountain people, intensely distrustful of outsiders. They had retreated centuries earlier to the hills to escape from the Muslims of the Syrian plain, who reviled them as heretics, and occasionally carried out murderous raids. The theologian Ibn Taymiyya had proclaimed in the early 1300s that the Alawis were "more infidel than Jews and Christians, even more infidel than many polytheists," and urged good Muslims to slaughter and rob them. Those words were invoked regularly. The Alawis retaliated with their own intense hatred. But even within their own community, the Alawis were so tribal and feud-prone that murder and robbery were constants of life. At times, the community stood close to extinction. One English clergyman who lived among them for several years in the mid-nineteenth century described a world of extraordinary violence and constant starvation, where "the state of society is a perfect hell upon earth." Alawis accused of banditry, when caught by Muslims, were given special treatment: impaled on spikes and left on crossroads as a warning.

Soleyman's story evoked great sympathy from his bearded American friend. Soleyman had come to doubt the truth of the Alawi faith after standing outside the house of a dying man and observing that no planet descended to the dead man's body, and no star rose from the house door. Other Alawi beliefs also seemed baseless. Disgusted, Soleyman converted to Islam. But after only a month of reading through the Koran, he found three hundred lies "and seventy great lies" in it. He decided to become a Greek Orthodox Christian. After a brief honeymoon, he found he could not bear the worship of holy icons or the idea of eating God in the form of a wafer. Next he became a Jew and taught himself to read Hebrew well enough to get through the Talmud. There, too, he found too much nonsense. He then discovered a Protestant tract attacking the pope and decided he had found the true path at last. It was then that the Turkish authorities threw him in jail and drafted him into the army. He escaped only after being marched six hundred miles to Damascus. There, a Christian scholar who had worked as an American consul discovered him and wrote the letter that brought him to Beirut.

Jessup was delighted that this bizarre, troll-faced polymath had finally found the true Christ. He got him a room to rent in Beirut. Soleyman was thrillingly exotic company for the Pennsylvania clergyman and his friends: he could recite whole chapters of the Koran from memory, along with much of the Hebrew Bible. He had an almost endless supply of mystical Alawi teachings. But Soleyman's wanderings were not over. He began roaming the region, preaching Protestantism with apocalyptic fervor, and one day he arrived on Jessup's doorstep again, this time reeking of liquor. When Jessup told him he could not allow him to enter the house if he drank again, Soleyman asked for a pen and paper. He wrote: "I, Soleyman of Adana, do hereby pledge myself never to drink a drop of liquor again, and if I do, my blood is forfeited, and I hereby authorize Rev. H. Jessup to cut off my head, and drink my blood." Jessup frowned at the "rather strong language" but was pleased with the pledge. It did not last long, however. Soleyman returned to his drinking habits and freely denounced all the religions he had abandoned. He married the daughter of a Greek priest and eventually moved back to Adana.

It was there that the Alawi sheikhs caught up to him. They had bided their time, believing that to kill Soleyman after the book was published would be taken for proof that all he had written was true. Years had now passed since its publication. Soleyman had fallen out of touch with his American friend, who was living hundreds of miles away in Beirut. Even then, the old sheikhs were cold and slow with their revenge. They invited Soleyman to a village feast, pretending to treat him as an honored guest, a son of the faith who had gained renown. He was on horseback, being led by young Alawi men who sang and fired their rifles in his honor. As his horse wove among the manure piles that ringed the village, the men suddenly grabbed his legs and flung him into a ditch they had prepared beforehand. They heaped dung onto him, ignoring his screams, until he was buried alive. Years later, when Jessup was passing through Adana in 1888, a local teacher told him that Alawi sheikhs had cut Soleyman's tongue out after killing him and preserved it in a jar. They would bring it out on special occasions, the teacher said, cursing him and consigning him to hell for his betrayal.

The Alawis, meanwhile, continued to live in wretched poverty in their mountain hideaways, at the margins of Syria's feudal economy. Many were forced to sell their daughters into indentured servitude as maids for wealthy Damascus families, where they were said to be treated as sexual slaves. The mutual hatred between mountain and city persisted even after the collapse of the Ottoman Empire and the arrival of the French at the end of the first World War. For a brief period, the French administered the Alawi mountain hinterland as a state of its own, and the Alawis were finally free from fear of their Muslim neighbors in the plains below. By the mid-1930s, the French were under pressure to recognize Syrian demands for a unified, independent state. The Alawis could see what was coming. In 1936, six Alawi notables sent a petition begging the French not to merge their northern enclave with the rest of Syria. "The spirit of hatred and fanaticism embedded in the hearts of the Arab Muslims against everything that is non-Muslim has been perpetually nurtured by the Islamic religion," they wrote. "There is no hope that this situation will ever change. Therefore, the abolition of the mandate will expose the minorities in Syria to the dangers of death and annihilation, irrespective of the fact that such abolition will annihilate the freedom of thought and belief."

One of the petition's signers was Sulayman al Assad, the grandfather of Bashar al Assad. When the French abandoned them, the Alawis rushed to embrace the Syrian nationalist cause. History was rewritten, and Alawi divines began declaring themselves Muslims. The young Alawi officer Hafez al Assad embraced Arabism like a new religion; he pledged himself to the destruction of Israel, he did everything he could to disguise his heretical roots, especially after he rose to the presidency in 1971. Syria's other minority groups—Christians, Druze, Ismailis, and the rest—did the same thing, rushing for the cover of Arabism and the Baath Party, its local political vehicle. But Assad needed more than just political cover. The stain of Alawi difference had to be explicitly cleansed. The word went out: the new strongman wanted fatwas. Several obliging Shiite clerics, eager for Syrian patronage, opened their arms and declared Alawis to be orthodox members of the Shiite fold.

Assad was grateful, but far too clever to mistake these bouquets for a wedding. He quietly positioned his Alawi kinsmen at the core of the expanding police state, like knives under a table. He knew he could count on them, and their fear, when the crisis came.

I remembered the 1936 petition signed by Sulayman al Assad when I first entered Aliaa Ali's family living room and saw a black-and-white portrait on the wall: her grandfather, in a stiff collar and tie. "He studied in France in the 1930s," Aliaa said brightly. Then she quickly added, as if someone had signaled a minor gaffe, "And later he fought the French in the struggle for independence—I think." You have to be careful not to stumble on your history if you are Alawi.

It was April 2013. After two years of fighting, the Syrian war had spun outward and was drawing in almost every country in the region and many beyond it. Hezbollah had soldiers and trainers on the ground, as did Iran. There were thousands of rebels fighting in the name of jihad from more than a dozen countries, bankrolled by intelligence services and militias and zealots of every kind. On the other side, Shiite volunteers from Iraq, Lebanon, and even Yemen were lining up to fight for Bashar. The jihad was irresistible to bored, frustrated young men who had been fed a diet of religion all through their schooling. I met a Saudi in Riyadh later that year who had gone to Syria eight times. He was a hospital administrator, a respectable forty-three-year-old who felt no shame in admitting that he relished a chance to kill a few Shiites. Sometimes he went just for a long weekend. Most of these people could not have cared less about Syria itself; they were there for the Apocalypse, the great battle between true Islam and its enemies that would shatter heresy forever and pave the way for God's kingdom. Or so they thought.

But there was always another way of looking at it, one everyone was at least half aware of: that this great battle between Sunni and Shiite was really just a cynical power struggle between the region's two biggest oil producers, Saudi Arabia and Iran, who fed their people sectarian slogans the way you might feed amphetamines to a tired boxer. One thing was certain: the Iranian and Saudi designs on Syria, like shifting gears, turned larger wheels in more distant capitals. Russia bankrolled Assad with an eye on its own Muslims in the Caucasus. China vetoed any efforts to authorize force in the United Nations. Qatar funded jihadis *and* American efforts to undermine them. Even Barack Obama became a proxy warrior, with deep reluctance. After resisting for a year, he signed a secret order for the CIA to arm and train "vetted" Syrian rebels just before I arrived in Damascus in April 2013. This was the first time I met Aliaa and her family, and heard her story of the revolution's unfolding in Jableh.

For me, it was an uneasy return to a country I barely recognized. I had been to Syria many times in the years before the revolution. I loved it the way you love an old abandoned junkyard, full of undervalued rusty relics that no one else has discovered. It was dim and depressing, with its collapsing old markets and decaying French mandate architecture, its medieval tunnels and dark silent bars, its dead cities full of crumbling stones and empty, lichen-clad cisterns. I made friends with film directors and Kurdish activists and Palestinian refugees, and we whispered furtively about the regime in bars, eyeing the Mukhabaraat men in leather jackets who pretended not to be watching.

Now that Syria was gone. Half the country was behind rebel lines, in a zone where Western hostages were bought and sold and beheaded. Most of my Syrian friends had fled and were living in Europe or Beirut or Dubai. Some of them were dead, or kidnapped God knows where.

I began my journey in Damascus and found one old friend on a Thursday night in Abu Rummaneh, a tony district. It was in a basement bar, a dark throbbing den of young Syrians dancing and drinking and making out. I pushed through the thicket of bodies until I reached the bar and found Khaled, who gave me a sweaty bear hug and bought me a beer. He is a novelist and a bohemian, a big man with a rowdy laugh and a massive head of steel-gray curls. He'd been a dissident ever since I'd known him, and a passionate protester in 2011. Two years had aged him visibly. We talked about mutual friends, all of them now gone. "I can't give up on the revolution," Khaled said. "I won't leave Damascus." He put his arm around a young woman and introduced her as Rita. "Khaled is the only optimist left in Syria," Rita said. When Khaled moved off to greet someone else, I asked Rita—we had to shout over the churn of Arab pop music—about the state of the peaceful opposition. "I am ashamed to say it, but the opposition has lost its meaning," she said. "Now it is only killing, nothing but killing. The jihadis are speaking of a caliphate, and the Christians are really frightened." There was a pause. "I waited all my life for this revolution, but now I think maybe it shouldn't have happened. At least not this way."

If the opposition had lost its meaning, so had the regime. The old masks were gone. The country that had defined itself as "the beating heart of Arabism" had been officially ejected from the Arab League, its leader scorned as a criminal.

On a quiet side street in one of Damascus's richest neighborhoods, a prominent lawyer with ties to the Assad family invited me to join him and his friends in an opulent book-lined study. There were soft leather couches and European chocolates on the coffee table. A sixteen-frame video screen showed every approach to the house. One of the guests was Father Gabriel Daoud, a handsome priest who sprawled on an armchair in his black cassock. The subject of Syria's minorities came up, and Father Daoud's face registered his irritation. "Minorities—it's a false name," he said. "It should be the quality of the people, not the quantity. It gives you the idea that minorities are small and weak. But we are the original people of this country." As for the protesters and their demands for freedom, Father Daoud smirked. "They don't want *hurriya*, they want *houriaat*." *Hurriya* is the Arabic word for "freedom," and *houriaat* is the plural of "*houris*," the dark-eyed virgins that suicide bombers are promised in the afterlife. Father Daoud chuckled at his little witticism, and then grew more serious. "They are barbarians, real barbarians," he said of the opposition. "They may have Syrian nationality, but not the mentality. We are proud of our secularism. We cannot live with these barbarians." When I raised the subject of Arab nationalism, Father Daoud winced. "We are Phoenician, not Arabic," he said. "We don't want to be Arabic."

Some other regime supporters took this idea further. One young Alawi filmmaker, the son of a high-ranking officer, hinted that it was time for the Alawis to stop pretending they were Muslims. "When the Alawi sect began, a thousand years ago, it was a rebellion against the status quo," he said, when I met him in a Damascus café. "The dictatorship at that time was Islam, so the rebellion against it naturally took a religious form. Islam is a lie, it is just a way to gain power and control crowds. This is what we should be rebelling against." When I asked him what—in the absence of Arabism of Islam—might inspire young Syrians or bring them together, he hesitated. "The Baath Party doesn't exist anymore," he said. "They are dinosaurs. Arab nationalism could be reconstructed, perhaps, on an economic basis . . ." His voice trailed off, and he grimaced. "I remember saying, when the first protests started in Tunis and Cairo in 2011, that if this happens here in Syria, it will never end. The moments of extermination are still too present in people's minds." I assumed he was referring to Hama, where so many Sunnis were killed by the regime's Alawi-led forces. But after a moment's thought I realized I was probably wrong: he had spoken earlier of the Alawis as rebels and victims. Everyone in this struggle was bent on portraying his own people as David and the other side as Goliath.

In some ways, life in Damascus was startlingly normal. There was fresh fruit in the market stalls, and crowds of shoppers in the Old City; sweet apple-flavored tobacco smoke drifted from the cafés. But checkpoints were everywhere, and I could not walk ten yards without a plainclothes member of the new National Defense Forces demanding my ID. Behind the comforting bustle of street sounds, the dull thump of artillery could be heard, like intermittent thunder. No one ever remarked on it, and in the spring sunlight it was hard to imagine that people were fighting and dying only a few miles away.

Only after taking the highway north out of Damascus did I see the war. On either side of us were houses pancaked to rubble or burned beyond recognition, posters bearing the faces of Assad and his clan shot to pieces. As we drove past the suburb of Harasta, where some of the worst fighting had raged, a huge column of black smoke rose from a cluster of houses a few hundred yards away. My driver glanced anxiously back and forth. The speedometer pushed past ninety miles per hour, and I wondered how our worn-out Hyundai would hold up. "This is a very dangerous area," he said. "We must go fast." Beyond the suburbs, the highway skirts the war-shattered city of Homs and turns west, toward the mountainous Alawi heartland along the Mediterranean. This was the route Bashar and his loyalists would take if, in the fantasy embraced by their enemies, they ever abandoned the capital and tried to forge a rump state in the land of their ancestors. The landscape along the highway grows greener the farther north you go, and the signs of war slowly fade. Magnificent snowcapped mountains rise to the west, and later, the glittering blue plane of the sea comes into view. The hills are speckled with olive and fruit trees, and the smell of eucalyptus mingles with the sea breeze.

It was there that I first met Aliaa Ali and found myself gazing at the photograph of her grandfather. The Ali family home in Jableh had the cozy look of a beach house, with shells on the walls and blue paint peeling in spots from the moist sea air. A picture of Hassan Nasrallah hung on the wall, and one of Bashar al Assad. On the shelves were some novels in English, including Dostoyevsky's *Crime and Punishment*. The bookends were oblong lumps of metal, which turned out to be bits of Israeli artillery shells, a memento from her father's years as a sergeant with the Syrian military in Lebanon. As we ate a lunch of fried fish and chicken, her father delivered a little lecture about the evils of Saudi influence; the seeds of terrorism had been sown in the '70s, he said, and they were flowering now. This was a constant during my time in regime-controlled Syria, as if everyone had received a little index card reminder of what to tell the American journalist: *We are facing Saudi-funded terrorism, just like you.*

Not everyone abided by the regime's sectarian script. After lunch, standing on the terrace in the warm spring air, I asked Aliaa what she thought of Alawis who joined the opposition, like the novelist Samar Yazbek, another native of Jableh. She grew wary at the mention of Yazbek's name. "I met her once," Aliaa said. "She told me I had a bright future in front of me. But I don't want a future like hers. I think Alawis who join the opposition don't realize that they are being used as tools. Or they think they can turn this jihadi war into a democratic revolution. But they will never succeed."

Samar Yazbek was also in Syria during the early months of the revolution. In her diaries of the revolt's first four months—later published in English under the title *A Woman in the Crossfire*—she describes the furious campaign conducted against her after she publicly backed the insurrection. Her family was forced to disavow her, and leaflets were passed out in Jableh denouncing her. At one point, she describes a terrifying encounter with the security apparatus. After being driven from her house in Damascus to an intelligence center, she finds herself with a scowling officer who spits on her, knocks her to the floor, and threatens to kill her. Guards then lead her blindfolded downstairs to one of the regime's basement torture rooms, where she is forced to look at bloodied, half-dead protesters hanging from the ceiling. The officer tells her that she is being duped by "Salafi Islamists" and that she must come back to the fold or die. "We're honorable people," he tells her. "We don't harm our own blood. We're not like you traitors. You're a black mark upon all the Alawis." When I spoke to Yazbek, who is now living in Paris, she told me she believed that the Alawi community had been the Assad clan's first victim, that they had been used as "human shields" to keep the regime in power. "They believe the regime's rhetoric, that they would be massacred if Assad falls," she said. "They are very afraid, and very confused."

Some Alawis inside Syria quietly make the same point, though it is far more dangerous for them to do so. Aliaa herself often seemed on the verge of conceding that much of what Yazbek said was true. She had read widely and absorbed the unforgiving Western view of Assad's regime. Once, she referred to him in passing as a "dictator." It was as if she wanted me to know that her mind was not captive to the sectarian label she'd grown up with. But these impulses were always followed by a gesture of anger at Europe and the United States: these were the governments that defined her people as an enemy. She might peer over the box of her loyalties, but she could not escape it. At times, Aliaa and her peers reminded me of Soleyman of Adana: struggling to escape the past, yet unable to speak too loudly lest their own people destroy them.

Most of the time, Syria's minorities—not just Alawis but also Christians, Druze, Murshidis—do not make such distinctions. All they know is that they are being hunted down and killed by an enemy that looks just like the one that killed their ancestors. By 2013, the rising death toll among regime soldiers had made funerals an almost daily affair in northwestern Syria. I saw at least half a dozen new war monuments in mountain towns near Latakia, often with hundreds of soldiers' names engraved on them. Paper flyers and colored posters cover the walls in Latakia and Tartous, all of them showing the names and faces of men (and some women) killed while fighting for Bashar.

Soon after I met her, Aliaa and her brother Abdulhameed took me to her family's ancestral home, in the mountain village of Dreikeesh. The road from the coast climbs along hairpin turns into a magnificent landscape of lush terraced hills and orchards that called to mind the hill towns of Tuscany or Umbria. After a twenty-minute drive, we reached the house, where Aliaa's uncle, Amer Ali, stood waiting for us, a sturdy-looking man of fifty with a hardened face and close-cropped graying hair. He led us upstairs to a large high-ceilinged room where sunlight splashed through two open walls. Dozens of people waited inside, some of them in uniform, sipping tea and coffee. Amer had gathered them to tell their stories of relatives or spouses lost to the war. I sat down and listened to them, one by one. They were working-class people: soldiers, construction workers, policemen, dressed in simple, worn-out clothes. All were Alawis, as far as I could tell. Some were probably *shabiha*, though none of them would have used that term. One of them, a middle-aged construction worker named Adib Sulayman, pulled out his cell phone and showed me the message he'd received after his son Yamin was kidnapped by rebels: "We have executed God's will and killed your son. If you are still fighting with Bashar, we will come to your houses and cut you into pieces. Never fight against us." None of the people I met in that room conveyed any arrogance of the kind I was used to seeing in Damascus. They all made clear that they felt their families, their homes, their whole way of life, were in terrible danger. I met a twenty-year-old man who had been shot twice in the head and had lost some of his memory and half his hearing. He told me he would go back to the front as soon as his wounds healed. His father stared at me and said, "I would be proud to have my son become a martyr. I am in my fifties, but I am ready to sacrifice my life too. They thought we would be weak in this crisis, but we are strong."

After lunch, Aliaa's uncle showed me around the house. On the wall was a Sword of Ali, an important symbol for Alawis, with verses in praise of Imam Ali engraved on the blade. There were old farming tools, a stick for catching snakes, hunting knives, and a century-old carbine—a kind of visual history of the Alawi people. There were ancient Phoenician amphorae, and a family tree in the kitchen, with names dating back centuries. Amer Ali led me to the roof, where we gazed out at the town where his family has lived for hundreds of years. The hills were lovely in the golden afternoon sunlight. You could see an ancient spring with a stone arch over it, and a mosque that had been built by one of his ancestors 240 years ago. Aliaa stood next to me on the terrace, looking out at the town with an expression of rapturous pride. I asked her how it made her feel to know that Western human rights groups had documented repeated atrocities by the Syrian regime—some, perhaps, by people like the ones we had just talked to. This was before the large-scale chemical weapons attacks on Syrian civilians that would bring the United States to the brink of military intervention in Syria in the autumn of 2013. It was before the Assad regime made "barrel bombs," the makeshift explosives dropped indiscriminately onto civilian areas, a household word. But already the litany of horrors was long.

Aliaa glanced downward. "Yes, there have been atrocities," she said. "You can never deny that there have been atrocities. But you have to ask yourself: What will happen if Bashar falls? That's why I believe victory is the only option. If Bashar falls, Syria falls. And then we, here, will all be in the niqab, or we will be dead." Before we climbed back down, Aliaa's uncle showed me a rusted white tripod, set in the center of the roof, under a gazebo. "It is for telescopes, for looking at the stars," he said, looking up at the cloudless evening sky. Then he glanced down the mountain, toward where the hills give way to the vast Syrian plain. "But we can use it to set up a sniper rifle and defend ourselves here."

Two hours' drive to the north, just beyond the lush green hill country of the Turkish border, Noura Kanafani and her family were living in an oddly parallel world of grief and encirclement. They showed me photographs of dead and disappeared friends and relatives, of bare skin marked by hideous bruises, welts, burns, the language of torture. I watched appalling videotapes of regime soldiers and paramilitaries shooting at funeral ceremonies in Sunni villages. Noura too felt that the world had abandoned her and her people: the Americans, the Europeans, the Arabs—all faithless. She had a job at an American-funded charity, and her mother, Zahra, was working at a nearby hospital. Aunt Maha was running a school for Syrian refugee children in a camp near the border. They were much better off than most Syrian refugees; with their jobs, they had enough money to rent decent apartments. But they were deeply unhappy in exile, and none of them believed they would ever see Jableh again. They had retreated into piety. Noura, who had always worn a simple hijab over her hair, told me she was thinking about donning the full niqab. When I first approached her, she refused to talk to me, because her husband, whose Facebook page was full of jihadi symbols and warlike slogans, did not approve of her talking to foreign men. Eventually, under the pressure of his in-laws, he relented. Noura and her relatives were all angry that the West was more focused on the crimes of rebel jihadi groups than those of Bashar al Assad. "It is not believable that a superpower can do nothing," Noura told me. "People are shocked by the world's silence." Her aunt Maha went further, saying that she suspected the United States was in league with Bashar, and it was all part of a war against Islam itself.

As their friendship receded into the past, both Noura and Aliaa began revisiting it in the light of a new wartime awareness. Each of them highlighted stray comments and anecdotes that had seemed innocuous at the time but now took on a sinister new meaning. Sitting in a Turkish café one night, Noura said something that amazed me: "I think Aliaa and her family became Shiites." When I asked what she meant, she said Aliaa had often told her about her parents' pilgrimage to Najaf and Karbala, the Shiite shrine cities in Iraq. And that Aliaa had often recited quotes from the Koran about Ali. Noura said she now remembered hearing rumors that Aliaa's family had once been poor, then suddenly became rich. This now made sense to her: the Iranians were said to pay people to become Shiites. As Noura thought about it, she began to feel that Aliaa had been subtly suggesting to Noura that she, too, should become a Shiite. "She wasn't very clear about it, but now I think maybe she was going to become more clear if I actually became Shiite," Noura said. None of this was true. Aliaa's parents had visited Najaf and Karbala, like many Alawis, but I found no evidence that they had ever contemplated converting to Shiism. But facts were not the point. It was as if the war had gradually cast its shadow over Noura's most intimate memories, reshaping them into a narrative that made Aliaa little more than a puppet in a sectarian morality play. Behind her friend stood the shadow of Iran, enemy of the Sunnis.

For her part, Aliaa also was combing through her memories of the friendship and had found all kinds of subtle but damning signs. She remembered Noura's mother having said something positive about Osama bin Laden. She remembered that Noura had almost married the old professor from Rastan, the one who was a hard-line Salafi, a Wahhabi. She remembered Noura having said something about "regaining the *Umma*," the Islamic nation. Once, Noura had said to her, "You don't understand, because you don't have a deep knowledge of religion." Most damning of all were the links to Saudi Arabia: one of Noura's aunts married a Saudi. And Noura's teenage brother, Kamal, had met with a Saudi jeweler, who was teaching him about the jewelry business. "It was just strange at the time, but now I understand why," Aliaa told me. Her friend had been a closet Wahhabi all along. This too was a fantasy, but it was a fantasy she needed, just as Noura needed hers. Their friendship belonged to a world that no longer made sense. They had redefined each other, little by little, as enemies.

4

— Prisoners of the Sheikh (Yemen) —

When I first saw the Ja'ashin peasants, they were standing in front of a tall iron gate in downtown Sanaa, a clutch of brown human figures so gaunt and unobtrusive they might as well have been made of dust. The younger ones looked starved. The older ones had cowed faces and brown, rotten teeth. They were dressed in rags. They shot fearful glances this way and that, as if the high walls and unfamiliar towers of the Old City might devour them. Then one of them stepped up and spoke to me. He had a vigorous face, with glinting eyes and a firm jaw. His name was Saeed. He was sixty-two, he said, but he looked older, with atrophied limbs and a pair of dirty white plastic crutches. He wore a rumpled brown suit jacket and a thin *futa*, a cloth skirt, over his sandals. His bruised legs were bare in the brisk winter air. I asked him what they were doing there. "It is because of the Sheikh," Saeed said. "He takes our land, kidnaps our children, and if we protest, he binds us hand and foot and puts us in his dungeons." Several of his companions held up lacerated wrists and ankles: shackle scars. Saeed said they had come almost a hundred miles from their rugged mountain home in a place called Ja'ashin, much of it on foot, to escape from this man. Some of the Sheikh's victims were tortured; others never came home. His soldiers—he commanded a private army—were merciless. The peasants had come to Sanaa, Yemen's capital, with the help of human rights activists, who had encouraged them to demand justice from a government that was scarcely more than a rumor to them.

The more Saeed and his friends talked, the more wretched and bizarre their tale became. The Sheikh had been oppressing them for decades, they said. He had prevented them from making the journey to Sanaa in the past, but this time they had escaped at night. They had trekked down steep mountain paths, meeting in villages, riding buses from one town to another as they made their way to Sanaa. But they feared his agents even here, in the capital. The Sheikh was a man of infinite cunning. He was not just a tyrant but also a renowned poet, famous for his seductive ghazals, and more so for the hymns of praise he wrote in flowery classical Arabic about his old friend, the president. And the president, in exchange for being compared with a god, granted the Sheikh his private fiefdom of some sixty thousand souls. There was no law in Ja'ashin, no state: everything belonged to the Sheikh. When I asked how long this had been going on, the old men looked baffled. They had never known any ruler but the Sheikh. And before him? Before him was his father, equally cruel. Did the government know? More baffled looks. These illiterate peasants seemed to live in a land out of time, a medieval landscape of high-walled castles, sadistic overlords, and backbreaking labor in the fields. Some seemed not to understand that they lived in the republic of Yemen, a nominal democracy. "All I know is that God rules above and the Sheikh rules here below," one broken-looking old man told me.

It seemed almost too outlandish to be true, an Arabized fable from the Brothers Grimm. I had spent the better part of a decade wandering the Middle East and never seen anything like it. Yet the activists standing alongside the peasants held up sheaves of documents and gruesome photographs, and said they could document it all. The Sheikh, moreover, was not some primordial figure from the Yemeni past, some cruel holdover. Granted, he might look that way to an outsider. But no, the Sheikh was all too contemporary. Sheikh Muhammad Ahmed Mansour, to use his full name, wasn't even a tribal leader in the traditional sense. The freedom-loving Bedouin of the desert would have been appalled by him. In a way, he was the quintessential product of the Arab old regime, its endgame and crowning indignity. He didn't just oppress the peasants; he delivered up all their votes to the president at every election cycle. In this way, he helped maintain the phony democratic veneer over Yemen's corrupt politics. He made himself so useful to the military men who ruled the country—clones, more or less, of the military men running all the other Arab republics, from Algeria to Iraq—that he'd become politically untouchable. He had won a tyranny over the people of Ja'ashin more complete, more demeaning, than anything his medieval ancestors had dreamed of. This was not the Middle Ages; it was a contemporary sadist's fantasy, bought with oil money.

This was in February 2010. You could argue that the uprisings in Yemen began right there, almost a year before Mohamed Bouazizi's burning body kicked off the Arab Spring. Half an hour after I first met Saeed, an angry young lawyer arrived. With the Ja'ashin peasants standing behind him like a screen, he began shouting through a microphone to the half-empty square: *Could there be a more glaring indictment of our rulers? We have had a republic since 1962, and now we have gone backward to feudalism. Is there a greater betrayal than this? You speak of fighting Al Qaeda, and our people are being turned into slaves?*

The Ja'ashin were the perfect foil for the self-dealing and criminality at the heart of Yemen's hollow state. Most Arab dictators have been corrupt and manipulative, but Yemen's ruler, Ali Abdullah Saleh, brought these traits to a whole new level of cynicism and mastery. In the Arab world's poorest country—where half the population lives on $2 a day or less—he managed to rake off tens of billions of dollars in public funds for himself and his family, becoming richer than Egypt's latter-day pharaoh, Hosni Mubarak. Saleh elevated blackmail into a tool of the state, redefining his country's worst afflictions as "investments" that could be used to bilk anxious donors like the United

States and Saudi Arabia. Al Qaeda was his greatest success: it put his country on the map and brought him hundreds of millions in military aid and cash. But Saleh's real currency was power, not money. His greatest talent was for corrupting other people. Saleh gloried in what Turks call the "deep state"—a subterranean world of proxy warriors who do the dirty work the ruler cannot be seen to do. He made sure that every potential opponent had dirty money or blood on his hands, or both. It was sometimes said that Saleh "retribalized" a country that was struggling to emerge from its tribal past. But that was unfair to the tribes, who at least had a code of honor. What he really did was to turn powerful sheikhs—and generals and politicians and jihadis and almost everyone else who mattered in Yemen—into criminals, and then, as often as not, set them against each other. In the end, no one was left standing to expose him except those at the very bottom, the people who had nothing to gain and everything to lose in this venal system: the peasants of Ja'ashin.

The Ja'ashin helped instigate the 2011 revolt in a literal sense, though few outside Yemen knew who they were or remembered them afterward. They were the first to set up the protest camp, at an intersection outside the gates of Sanaa's main university. Scores of people moved in, despite the heat and the filth and the police harassment. They had already been there for months when Tunis fell, in January. Their camp quickly expanded into Change Square, Yemen's version of Tahrir. Their cause seemed to merge with that of the 2011 uprisings, thanks in part to a young activist named Tawakol Karman, who'd been promoting their cause for years. Hers was the face of the Yemeni revolt as it reached the rest of the world, via al Jazeera: a brave young woman leading an unlikely protest in a remote corner of Arabia. Yemen had always been known by its exotic façades. Sanaa's Old City, with its rectangular medieval towers clustered densely together, like drip-castles on a beach; long-haired tribesmen lurching around, their mouths bulging with qat, the national addiction that consumes Yemeni afternoons; women covered head to toe in black niqab. The 2011 revolt made many people look more closely for the first time. Tawakol, with her colorful head scarves and the perennially thrilled expression in her wide-set brown eyes, was their symbol. When she won the Nobel Peace Prize later that year, it seemed to put Yemen on the map as something more than the stock phrase used by all the wire services: "the ancestral homeland of Osama bin Laden."

But the figure who embodied the Yemeni revolt to me was Saeed, the bandy-legged man I'd met on that winter day in Sanaa. His battle had begun not in 2011 but almost four decades earlier. He had spent most of his adult life fighting for the same cause, and unlike the young protesters who flooded the squares in the wake of Tahrir, he did not become discouraged when the revolts failed. He had seen far too much for that.

When I first asked Saeed what he had been fighting for all that time, his reply was deceptively simple: *dawla*, a state. "I don't want an Islamic state, I don't want a Socialist state, I don't want a one-party state," he said. "I just want a modern state, the kind they have in Britain and Europe." In a sense, that was what all the protesters of 2011 wanted: a state where citizenship meant something, where the rule of law was respected. But in Yemen, the bar was lower and the absence far more literal. This was a country where the state had never really risen above the tribe. Partly, it was a matter of geography: the southwest corner of Arabia is stippled with arid mountains and remote deserts, and much of it is so inaccessible that no foreign conqueror has ever held it for long. Even today, most Yemenis live in rural villages where local clan leaders have far more control over their lives than anyone in the capital. These people do not read newspapers, and few have access to the Internet. Other Arabs often resort to the same word when talking about Yemen: *mutakhalif*, backward. But its backwardness is not just a fact of nature. Many people who grew up in northern Yemen can remember a time when their nominal ruler was a xenophobic king who deliberately kept the country in a state of preindustrial misery. There were almost no roads, cars, schools, or modern medicine. No airplane landed, no visa was granted without his personal approval. His name was Imam Ahmed, and he was the last of a dynasty in North Yemen that had ruled intermittently—often fighting with the Ottomans, who saw Yemen as part of their empire—for a thousand years. He lived in a palace, but he depended on the warlike tribesmen of the highlands to maintain his rule, and he cleverly played them off against each other.

This was the world Saeed grew up in. Life in Ja'ashin in the 1950s was almost exactly as it had been a thousand years earlier. Men worked long days in the Sheikh's fields, while women collected firewood and ground wheat on stone. Donkey carts rolled slowly along muddy lanes, the only means of transport. There was no electricity, no radios, no way to know what was going on outside the valley. "Hunger was in every house, disease in every house," Saeed told me. "Some days we did not eat." There was no school, only an old man who sat under a tree with children and taught them the Koran from memory. When Saeed was nine years old, his parents sent him down to live with an older brother in Aden, then the capital of British-ruled South Yemen. He was so new to modern life that on his first day, entering a store, he walked right into the glass door, smacking his forehead against it like a bird on a window. He had never seen glass before.

The city struck him in more ways than one. It was there that he first realized how poor his village was, and what a *dawla* might mean for him and his family. Aden at that time was a model of urban prosperity and order, at least by Yemeni standards. It had been a British colony since 1839, and it was an ancient entrepôt for trade with the East. There was a thriving port and a polyglot population of Indians, Chinese, Africans, and Arabs. The British had built good roads, schools, factories, and hospitals, along with a thriving port and a modern judicial system. There was a miniature replica of Big Ben and a statue of Queen Victoria presiding in a gated park. Queen Elizabeth had visited in 1954, laying the foundation stones for an oil refinery and for a hospital named after her. Aden was a place where Yemenis could find good jobs and a free first-rate education for their children. But they resented living under foreign rule. At the school Saeed attended, most of the teachers were ardent Nasserists, and they dreamed of building their own nation, an Arab republic that would open Yemen to the West and free it from colonial tutelage.

Saeed was fourteen years old when that dream was officially declared. He remembers the moment in near-photographic detail, like many other Yemenis who were alive at the time. There had been rumors of a coup against the imam in North Yemen for days, and no one knew for sure what was happening up in the capital. He was sitting in a smoky café when the news broke, his book bag on the table and his school friends packed in tightly around him. It was around dusk, after evening prayer. Suddenly there was shouting, and a group of men crowded around the café's primitive transistor radio. An urgent broadcast from Sanaa was coming on. The Egyptian music stopped abruptly. Static buzzed, and then a voice sailed out confidently over the smoke and the murmurs:

> In the name of God and in the name of the free independent Yemeni people, and in the name of the Yemeni Arab Republic, the leadership of the revolution announces its goals and its general policies with regard to internal and nationalist and international affairs. The goals of the revolution are: One, to annihilate absolute monarchical rule, and to annihilate foreign influence. Two: instituting republican, democratic, and Islamic—

The speech went on, but no one heard it. Cheering, screaming, laughing: ecstatic voices drowned out the radio, the tables clattering with pounded fists and dropped glasses, the clang of cutlery on the floor. Women began ululating from the windows of all the buildings nearby. Men and boys gathered in the street, their eyes wild with joy, chanting together: "No more going backward after today! No more colonialism after today!"

Thawra. Revolution. North Yemen had finally thrown off the imamate and joined the modern age. It was September 26, 1962. Young officers inspired and aided by Egypt's Gamal Abdel Nasser had pulled off a coup, in a carbon copy of Egypt's own 1952 revolution. Things always took a little longer in Yemen. After a few heady days of celebration, Saeed talked his way onto a rented bus packed with excited young men. He had ignored the pleas of his older brother and teachers, and was on his way to Sanaa, the north's capital, to be part of the revolution. They were southerners, but the fever of revolution encompassed all of Yemen, and people in Aden felt sure the country would soon be united. The boys sang revolutionary songs as the bus made its way northward across the unmarked border of the British colony. After two hours, they stopped on a hilltop just above the city of Taiz, about a third of the way to Sanaa. A group of soldiers in natty brown uniforms stood outside, and one of them shouted for everyone to step off the bus. His accent was unmistakable: these were Egyptians, part of the advance guard sent by Nasser to help secure the revolution. The soldiers demanded to see everyone's ID card. Saeed stepped down into the crowd, and after waiting his turn, handed over his school card. The officer examined it and looked down at Saeed. "You're only fourteen," he said. "That's too young. You've got to go home." Saeed protested, but the officer shook his head and told him it was no use. Then he smiled. "Don't worry, you'll get your chance," he said. "There's going to be a revolution in the south very soon."

The officer was right. Saeed got a ride back home from a qat dealer that afternoon and resumed his schoolboy's life, but the peaceful British colony of Aden was changing. One afternoon in 1964, Saeed had the chance to meet one of the southern rebel leaders, a small-bodied man with a huge quiff of curly hair who was gaining a reputation as a Yemeni Che Guevara. Saeed shook his hand and told him he wanted to help make South Yemen independent. The older man smiled and told him, "The important thing is not getting rid of the British. That will happen very soon. The important thing is to get rid of those who helped the British and oppressed us for so long, the sultans and the tribal sheikhs." Saeed felt a bolt of kinship on hearing those words. He thought instantly of the Sheikh back in Ja'ashin, who was a feared and hated figure even then. He volunteered that same day to join the resistance against the British.

Saeed spent the next ten years with a gun in his hand, first as a rebel against the British in the south, then as a recruit up north, fighting the Saudi-backed royalists who wanted to defeat the revolution there. He defined himself variously as a Socialist, a Baathist, or an Arab Nationalist—Yemen was a stew of ideologies in those days—but all those labels meant the same thing to him: freedom from the Sheikh and all the other tribal tyrants. He never forgot his village in Ja'ashin, though he did not see it for a full decade, even when his mother died there. He came close to death several times. But the experience that marked him most, he told me, was falling in love with a British nurse. It happened in 1966, after he was badly wounded in a botched raid on a British base. He woke up in a British military hospital, his body covered in bandages. He'd been through one operation already, and now he found himself alone, in a white room, with a fan circling slowly overhead. An hour went by with almost no human sound, and the unaccustomed solitude terrified him. "I had never been so scared," he told me. "I felt death was near." It was then that she came into the room, a pretty young blonde woman in a white hospital gown. She spoke to him in fluent Arabic and told him not to be frightened. When he implored her not to leave, she looked at him gently and said he could call on her anytime if he needed her, and she would come. Over the following weeks and months, as she tended him through several more operations, a flirtatious energy crept into their banter. Once, as she was cutting bandages on his thigh, she gestured with the scissors toward his penis. "You want me to cut that off too?" she said. "Sure," he said. "You can do anything you want to me." She slipped him cigarettes, in violation of the hospital rules. By the time he was well enough to walk, it was autumn of 1967, and the British were about to leave Aden for good. On his last day she came to him and urged him to come back to Britain with her. "There's a civil war going on here," she said. He said he could not. She kissed him—his first kiss from a woman other than his mother—and they both wept.

When he recalled that moment to me, almost a half century later, he was so overcome with emotion that he could not speak for more than a full minute. He never saw her again. But her memory merged, in his mind, with the meaning of a real *dawla*: a place where people can treat even their enemies with kindness.

By the early 1970s, Saeed was done with soldiering. He had no desire to go back to Aden, where a radical Marxist faction had taken power and declared a new state called the People's Democratic Republic of South Yemen, allied to the Soviets. He moved back to Ja'ashin at last, eager to start a family and reap the fruits of the revolution at home. But he found people there as miserable as ever. The revolution of 1962, meant to turn all North Yemen into a republic, had still not reached them. When he asked his cousins about the Sheikh, they put their fingers to their lips, too frightened to speak. Most of the peasants were slaves in all but name. Their few possessions—a cow, a donkey, a patch of ground—could be snatched away by the Sheikh at any time.

Saeed began a campaign for peasants' rights, the first of its kind in Yemen. He contacted a group of wealthy Yemeni expatriate businessmen in Saudi Arabia who had roots in the village and persuaded them to fly back to Sanaa to lobby on the peasants' behalf. His timing was good: North Yemen had an ambitious new president named Ibrahim al Hamdi, who had begun cutting back the power of the big tribal sheikhs. Hamdi declared again and again that no one could be above the law if Yemen were to build a real state. He even dared to disarm some of the most obstreperous sheikhs and throw them in jail. One of them was Sheikh Mansour. Relief seemed to be on the way for the peasants of Ja'ashin. But President Hamdi was gunned down by assassins in his house in 1977, probably at the behest of his tribal enemies. A year later, his successor opened a briefcase that was supposed to be full of money. It exploded in his face, killing him. In 1978, North Yemen's third president in as many years came to power, a young and relatively unknown military officer named Ali Abdullah Saleh. No one expected him to last long.

Saleh proved them wrong. He was a tribesman from a poor family with an elementary-school education, and he made up for his lack of sophistication with guile. He soon reached an understanding with the big sheikhs, who became part of a Mafia-style spoils system that substituted for governance. The country's young institutions began a slow slide toward irrelevance. The Sheikh of Ja'ashin became more powerful than ever. Saeed soon found himself in a dungeon, where he spent a week on a mud floor, his hands and feet shackled, in total darkness. When they released him, he fled to Marxist South Yemen and joined a rebel group, hoping to build a military force that could challenge the Sheikh. He ended up staying there for a decade, missing his children's youth. By the 1990s, he risked a return home and was imprisoned again in the Sheikh's jail. The collusion between President Saleh and the Sheikh became more flagrant as the years went by. In 2005, after Saeed had published an article in a southern newspaper excoriating the Sheikh, a group of thugs beat him mercilessly and then drove him six hours north to a prison in the capital. There, still badly bruised, he was given a bed and decent food and left alone for two full days in a windowless room. Finally, a well-groomed man in a suit came to his cell and made an offer. If he signed an agreement to stop insulting the Sheikh, he would be rewarded with a job as a cultural attaché at one of Yemen's foreign embassies. Saeed pondered for a moment, and then answered, "Why would you want to hire a liar as a cultural attaché?"

Saeed was transferred to an ordinary prison, on trumped-up charges. It was not until two years later, in 2007, that his case began to attract attention. Yemeni human rights groups demanded his release and echoed his calls for the Sheikh to be brought to justice. When Saeed got out of prison later that year, a crowd of supporters accompanied him part of the way back to Ja'ashin, chanting, "No more sheikhs after today!" as they marched along. It was then that he gained the confidence to start leading groups of peasants to the capital to stand in front of the Parliament building and make their case to the nation. By mid-2010, those periodic pilgrimages had turned into a permanent sit-in.

In early January 2011, Saeed was living in a tent in the Sanaa square that the Ja'ashin delegation had called home for months. After four decades of protest and intermittent exile, he was so poor that almost all his earthly possessions could fit into a couple of plastic bags. His crutches lay next to the thin pallet he slept on, and he'd pasted posters of his lifetime heroes on the tent's canvas walls: Hamdi, the murdered Yemeni president; Abdelfattah Ismail, the southern rebel who'd told Saeed about the need to fight the tribal system; Che Guevara. He ate almost nothing—a sandwich of bread and eggs for breakfast, some tea, and the occasional bit of grilled chicken. Almost all of it was donated.

His children were all grown, and they dropped in to see him now and then. His wife was still living in their house in Ja'ashin. With his frequent absences and prison stints, she had done all the hard work of child rearing. "She is a thousand times stronger than me," he told me.

But by the end of January, with the revolts spreading from Tunis to Cairo and beyond, Saeed looked out of his tent and found himself surrounded for the first time by tens of thousands of people. Suddenly the dream he had been working for through most of his adult life seemed close to coming true. The banners were everywhere: NO TO CORRUPTION, NO TO TYRANNY, THE PEOPLE DEMAND THE FALL OF THE REGIME. "It was a feeling like nothing else in life," Saeed told me. The Ja'ashin tent was treated with great respect by the young protesters. Tawakol had publicized their role, and they were given the status of ancestors. But they were soon swallowed up by the inrush of people from all over the country. Change Square quickly took on a distinctly Yemeni feel. It may have been inspired by Cairo's Tahrir Square, but it was unmistakably different: larger, dirtier, wilder. It stretched on for blocks in several directions, an unbroken mass of canvas tents pitched on the pavement with a big central stage for speeches. Vendors hawking melon and popcorn and cotton candy rolled wooden carts through the crowds. The place stank of sweat and urine and cheap roasted corn, and within a few weeks there was a thick slurry of newspapers and food and plastic bags underfoot, almost obscuring the pavement.

What did the protesters want, apart from the fall of the regime? It was hard to say. Yemen was a country with almost no middle class, and half of its people were illiterate. To some extent, the protest became an end in itself. "New values are being formed," I was told by an old Yemeni friend, as we toured the square. It was true. Most Yemenis live in the countryside, their lives constrained by tradition and the backbreaking work of subsistence in the desert. Suddenly they were packed into an urban space that forced them to confront each other in new ways. The protesters built makeshift medical clinics, as in Tahrir, but because Change Square lasted so much longer than eighteen days, they went much further. There were primary and secondary schools for all the children whose parents were living in the square full time. There was an "academic forum," a kind of open university where classes on various subjects were taught, the schedules posted outside roped-off classrooms. Some of the people sitting there in folding chairs were illiterate peasants, staring wonderingly at the whiteboard. There was at least one full-scale restaurant, where chefs cooked meaty stews in big metal vats and handed out plastic bags full of freshly baked bread, often for free. Tribesmen swaggered around, with their long unkempt hair, a curved *jambiyya* dagger in their belts, their cheeks often packed with thick green wads of qat. Sometimes they'd perform dances, holding hands and clapping and shouting while a drummer squatted next to them, beating out a loud and furious rhythm.

In a sense, the entire protest was directed at Saleh himself. After thirty-two years, he'd become almost synonymous with Yemen. His picture was everywhere, on billboards, in shop windows, in banks, always with the same arrogant expression: chest thrust out and eyes glinting, as if to confront a challenger. His ruling style had filtered so deeply into the country that people had almost forgotten there was anything else, and wondered if it was just fate. Saleh knew better. He called his method *tawazzun*, balance. It went like this: if a northern tribe is giving you trouble, you give some weapons and money to their enemies in the next village. If that second tribe gets too powerful, you give a little something to the first one. Keep them shooting at each other, so long as they don't shoot at you. If an Islamist leader or a general is gaining power and influence, dole out money to his rivals—or, better yet, promote an alternative leader, and set them against each other. Saleh was behind the creation of Yemen's largest opposition party, and he packed it with old allies who were always amenable to a deal. In this way Saleh made sure that everyone who mattered could be bribed or blackmailed. His nimble deal-making dragged the country backward, even as he passed landmarks of apparent progress: the unification of North and South Yemen in 1990, and the establishment of a nominal democracy. Yemen became a landscape of brushfires, all of them requiring constant management, and only one man could do it. He was the linchpin of this enlarged system of tribal feuds, the one who held all the strings and knew how to manage all the players. When people called him out on these cynical tactics, he would reply that it was Yemenis themselves who were to blame, and his wiliness was merely pragmatism. "Ruling Yemen is hard," he told me when I first met him in 2008. "I always say it is like dancing on the heads of snakes."

This dance worked very well—up to a point. It kept Saleh in power, and there were no more coups. But after thirty-two years of one-man rule, the little fires Saleh had been setting and managing had grown beyond his control. He'd funneled almost all the country's money into payoffs and patronage. The rebels and sheikhs and gunmen had seen through his game. Some of them were starting to recognize that *tawazzun* had eaten up all the money that should have gone to building schools and hospitals and dealing with Yemen's terrible poverty. The country was an economic time bomb, with a fast-growing population of twenty-four million. If not for the government subsidies on oil and food, many of Yemen's poorest would starve. Most people still lived in the countryside, scraping out a living from livestock or crops. In a country with so little rainfall, they depended for survival on illegal drills that pumped water to the surface, but the drills had to go deeper every year, and in some places there was nothing left of what Yemeni farmers once called "the underground sea." The World Bank projected that Sanaa would soon be the first global capital with no more water supply. The discovery of oil in eastern Yemen in 1984 had thrown Saleh a lifeline, but that too was running out. The government ministries tasked with addressing these crises had been hollowed out by corruption. Even the army, the only sacrosanct institution in most Arab regimes, was so corrupt and mismanaged that soldiers walked off the field in droves and sold their weapons to the rebels, or to Al Qaeda.

Many Yemenis were starting to recognize these things, and the Ja'ashin helped crystallize the discontent. They made it plain that Saleh had betrayed the 1962 revolution, the revolution he constantly swore to uphold. He had brought back and amplified the worst elements of the tribal system. This had almost nothing to do with traditional tribal life, the kind you encountered if you drove out to the highlands of northern Yemen. The tribesmen there were mostly dirt-poor, and they treasured their independence. They had an ancient code of law, known as *'urf*, that regulated their lives and protected them in times of war. But some of their sheikhs had been lured into the city and corrupted with money and houses and guns. Starting in the 1980s, Saleh—like other Arab dictators—perverted the tribal system, discrediting sheikhs who threatened him and anointing new ones with cash to suit his purposes. Saleh liked to play the sheikh himself, to arbitrate in feuds he'd provoked and then claim the mantle of the peacemaker. A sociologist friend of mine who spent years studying Yemeni tribes put it like this to me: "In Yemen, the state acts like a tribe and the tribe acts like a state."

It wasn't so surprising, then, that the Yemeni revolt of 2011 soon spread to the tribesmen themselves. It was as if they wanted to prove that Saleh's thuggish version of tribalism was false, that they were not just snakes to be danced on. Thousands of them embraced the square's peaceful ethic with a vigor that surprised everyone. One of the most zealous was a paunchy thirty-six-year-old named Abdullah bin Haddar. I met him in his tent in Sanaa's Change Square, not far from where the Ja'ashin were still living. I was struck instantly by his appearance: he wore no belt or *jambiyya*—the dagger that is the symbol of a tribes-man's martial honor. "I stopped wearing it since I came to the square," he told me with a wry smile. His head was bare, too—he had disdained the patterned cloths most tribal men wear—and though he spoke in a thick Bedouin accent, he wore rimless glasses that made him look more like an ill-shaved salesman than a feudal warrior. When the Sanaa pro-tests had ramped up in February, Haddar told me, he had been at home in Marib, a lawless province east of the capital, surrounded by his family and a vast armory of weapons. "I used to sleep with guns all around me," he said. "It always scared my wife." He needed them. His life, he explained, was dominated and constrained by tribal feuds. The feuds are almost constant in Marib, and because they are collective, any member of the tribe is fair game. Tribal boundaries are closely watched, so that walking or driving into enemy territory can instantly endanger your life. Sanaa is often just as dangerous, because your enemies can catch up to you at any time in the anonymity of the crowd, and it is harder to see them coming, Haddar told me. "This is why I never learned English," he said. "The class is always at a certain time and place, so people know where to find you."

Haddar had long nourished a deep hatred for Saleh's government, which he blamed for much of the misery in Marib. So when the uprising started, he drove straight to Sanaa and sought out Khaled al Ansi, a forty-six-year-old human rights lawyer and colleague of Tawakol Karman's who had emerged as one of the movement's leaders. When I met with Ansi in Sanaa, he recalled the encounter, smiling at the memory. "Abdullah Haddar told me, 'I will bring my tribe, we will protect you, we will fight for our dignity,'" Ansi said. The uprising was still young, but Ansi, an eloquent critic of the Saleh regime and a pillar of Sanaa's small circle of civil society activists, had his priorities set. "The most important thing for us is not getting rid of Ali Abdullah Saleh, or even building a civil state," Ansi told me. "It is changing the mentality of violence, this culture of the military and of the tribes." So he offered Haddar a firm rejoinder. "I told him, 'Thank you, but we don't want protectors or supporters. We want partners. If we wanted to be safe, we would have stayed home. We hope you will join us.'"

That message struck Haddar with the force of revelation. As a tribesman, he had expected his role to be that of hired muscle, an enforcer. "The government has always treated these people as tools," Ansi told me. "Yes, they give them money and weapons, they talk about dignity, but they never really treat them as equals. They don't respect them." Haddar brought the zeal of a convert to his new role as a protester. "I had never imagined this would be possible, giving up violence," he said, staring at me with large, earnest eyes. "It is something heavenly, not earthly." Within days, he had been beaten up badly in a street confrontation with plainclothes government thugs. He wore his new badge proudly, and al Jazeera broadcast footage showing his bare back covered with scars. Members of his tribe in Marib saw it, and one of them called him right away. "They said we are coming to take revenge," he told me. "They were heavily armed. I refused. I said if anyone wants to join me, he must leave aside all weapons, and not even carry a dagger. I told them, even if I am killed, they must not retaliate." This was a violation of one of the fundamental tenets of tribal life. Haddar's fellow

tribesmen, baffled and wondering about his mental health, sent a delegation to see him and explore the sit-in. There were about twenty-five
of them, he said, and on the first day in the city, a group of government
thugs recognized Haddar and attacked him. "The tribesmen tried to
protect me, but I said no, each one protect himself."

The following weeks were not easy ones. Haddar got angry calls from
family members, who said he was dishonoring them. Government
officials tried to bribe him away, with offers of money and jobs. And he
was still frightened of vendettas, even in the protest square. "One man
had been trying to kidnap or kill me for two years," Haddar told me.
"I saw him in the middle of Change Square, and I was afraid. But he
walked right up to me. He said, 'Yes, I was planning to kill you. But
that's all over, I'm with the revolution.'" Stories like this one sounded
almost too perfect to be true, but Haddar made them sound plausible.
His life had become a fairy tale of transformation.

As word spread along tribal networks, more and more men from
the provinces came to Sanaa and other cities to join the protest. Even
in provincial capitals, sit-ins were established, sometimes with elaborate deals being struck to suspend feuds so that people could attend
without fear of being ambushed. In Sanaa, tribesmen were invited to
sign a document suspending all feuds, I was told by Ahmed al Zaydi, a
twenty-three-year-old activist from Marib. But after getting hundreds
of signatures, the papers turned into a thick, unruly shuffle, and Zaydi
and other organizers decided to just announce a pan-tribal amnesty on
the microphone at the main soundstage at the Sanaa protest square.
When I met Zaydi, a lanky man with long hair and dark skin, he was
living in a "tribal tent" in the square with six other young men from
Marib, including some with whom his tribe was officially at war. "These
feuds are something we learned from the elders," he told me, as he sat
Indian-style at his laptop, drafting a new communiqué. "But enough,
we don't want it. The youth are our only hope for getting out of this
cycle of violence." Zaydi added that there had been no serious fights
among tribesmen in the square, although there had been brawls involving members of opposition political parties. "It's the ones who are

supposedly civilized who have had problems," he said with an amused smile.

But even as the tribesmen of Marib laid down their weapons, others were picking them up. The breaking point for Ali Abdullah Saleh, the moment *tawazzun* finally failed him, came on March 18, 2011. On that day, a Friday, the protesters in Sanaa gathered en masse for prayers. Afterward, they began gathering for a march out of Change Square toward the presidential palace. That was when it began: shots, sporadic at first. No one could see where they were coming from. People in the crowd began screaming and collapsing to the ground. Before long it became clear that sharpshooters were firing from roofs near the stage. Young men began ripping up the pavement and throwing rocks at the gunmen, and the pace of the gunfire increased. The square turned almost instantly from a carnival into a war zone, full of wailing women and bloodied protesters being carried out by their friends. The mosque alongside the square became a makeshift clinic and morgue, its carpets drenched in blood. By the time it was over, at least fifty-two people were dead and hundreds injured. Saleh tried to mollify the crowds, saying in a televised speech that night that the dead were "martyrs of democracy" and that the shooters were not his men. No one believed him. Within days, Yemen's most powerful military commander— who'd been Saleh's right-hand man for decades—declared that he and his troops were defecting and would now serve only as protectors for the protesters. A wave of defections of high-ranking generals, ministers, and ambassadors followed. The regime had split, and from that point onward, the protests became the noisy backdrop to a power struggle inside the Yemeni elite.

The rift was partly tribal: Saleh's most powerful enemies were the al Ahmars, a clan within the north's strongest tribal league. The Ahmars were also leaders in Yemen's main opposition party, an Islamist group called Islah that had supported the sit-in from the first. Saleh became convinced that the entire revolution was a plot by the Ahmars and their Islamist allies—Tawakol, as it happened, was a member of Islah's liberal wing—to take power from him. He told friends that he would rather see Yemen burn than let them succeed. He kept all his best troops, and even the American-trained counterterror corps, in the capital, girding for battle. Nothing else mattered. Out in the hinterland, local administrators and military commanders saw that they would be forced to take sides. Many of them took off their uniforms and went home.

Saeed and many others saw this as a moment of opportunity, a crisis that would unify Yemenis against the regime. The blood of the martyrs, Saeed said, would strengthen the revolution's cause, just as it had in Tunis and Cairo. Only years afterward did they come to see it as their revolution's most painful irony. A movement that championed the idea of *dawla* had unwittingly helped destroy what little there was of a state in Yemen.

It was in late March, just after the Yemen uprisings turned violent, that a news bulletin flickered on the many TVs hooked up in the tents of the sit-in. "URGENT NEWS!" the screens declared. "Armed men have taken over a town in South Yemen." A newscaster provided details: the attackers were from Al Qaeda, and they were declaring a new Islamic emirate in the town of Jaar, not far from the southern Yemeni coast. It was afternoon when the news broke. Most of the protesters who saw it probably glanced up from their qat chew, said a few dismissive words, and moved on to another subject. It was a sideshow, they felt. The jihadis were the past, the revolution was the future.

But scattered among the protesters in those tents were a number of Al Qaeda members and sympathizers. To them, this announcement was so momentous that the hum of Change Square, with its constant songs and speeches and drifting smells of smoke and street food, must have faded into the background. Al Qaeda had finally declared its emirate. This was their answer to the Arab Spring. Perhaps a few of the young jihadis had been impressed by the revolutionaries and their Gandhian vows of nonviolence, at least at first. But by late March, it was pretty clear that President Saleh was not stepping down anytime soon. And even if he did, this clamoring crowd full of students and peasants could never agree on how to run the country. After all, why had Mubarak been overthrown in Egypt? Not because of the protesters. It was the army. And behind that army, the United States. This was the way Al Qaeda's leaders saw it: armed insurrection—not sit-ins—changed regimes. Change Square was street theater, nothing more.

For some of the young Arab journalists in Change Square, the news from Jaar was just as exciting. They had grown a thick skin of cynicism about the West's interest in Yemen. If you could show the Americans and British a few mad bombers with beards and black flags, you had a story, one they would pay for. If you had a thousand starving children, or a collapsing economy, or a political crisis—your call might not be returned. Some of these young journalists were my friends. One of them told me that he remembered a sentence forming in his head in the moments after he first heard about the jihadi takeover of Jaar: *What's happening in Jaar will determine what happens in Sanaa, and not the other way around.* This ambitious twenty-seven-year-old newspaperman was soon on his way to Jaar to ingratiate himself with the gunmen and document a new phase in the unraveling of Yemen's feeble state.

This is the story he and other Yemeni reporters heard when they got there. Just after sunrise on Saturday, March 26, townspeople in Jaar woke up to gunfire breaking through the familiar sound of the call to prayer. Stumbling from their houses, they saw something amazing. Hundreds of bearded, long-haired fighters were storming into town, many of them carrying heavy weapons and ominous black flags. The townspeople stared in wonder as the intruders broadcast their message on the loudspeaker of the town's biggest mosque. *In the name of God, we greet you, oh people of Jaar. We aim to make of Jaar the capital of an Islamic emirate that will stretch to Aden, to Riyadh, to all the Islamic world.* The gunfire had subsided. There had been no real battle, only warning shots. The government soldiers had all fled. Before long, the jihadis—a mix of local boys and foreigners—were handing out free bread and cutting off the hands of thieves, in the manner of the Taliban.

In some ways Jaar was a natural place for Al Qaeda to declare its new project. It is a town of about ten thousand people, surrounded by low acacia-covered hills that mark the start of Yemen's tribal hinterland. To the south, the hills slope toward the sea, about twenty miles away. The people of the town, like most people in South Yemen, have bitterly resented the national government for many years, seeing it as a hostile northern occupier. Jaar in particular had a reputation for Islamist militancy and had been a big recruiting spot for the Afghan jihad during the 1980s.

But if you looked a little farther back, there was a sad irony in Jaar's new role. A few decades earlier, when South Yemen was still a British colony, Jaar had been one of the area's most peaceful and promising places. The British had built a cotton mill there in the early 1960s that employed hundreds of Yemenis, along with a hospital and a school. These were rare and enviable institutions in Yemen at that time. The Brits declared Jaar a "model town" and hoped to replicate it elsewhere. I met the British officer who lived there at the time, now a white-haired man with crystal-blue eyes named Stephen Day. He remembered his time there fondly: "It was an orderly, well-run place, very quiet." The Yemenis were in charge, but there was a small group of British engineers and their families, who mostly kept to themselves. Day told me he could remember only one episode of trouble when he lived there. It happened in 1965, when the local sultan showed up at Day's house one morning fuming and cursing, threatening to evict all the infidel British from his lands. The sultans enjoyed a hereditary right to local rule that the British respected, so this was a serious matter. Day asked him what was wrong. It turned out that the local British expats had organized a film society, screening European and American movies with a 16 mm projector on Thursday nights. They had declared their society British-only and had not invited the sultan to join. Day listened respectfully and later that day secured a promise that the sultan would be invited to all future movie nights. Peace was restored.

The town's decline since then was a familiar story: battered and convulsed by war and revolution and economic blight, like so many other towns in the Arab world. The cotton mill was in ruins. There were no more jobs, and scarcely any water in the depleted wells; many of the farms encircling the town had dried up and blown into dust. The

British had long since fled, a rushed withdrawal from their last real colony, with a military band playing "Fings Ain't Wot They Used to Be" as the last officers boarded ship and steamed away in November 1967. The locals had cheered their departure. But by 2011, after so many years of suffering and tyranny, people spoke of the colonial era with deep nostalgia. The rule of President Saleh, they said, was worse than any foreign occupation they had known. In this atmosphere of despair, the jihadi recruiters, with their talk of martyrdom and paradise, found many listeners.

By the time I got to southern Yemen in June 2011, the jihadis had extended their rule from Jaar and were literally just outside the city limits of Aden. The Yemeni military, demoralized and unpaid, had melted away before them. On my taxi ride into town from the Aden airport, I scarcely saw any cars or people: the city seemed to have been abandoned. Even the weathered old British expats were afraid. These were men who had lived in Aden through decades of war and revolution, and now they were joking nervously about escaping on a dhow across the Red Sea to Djibouti. At the hotel where I stayed, an eight-story building with tall iron gates and at least one hundred rooms, I saw only three or four other guests. One of them was the governor of Abyan province, just to the northeast. He told me he'd been forced to flee his provincial capital, Zinjibar, when the jihadis stormed it. He was a squat, anxious-looking man with a widow's peak and a thick mustache, and when I said I was a journalist, he looked at me pleadingly, his eyes wide. "They will take over Aden and they will have their own state if there is not immediate international assistance," he said. There was no air-conditioning in the lobby, and sweat was running down his forehead. A Muzak version of the *Titanic* theme played in the background. I asked him what had happened to the Yemeni army. "It was a war," he said. "The Qaeda people came with a huge number of armed men. There is army there, but they are exhausted from so many attacks. The fighters knew the army's weak points. Besides, everything is divided now, the government, the army. They took advantage of this."

Soon after I arrived at the hotel, I met a man who seemed to embody the state's collapse. He was a tribal mediator, and the Yemeni government had hired him to negotiate a cease-fire with Al Qaeda. He was a big, powerfully built man of forty-nine, who went by the nom de guerre Mullah Zabara. I could hear him coming a long way off, because he refused to take off his dagger as he walked through the metal detector, and the hotel staff, frightened, backed off and let him pass. He had a strong jaw, steel-gray glasses, and a scar on his right temple that gave him a fearsome look. He saw me across the empty lobby, bellowed a greeting, and walked up to kiss me on both cheeks, grinning mischievously. He stank of whiskey. We sat down, and within minutes he was asking me how much I would pay for the interview. He said he had information that the CIA would pay a lot for. I told him I couldn't pay anything. He had a sidekick with him, a skinny young tribesman named Taha, who seemed wearily familiar with this routine. "Okay, that's enough, drop it," Taha whispered several times.

He dropped it and began telling me about his meetings with Al Qaeda leaders in a farmhouse about an hour outside of town. After the first trip, he had exchanged messages with a top Al Qaeda figure named Fahd al Quso, wanted by the United States for his role in the bombing of the USS *Cole* in 2000. Al Qaeda leaders never talk on the phone, Zabara explained, because Yemen's government has voice-recognition software provided by the United States. He showed me the text messages on his cell phone. They were written in highly formal Arabic and referred briefly to Zabara's having "protected" Al Qaeda leaders in the past. The writer of the message expressed his appreciation for Zabara's mediation efforts but said the government had lied and refused to suspend their fire during the negotiations. "These people cannot be trusted," the message said. "We will defeat them, and God willing, we will conquer Aden."

After his story was over, Zabara seemed to undergo a strange process of deflation. He sank back in his chair, and his voice subsided to a mumble. He told me tribalism was Yemen's downfall. "People have reached the moon," he said. "But we can't even build a car, because of our feuds." He began telling me about his family. His father's great ambition had been for Zabara to get a Western education and become a doctor or a professor or an engineer. But the family was blacklisted by the Socialists, because his father had worked for the British colonial administration in the 1950s and '60s. They'd been forced to flee Aden after the Marxists took over in 1967, and Zabara grew up illiterate in the Shabwa desert. His father had died a broken man. Zabara went silent after that. We sat in our lobby chairs, and finally he shook my hand and left. As my plane lifted off the runway a week or so later, I thought of Zabara, with his bravado and his whiskey breath. I wondered what Al Qaeda would do with him if they captured Aden and felt no more need for drunken mediators.

Back in the capital, people seemed certain that the whole jihadi fiasco in the south was a deliberate ploy, engineered by Saleh and aimed at the West. *You want a revolution? This is what you'll get.* There may have been some truth to it. He had been dancing on snakes for so long that it was hard to tell myth from reality. In the north, too, the revolution was taking its toll: cars waited in mile-long lines for gas, and power cuts were more frequent. Water was getting scarcer. It was easy to find people who believed these trials were yet another "message" from Saleh about the price of disobedience.

The protest camp in Sanaa persisted all through the summer and fall of 2011, despite the heat and the torpor and the daylong fasts of Ramadan. Bursts of violence came and went, and the list of martyrs multiplied, but the tents remained, along with the speeches and the prayers and the ever-expanding graffiti on the walls. In September, Saleh appeared in public for the first time in three months. He'd been in Saudi Arabia, recovering from his injuries after an assassination attempt in his palace mosque. When he stepped out of the airplane from Riyadh, he was clutching a cane. You could tell right away he would never be the same. The skin on his face and neck looked mottled, and his movements were slow and tentative. American and Saudi diplomats had been pushing hard for his resignation since the spring, and he held them off for two more months, always finding new reasons. He might never have signed the transition document if the UN Security Council had not threatened to impose sanctions on him and his family. Watching the endgame in Libya may have helped too, with that gruesome TV footage of Qaddafi's bloody corpse.

When the day finally came and Saleh signed the papers in November 2011, sitting next to the Saudi king in a palace in Riyadh, governments in the West hailed it as a breakthrough, even a model. Here was a peaceful, negotiated transition in an Arab Spring that had devolved into civil wars across the Mideast. But back in Yemen, the reaction was mostly unhappy. The deal gave Saleh and his family immunity from prosecution. Tawakol Karman and her friends lost no time in declaring that their revolution had been betrayed and they would stay in the square and keep protesting. The square, meanwhile, had become a more overtly political place. Street battles broke out between northern tribesmen and members of Islah, the Islamist party to which Tawakol still belonged. After nightfall, the chants in the square were drowned out by loud explosions. Saleh's loyalists were shelling their rivals in the Ahmar clan, the leaders of the Islamist party and of Yemen's strongest tribal federation. The transition was not a transition. Yemen's tribal players were all still in place. The new president, Abdu Rabbu Mansour Hadi, was a short, smiling man whose talk of consensus meant nothing. He had been Saleh's obedient flunky for almost twenty years. He would inherit the office of president, but everyone sensed that the unfinished business between the Saleh and Ahmar clans would smolder under the surface until the time was right. It was the same revenge plot that had fueled Yemeni politics for decades, and nothing that had happened in the square would alter it. Those who stayed on in the protest camp, like Tawakol Karman, seemed to sense that their moment was over, that the country was no longer paying attention. The graffiti on downtown walls took on a sour, embittered cast. YEMEN REVOLUTION 2.0, wrote one artist over the spray-painted image of a blue computer screen, with a black cursor hovering over a key marked "DELETE?"

Even then, in late 2011, some people were predicting the direction Yemen's next war would take: Saleh would team up with the Huthi rebels. It sounded crazy at first: the Huthis were a rebel movement in the far north that had fought an intermittent war against the state for years. They hated Saleh. But the old man understood his country's rivalries better than anyone else. He knew that the next great fault line was between Yemen's ambitious Sunni Islamist movement, Islah, and the Huthis, who belonged to the Zaydi religious minority, an offshoot of Shiite Islam. This religious distinction had never mattered much in the past; Yemen had always been free of sectarian rancor. Most northern tribesmen were Zaydis, including Saleh himself. It hadn't stopped him from fighting brutal wars against the Huthis, or making deals with Sunni jihadis. Few Yemenis had ever cared much about sect. What mattered was your tribe.

But the virus of religious hatred was spreading. Iran and Saudi Arabia—the region's two great Shiite and Sunni powers—were nurturing it with their rivalry and sending young zealots to fight on opposing sides of the war in Syria. Saleh always had his nose to the wind, and now he wasted no time in changing camps. He hated and feared Islah, Yemen's most organized political party, and he blamed them for the uprising of 2011. So he allied with their enemies. He didn't care that the Huthis were allied with Iran. He cared about power, and the Huthis had proved their value on the battlefield. In this way, Yemen's old man made his country the next great proxy battleground of the Middle East. It was only a question of time. The same Saudis who'd hosted Saleh in 2011, and applauded as he signed the transition agreement, would—almost three and a half years later—launch a devastating bombing campaign against him and his Huthi allies. The Iranians, seeing an opportunity to score points against the Saudis, would jump on the Huthi bandwagon, sending more money and arms. The region's poorest people would be forced from their homes en masse, some of them so desperate that they fled on boats to Africa.

Saeed was not discouraged, not yet, anyway. I found him in Taiz, four hours south of the capital. He was living in that city's version of Change Square, in a tent. It was a desolate place by that time, abandoned by all but a few stalwart protesters. Saleh's troops had burned the entire square back in May, killing a dozen protesters and maiming many others. You could still see the evidence: the trees had blackened trunks and dead leaves. The ground was still littered with rubble and charred shreds of canvas and clothing. Saeed was as cheerful as ever. He insisted on showing me his canvas tent, with its miserable little sleeping pallet and the same old posters of his heroes on the walls. He offered me a glass of cloudy brown tea and we sat on plastic crates. Taiz is a beautiful city, surrounded by dry wooded hills and coffee-tree groves, a little like San Francisco, with the ancient port of Moka not far away. But it had been neglected for decades, and now it was suffering a total vacuum of authority. Huge heaps of reeking garbage stood uncollected in the streets, and trucks full of long-haired militia fighters rode through town. Saeed clutched my forearm and showed me where the protest stage had been, where they had sung the Yemeni national anthem together, where the brave young men had died under the guns of the regime. "The young people are suffering," Saeed said. "But the revolution will succeed, God willing."

Most of Saeed's fellow Ja'ashin peasants had gone home, and I decided to follow them. I wanted to see the place where their journey had begun. The Sheikh had become an almost mythical figure for me, and I wanted to see him in the flesh. It was not an easy trip. Driving out of Taiz, you travel northward through the hills, past a town called Al Qaeda, named not for the jihadi group but for an old Ottoman military base. After that, the paved road ends, and there is a long journey into the countryside over increasingly steep and lumpy tracks. Some local people had warned me to keep my travel plans secret, because the Sheikh could easily have me murdered with total impunity. "He knows how to disguise it as a car accident, or a stray bullet," one man warned. Others said there was no point in trying to disguise my plans, because the Sheikh would know everything the moment I set foot in his realm. It was hard to know what to believe. It seemed clear, though, that the 2011 uprising had not done much to rein him in.

In the end, I went with a local man who sat in front next to my driver, with an AK-47 at his feet. We set out before dawn from Taiz so as to avoid meeting too many people; even so, he scanned the road and the hills above it hawkishly as we drove. My own nervousness gradually melted in the unearthly beauty of that landscape. Yemen is a desert country, but Ja'ashin is spectacularly, voluptuously fertile. It was easy to see why the Sheikh had clung to it so fiercely. The green hills curl around each other in sudden, jungly escarpments, often with ancient stone houses perched on top. Your eyes, accustomed to Yemen's arid mesas, are overwhelmed by thick tussocks of saw grass and sprays of luminous magenta wildflowers. Ancient crop terraces decorate the slopes, bursting with bright green rows of coffee plants, figs, apricots, medicinal herbs, and qat. The road soon gave way to a muddy dirt track, its deep red soil torn by rivulets and gullies. We lumbered along at a donkey's pace. We stopped in a little village market at the valley's bottom, where goats munched on garbage piles littered with blue and pink plastic qat bags. One of the Sheikh's houses loomed on a hilltop, high overhead. I asked a local farmer, a skinny, bald man of about forty with a rosy, wizened face, if anything had changed over the years. He shook his head dismissively. "The sheikhly system will never go away, not in Ja'ashin, not in Yemen," he said, gesturing at the hilltop. "We'll never be free of them." My guide tapped my shoulder: it was dangerous to stay any longer.

Later I received an invitation to see the Sheikh, at his home in Taiz. He knew I'd been trespassing but apparently chose to treat me as a guest. One of his eldest sons arranged for a car to take us there. His house stood out in the city's cluttered streets: a castle of a place, surrounded by long stone walls decorated at regular intervals with a palm motif. Inside, we were led down a pathway to a small garden house with glass walls and magnificent *gammariyas*, the translucent alabaster carvings that adorn traditional Yemeni windows. Inside, a dozen men sat on floor cushions in the Yemeni fashion. In the corner, apart, was the Sheikh. I had heard so much about him that I expected someone vast and forbidding, an Ozymandias figure with glittering eyes and a long beard. This was a man who had been tyrannizing tens of thousands of peasants for decades. His men had actually fired artillery at the villages of rebellious farmers, smashing their homes into rubble (one of the victims showed me the aftermath on his cell phone camera). But here in front of me was a frail old man of near ninety, reclining on pillows in an attitude of languid repose, with a water pipe at his lips.

He had a pale face, strangely unlined and perfectly clean shaven, and a remote, cold gaze. His head was wrapped in a gray-and-blue silk cloth, and he wore a sweater and a gray wool blazer. On his wrist was a gold and silver Rolex encrusted with what looked like diamonds. As I entered, the other men stood up quickly to greet me. The Sheikh did not move. He merely glanced up and then made a small hand gesture signaling for the rest of us to sit down. The men resumed their small talk, and the Sheikh said nothing. At times, he seemed only half aware of what was going on around him, though his eyes remained shrewd, like a stuffed hawk on a mantel. I had thought of asking him about the private prisons and the torture and the whole litany of grievances. But as I looked at his old, absent eyes, I decided it was pointless. After a while, one of his sons suggested that the Sheikh read a poem to us. He paused, looking down at a book of his collected poems with a baffled expression. At length he opened the book and began reciting in a voice so soft I could scarcely hear it. The poem was a ghazal about the charms of women titled "Spells and Sahar."

In the silence that fell afterward, I asked him to tell me about some of the changes he had seen in his long life. I mentioned that he had witnessed the imam's rule, the revolution of 1962, the rule of Saleh, and the present turmoil. "Where is Yemen going?" I said. The Sheikh puffed on his water pipe and stared into the distance. The room was silent for more than a full minute. The other men shifted in their seats and darted uneasy glances in his direction. Finally he spoke. "Yemen," he said slowly, "is going to Yemen."

— PART II —

Restorations

The Ruler is the shadow of God on earth.
—Saying attributed to the Prophet Muhammad, inscribed on a
wall of the Topkapi Palace, Istanbul

5

— Brothers (Egypt) —

By the autumn of 2011, one group seemed poised to inherit the mantle of democracy across the Arab world: the Islamists. Their long wait was being rewarded. Men who had spent decades cultivating secrecy and paranoia were emerging, and old mosque networks were transforming into disciplined electoral machines. In October, the main Tunisian Islamist group, Ennahda, won 41 percent of the vote, enough to form a government. A month later, Egypt's Muslim Brotherhood and its allies won a crushing majority, more than 70 percent of the new Parliament. Morocco's Islamists won landmark victories in the same month. Even in countries where the guns were still firing—Libya, Syria, and Yemen—Islamists seemed confident that they would dominate the aftermath. But electoral victory was far less important than what would come afterward. The legacy of the 2011 revolts, it seemed, boiled down to a single question: Would the Islamists succeed in building a new political order?

Many of them had spent years in exile—or in opposition—insisting that all they really wanted was freedom, democracy, a chance for the people's will to flower. Now the moment had come. What would they do with their new powers? The question was being asked all over the Middle East, and even beyond—in Washington, in London, in Moscow. It was easy to get different answers, because the spectrum was so wide, from the puritanical Salafi sheikhs with their shovel-shaped beards to mild-mannered Islamists with British university degrees and nice suits. Some outsiders said these guises were a ruse, good cop/bad cop, differing faces of the same totalitarian vision. Others said the Islamists had no vision at all, that their years in opposition had turned them into opportunists who craved power but were armed only with slogans. One thing seemed clear: much would depend on their ability to earn the trust of those outside the movement.

In Egypt, some people said there was only one man who could earn that trust. His name was Muhammad Beltagy, and he was a rising star in the Muslim Brotherhood, the Arab world's largest Islamist group. Beltagy was a rare bridge figure: a doctor and former Parliament member with a vast working-class base in the slums of Cairo, he also had old and close friendships with some of Egypt's best-known liberal politicians. He'd been prominent for years, but it was Tahrir Square that really made him. He'd gone there on the very first day, bucking the Brotherhood leadership, and soon gained the trust of all the political cliques. Even the Socialists loved him.

At forty-seven, Beltagy was just young enough to appeal to younger protest leaders and old enough to carry weight with the Brotherhood's top men. He was tall and broad shouldered, and his face—with its jutting nose and dark, haggard circles under the eyes—had a kind of Kabuki grandeur, full of shadow and light. He always looked as if he'd been up all night negotiating a truce and emerged victorious at dawn. The camera loved him. His face had become an icon of the revolution, like that of Wael Ghoneim, the young Google executive and Facebook organizer. Beltagy lived in Tahrir through all eighteen days, usually with his wife and children sitting alongside him. He was the only senior Brotherhood figure there. The younger protesters treated him with awe, perhaps because he seemed to have all the Brotherhood's street credibility and little of its baggage. He had no formal position in the group, and he was willing, on occasion, to openly criticize its timidity and opportunism. When people asked him what he stood for, Beltagy spoke of a social and political compromise: a government with mildly Islamist social policies and a free-market economy, "on the model of Turkey." It was a phrase you heard pretty often in 2011, but Beltagy was one of the few Islamist leaders who seemed capable of acting on it.

Beltagy clung so tightly to the vision of unity he witnessed in Tahrir that he literally refused to leave. Two days after Mubarak's fall, long after the crowds had dispersed, he was still there on the cold, muddy ground with two of his sons. They stood by their tent in the winter sunlight, urging other protesters to come back and demand a civilian transitional government. The military council that had ousted Mubarak was not good enough, Beltagy said. It would exploit Egypt's divisions, just as the old regime had. Most people nodded and moved off, impressed but baffled. Eventually, the cops and thugs began to harass him, and even his friends told him to let go. It was a strange sight: one of the country's new celebrities standing in dirty clothes amid a half-empty traffic circle, talking back to the police who were telling him to go home. Beltagy wasn't holding onto Tahrir for just sentimental reasons. He had friends at both ends of Egypt's political landscape, and he could feel their fears rising like gusts of wind in the dictator's sudden absence. He said he wanted to build a political center in Egypt. His refrain, repeated again and again from before Tahrir until the end of his career, was, "I am for political enemies being forced to work together." It was not something you heard other Egyptian politicians say.

It didn't take long for the bliss of Tahrir to wear off. On March 19, Egypt held its first postrevolutionary vote, and the Islamists organized a campaign casting their choice on the constitutional referendum as a "Yes to Religion." At about the same time, some Brotherhood leaders began sounding arrogant, triumphal notes. Sobhi Saleh, a popular former Parliament member from Alexandria, said in May that the Brotherhood would dominate the next government and would implement Islamic law. He also said Brotherhood men should marry only Brotherhood women, to ensure that their children stayed within the fold.

Mohamed ElBaradei and other liberal leaders began to complain that Egypt was sliding toward Islamist tyranny. Each side accused the other of aiming for a secret deal with the military council.

This degree of polarization was new. Prior to the 2011 uprisings, the distrust between Egyptian liberals and Islamists was muted by a sense of common oppression by the state. Most liberals had either avoided politics altogether or made an uncomfortable accommodation with the Mubarak regime and its official political organ, the National Democratic Party. The handful of liberal opposition parties were much weaker and less organized than the Brotherhood. Only a small minority from either side dared to speak out against the regime's corruption, autocracy, and jailing of dissidents. Those who did usually paid the same price: prison. This shared experience fostered occasional tactical alliances, despite the fact that the secularists were mostly on the left economically, and the Brotherhood preferred probusiness policies. (Some Arab leftists derided the Brotherhood as American-style capitalists with prayer beads.) Things began to change almost immediately after Tahrir. The prospect of real Islamist dominance was frightening to many people who had never cared much about politics, and they began to band together, ignoring their old feuds. A new line was being drawn, with Islamists on one side and their opponents on the other.

The differences were less a matter of any specific Islamist project than of a gulf between cultures. The Brotherhood's top leaders were old men who'd spent too many years of their lives in prison, suffering terrible isolation and torture. They had little understanding of the world beyond Egypt. The group's turn toward democracy in the 1990s had come too late for them. They knew the Koran by heart, but read little. They were intensely paranoid, seeing spies around every corner. They were not always wrong about this, but the suspicions prevented them from gaining valuable allies. The opacity of the Brotherhood's decision-making process—and the rigid discipline imposed on ordinary members—induced a corresponding suspicion among many Egyptians, and not just devout secularists.

The rift was also partly about origins. One way to take its measure was to go to Beltagy's medical clinic in Shobra al Khaima, eight miles north of Tahrir Square. It is one of Cairo's "unplanned suburbs," a euphemism for the crowded slums that have accreted on the capital's edges over the past century. Streets emerged there willy-nilly in the mud alongside old irrigation canals, and sewage and electricity were an afterthought. Tall smokestacks loom like nineteenth-century mills over a landscape of ugly concrete tenements, spitting gray clouds; the air is noticeably sootier there than in the rest of Cairo. More than a million people live in Shobra al Khaima, and they are more densely packed than in any other city in the world except Manila. Many of the lucky ones with jobs work at textile plants, for dollars a day. None benefit from the patronage networks Mubarak built up during his long reign. Their lives illustrate the great migration that took place across the Arab world in the middle decades of the twentieth century, as poor and mostly illiterate peasants streamed from the countryside into the cities in search of work. Many of them settled in newly built housing at the city's edge, places like Shobra al Khaima, but also like Dahieh in Beirut, and al Thawra in Baghdad. Over time, these slums grew as more migrants from the country flooded in, living in crowded cinder-block towers that stank of raw sewage and uncarted trash. In the misery of these new surroundings, populist preachers gradually transformed Islam from the traditional religion of the migrants' ancestors into something new. It became a bulwark for their lost dignity in that foul-smelling slum. It became a shield they could rattle at infidels at home and abroad. It made them feel they belonged to something higher and better than the Westernized urban elite who despised them.

The reigning Islamist faction was different in each place, but Egypt was home base to a group with tentacles all over the Arab world: the Muslim Brotherhood. The movement's founder was himself a migrant from the Nile Delta, the agricultural heartland to the north of Cairo. Hassan al Banna first came to Cairo as a young man and took in the political scene, as he later wrote, with "the eyes of a religious villager." He founded the Brotherhood in 1928, preaching faith as the key to social and economic justice and sinking deep roots in Egypt's powerful labor unions. In the wake of the Ottoman Empire's collapse at the end of World War I, Banna feared that Muslims were losing their sense of religious and cultural identity. But the Brotherhood's aims were also implicitly political, and its rapid growth set it on a collision course with the Egyptian state. In 1949, Banna was murdered by government agents. In 1954, after a failed assassination attempt against him, Egypt's new leader, Gamal Abdel Nasser, legally banned the movement, throwing thousands of its members in jail. From then on, it would pursue a policy of accommodation, though many of its members turned inward. It was torn between two roles: a religious movement seeking democracy, and a more secretive element—with radical spin-offs—bent on implementing Islamic law. By the early 2000s, it operated a vast network of charity and social services but remained in a legal shadowland. Its members were allowed to run for office as independents but were subject to mass arrests at any time.

Beltagy's clinic was on the third floor of a ten-story tower full of medical offices. When I arrived on my first visit there, at 9:30 on a moonless Wednesday night in the fall of 2011, a single yellow lightbulb illuminated the crowd waiting for the elevator in the mud-spattered foyer. I climbed a dirty, half-lit stairway, passing parents carrying sick children in their arms and hobbling old men. Colorful signs advertised medicines for everything from hair loss to cancer. Even inside the building, the din of honking horns coming from the street was so loud that I had to ask one of the doctors if something unusual was going on. Election enthusiasm, maybe? He shook his head and gave me a weary smile. "Welcome to Shobra al Khaima," he said.

The mention of Beltagy's name here was like a password, eliciting an instant welcome. "Dr. Beltagy has always been outstanding, ever since he was a child," I was told by Anwar Hamid, a nutritionist who worked in a clinic on the building's ninth floor. Hamid, a thin, middle-aged Brotherhood veteran with a huge prayer bruise in the center of his forehead, sat at a battered metal desk in his modest office. He had known Beltagy for decades, and he made him sound like a kind of Egyptian Jay Gatsby. As a young man, Hamid said, Beltagy "always used to read newspaper articles with a pen in his hand, to outline them and take notes. He wanted to make sure he understood everything clearly. He was always first in his class. As a doctor, he has done so much good that people here trust him—he has a balance in their hearts."

Beltagy established his office in Shobra al Khaima soon after graduating from medical school, in the early '90s. He came for professional reasons; people told him he'd build a client base, a reputation, and then perhaps move into a more moneyed address. But he soon discovered that working in that slum was not just about medicine. "There is no government there," I was told by Hamza Zawba, another Brotherhood doctor who began working there at roughly the same time. "You are not just a doctor. If people are fighting, you must intervene and resolve it. If someone is jumping off a roof, you must persuade him not to jump. The police? They'd take three or four hours to arrive. Beltagy understood this right away. He got to know every corner of that place, every street. He worked night and day." The Brotherhood *was* the government in places like Shobra al Khaima, and Beltagy quickly became one of its most important players.

He had always had a hunger for politics. He got it from his father, a floor worker in a textile factory. The family lived in Kafr Dawar, an industrial town in northern Egypt not so different from Shobra al Khaima. Muhammad, born in 1963, was the sixth of seven children. "My father was a simple worker, not a boss," Beltagy told me. "But he always stood up for the rights of workers, no matter what the consequences. This had a big influence on me. When we got home from school, he was always talking about the other workers at the factory, and their struggles. This was the constant of our lives." In the dedication to his book, *Egypt: 2010: Is the Clock Going Backward?*, he wrote: "To the spirit of my father, who instilled in me the importance of telling the truth, even if it is bitter, and of standing up against falsehood, even if I am alone." When he got to university in Cairo, Beltagy told me, he was not sure where he stood politically. His parents were not members of any party. He explored several of Egypt's secular and leftist parties, which had a presence on campuses, before joining the Brotherhood. In talking about his decision, Beltagy said nothing about any religious epiphanies, or any clear conviction about the Brotherhood's Islamic message. Instead, the Brotherhood seems to have appealed to him because of its grassroots reach and organizational power. "It is a human fortune, and a blessing for the country," he told me. "It has so many capabilities in so many fields."

It was Beltagy's reputation as a working-class hero in the tenements of Shobra al Khaima that led the Brotherhood to nominate him for Parliament in 2005, and he won in a landslide. The group's members— running officially as independents—won a substantial number of seats that year for the first time, partly because Mubarak wanted to warn the United States about what democracy might look like in his country. The Islamists had no real power; most lawmakers treated Parliament as little more than a patronage mill. But Beltagy took to his new role as a government scourge. He railed against corruption, against tax laws privileging the rich, against the government's neglect toward the poor victims of a ferry disaster. He organized a weekly protest against a garbage-collection tax that hurt the poor in his district, and attended countless other sit-ins of one kind or another. "We did what we could," he told me. "But the old Parliament was like acting in a comedy. There was no real use." Later, he handed me a copy of his book, which summed up his feelings about the Mubarak-era Parliament and his efforts there. It was published in January 2011, just two weeks before the first protests in Tahrir Square. He gave me a knowing smile. "All the indicators were going in the other direction," he said. "None of us knew the revolution was coming."

By November 2011, the frenzied unity of Tahrir Square was a distant memory. As the parliamentary elections drew closer, Egypt was sinking into a cold war of thinly veiled hatred between the Islamists and their secular rivals. Then, at the last minute, something happened that had seemed impossible since Mubarak. The military council conjured enough stupidity and arrogance to bring the whole country together again, if only for a moment. In mid-November it issued a document, through a civilian proxy, declaring that it alone would be responsible for "the protection of constitutional legality," no matter who won the

Parliament or the presidency. The details were arcane, but the military's intention was clear: to dominate Egypt's politics on a permanent basis. Instantly, opposition broke out everywhere. Liberals and Islamists hit the streets together for the first time in months. The Brotherhood organized a vast rally in Tahrir Square on November 18, its first planned appearance there since February. With the leaders of the movement standing at either side of him, Beltagy took center stage, delivering a long speech before a crowd of tens of thousands. From the crowd rose chants of "Down with military rule!"

It took almost twenty-four hours for the military to strike back. Just after dawn, police flooded into the square and began brutally beating a few hundred stragglers who had stayed overnight. The news spread quickly, and thousands of people surged back into the square to join the battle. Beltagy headed straight for the square as soon as he found out, issuing a call through his campaign staff for others to join him. He found a chaotic scene reminiscent of the early days of the revolution ten months before, with clouds of tear gas and hundreds of young men squaring off against helmeted riot police. Television images of the violence spread a renewed sense of outrage across Egypt, and protests began in Alexandria and other cities.

Beltagy returned to the square the next day. This time he was on his own: the Brotherhood issued no call to its members. Instead, it released a statement on its website saying that it had only one spokesman, and it was not Beltagy. The leadership did not want any more distractions that might interfere with their looming electoral victory. Beltagy was furious, and he said so, in a statement carried on the group's website that took his conflict with the leadership into the open. "You have a right to be angry," he wrote to the protesters. "We, the Brotherhood, have to reconsider our position." But it did not. Instead, the group told its supporters on Tuesday to stay away from the square, even after almost every other political party in Egypt began calling for a "million man march" against military rule. Rumors spread that the Brotherhood had made a "deal" with the military to stay away from the square, in exchange for new promises to hold presidential elections sooner.

On Monday evening, sick with anger and frustration, Beltagy met with a number of secular party leaders at the headquarters of the liberal Ghad Party, led by his friend Ayman Nour. They called a high-ranking Interior Ministry official and pleaded with him to call off the troops; when that didn't work, Beltagy walked to the square and toured it three times. On the third tour, a dense crowd of young men attacked him, shouting curses about the Brotherhood. His aides formed a human barrier, shielding him from the punches and hurrying him toward a side street. Beltagy had a tight smile on his face as he stumbled through the scrum, as if he were trying to laugh it off. But there was nothing funny about it: you could see the rage on the faces of the men leaping at him, and the desperation among the Brotherhood guys pushing them back. The whole thing showed up on YouTube hours later, a shocking humiliation for the man who had once embodied the spirit of Tahrir. "Beltagy Thrown Out of the Square," was the heading.

One of the men fighting his way through that crowd had tears streaming down his face. Khaled Abdulhamid, a Socialist who had come to idolize Beltagy back in January 2011, had tried to warn him that this crowd was out for blood, but he was too late. Now, seeing his friend being cursed and beaten like a criminal, it broke his heart. He wanted to grab the kids who were attacking Beltagy and tell them: *This man is the only politician in Egypt willing to come here and face your punches, the others don't even care.* But the other voice in his head told him Beltagy was still with the Brotherhood. And the Brotherhood had betrayed the revolution with its refusal to show any support for the protesters. Abdulhamid stood watching the tangle of struggling men reach the edge of the square, slowly dispersing like a gaggle of street cats. Then he turned back, wiping the tears from his cheeks.

When I caught up to Beltagy three days later, he was still raw from the encounter. He sat in an overstuffed chair at the Brotherhood party offices, the skin around his eyes looking darker and more owlish than ever. "Yes, I had a difference of opinion with the Brotherhood," he said wearily. "I thought we should send thousands of members to the square to protect the protesters. There is a conspiracy against the revolution, and

I thought we should defend it." I was struck by his frankness. At around the same time, a former Brotherhood member told me he was sure Beltagy would leave the party, or be thrown out.

But when I next saw him, just after the first round of elections, he seemed almost to have forgotten the trauma of the preceding weeks. Beltagy and his Brotherhood colleagues had won their majority—their total would be about 47 percent, plus another 24 percent for their main Islamist allies—and would soon be running Egypt's first freely elected legislature. Many liberals had stayed away from the polls, out of anger at the military. This didn't seem to bother Beltagy anymore. "It's a democratic landmark," he told me, his face flushed and relaxed. "The whole country was out in the street, old and young, men and women, but nothing went wrong. It should go down in *Guinness World Records*." At moments like this, I had a strange feeling that he was drifting away, that some tidal religious force had greater power over him than even he understood. Would he fight for the liberal friends he'd made in Tahrir, or would he wave to them reluctantly, like a passenger on one of those great old ocean liners, borne away by the Islamist victory?

At times, it seemed as if an invisible film separated him from me, like the barrier that separates warm and cold currents underwater. Even when I thought I was hearing his most unfeigned self, the barrier hovered. It was there when I first visited him at home with his family, despite all my efforts to set them at ease. He lived on an unpaved street in a newly built middle-class area of eastern Cairo where the houses were ugly cinder-block stacks with battered, cracked doors. When he greeted me at the landing and led me into his home, the contrast was striking: it was warm and elegant, with a big reception room where the walls were painted a two-tone pattern of red and gold. There were two couches and a few easy chairs, but little else in the room besides a cabinet full of his medical books. His wife and sixteen-year-old daughter joined us. We spent more than two hours talking about his childhood, his career, the Brotherhood. He seemed relaxed and unguarded. Yet all the while, the curtain was there. I found myself wondering whether things would be different between us if I were Muslim. Would Beltagy then confide a different, truer version of himself and his history, his plans for the Brotherhood and the country?

One morning in early February 2012, Beltagy and one of his colleagues from the new Parliament were ushered into the cavernous office of Egypt's interior minister. After handshakes and formalities, the two parliamentarians sat down on the Louis Farouk–style gilt chairs and explained that they were there to ask for information. At a recent street protest, hired hoodlums had appeared and started beating up the demonstrators. Who, they asked, were these *baltagiyya*, these thugs? Why were they still being sent to disrupt protests, just as Mubarak used to do, a full year after the revolution? Who was sending them?

The minister, a shrewd-looking man with a small head and hard, chiseled features, gazed unsmilingly at the two men from behind his big desk. He asked if they had evidence. Beltagy said yes, the protesters had taken pictures. He offered to share them. The minister nodded gravely. Then he took out his cell phone and made a call. "Listen," he said, when a voice answered, "your people have been seen in the square. They've been photographed. Deal with it." He hung up without saying goodbye, put the phone down on the desk, and directed his gaze back to his guests.

The two parliamentarians stared at him, too stunned to speak. Finally Beltagy said, "You're warning the thugs? You're supposed to arrest them!"

The minister shrugged. "That man doesn't work for me," he said. Beltagy and his colleague looked at each other.

"Who does he work for?" Beltagy asked.

"It's a long story," the minister said. "What else can I help you with?"

Another long pause followed as the men struggled to make sense of what they had just heard. Finally Beltagy said, "We have heard about a man called Nakhnoukh, someone connected to these thugs. Who is he?"

The minister nodded, his face still registering no emotion or surprise. "Yes, Sabry Nakhnoukh. He's sort of a dealer for the thugs, he pays them. Very powerful. He's been in it for a while. Started out on Haram Street years ago, supplied bodyguards for actors and other people. We're looking for him. But be careful, he's an extremely dangerous man."

Beltagy asked some more questions, but the minister seemed reluctant to say much more; he began looking at his watch, and soon he told them he had to go. He ushered them out, muttering the usual niceties: stay in touch; thank you, gentlemen; goodbye. And that was it. Beltagy and his colleague took the elevator down, still in shock. They walked out the front steps, past the stacked concrete barriers and the barbed wire, talking the whole time: *What was that about?* And was the warning about Nakhnoukh intended as a threat to them? How could they trust a minister who was still working with criminals?

For Beltagy, the ministry visit drove home a painful lesson: so little had changed since the revolution. The whole drama of Tahrir Square had been about getting rid of one eighty-two-year-old man. Beneath him, the vast apparatus of brutality and corruption was still in place. Uprooting this system, whether in Egypt or anywhere else, would mean confronting a web of state-supported Mafia networks that thrived on intimidation and payoffs and secrecy. Cooking the books on election day had been only one of the Interior Ministry's jobs under Mubarak. These were people who specialized in acquiring dirt on their enemies—or arranging "accidents" for them—and they would not go down easily. The expression "deep state" had originated in Turkey in the 1990s, where the military colluded with drug traffickers and hit men to wage a dirty war against Kurdish insurgents. But it was just as apt for Arab regimes. The Assads of Syria had long worked with smugglers on the coast, and later mastered the art of deploying jihadis and suicide bombers against various enemies. The generals running Algeria had carried out atrocities using men disguised as jihadis during their brutal civil war in the 1990s, in an effort to bring the population to their own side. Yemen's strongman, Ali Abdullah Saleh, needed help during the 1994 civil war, so he recruited an irregular army of jihadi veterans of the Afghanistan war and later rewarded them with huge tracts of stolen land.

Beltagy was convinced that Egypt would never progress unless he got to the bottom of this swamp. He pressed all his contacts in the government for information, and a picture of Egypt's most powerful thug began to emerge. Nakhnoukh had started off as a nightclub bouncer and quickly graduated to providing bodyguards for VIP actors and policemen, all while running a prostitution business on the side. He videotaped his clients in flagrante delicto with his hookers and leveraged the dirt into bigger deals, better access. You could see his sense of invulnerability on his face: he stares out from photographs with a knowing sneer, a man with a meaty face and a huge chest, dressed in a tracksuit. Before long he commanded an army of street hoods, recruited through his own networks and through backroom deals with his friend Habib al Adly, Mubarak's interior minister from 1997 onward. Mubarak's fall had damaged him, but even so, the cops didn't dare touch him until the late summer of 2012. By then Beltagy had been harassing them for months to do something, and getting regular death threats.

The cops who finally broke into Nakhnoukh's high-walled villa outside Alexandria found a palace to rival one of Saddam Hussein's. There were five lions in cages and an ostrich wandering the compound. There was a pleasure garden surrounded by thick trees, and a disco with mirrored walls and leather lap-dance couches. They found a huge cache of automatic weapons, grenades, and machetes; there were bundles of hashish and cash, and evidence of a wide prostitution ring. Even after he was in jail, with his name in the papers, Nakhnoukh seemed confident that his friends at the ministry would spring him. He boasted smilingly of having sent hundreds of thugs to beat and intimidate voters during elections, insisting he was a patriot and had done it to keep the Brotherhood out of power. When his trial began, he still had people on the payroll: supporters showed up carrying signs with WE ARE ALL SABRY NAKHNOUKH written on them.

Beltagy was pleased with the arrest, but he knew it was a symbolic victory. Seven months as a parliamentarian had given him ample proof that Egypt's nominal legislature was still window dressing for a military regime. It didn't matter that he was elected, or that he belonged to the committee tasked with reforming Egypt's Interior Ministry: the old regime *feloul*, remnants, who ran the administration ignored his requests. Still, he redoubled his commitment. He started coming home from work at night with thick stacks of documents about administrative corruption and potential reforms. His wife worried about how little sleep he was getting. During his years as a doctor he'd been a workaholic, getting up for dawn prayers, spending hours a day at the university and at his clinic, getting home close to midnight. But now it was worse. This, he told younger friends who'd left the Brotherhood, was why he was staying in the group: to root out the culture of corruption. It was a crusade his fellow Islamists supported, at first. Then, as the momentous presidential election of 2012 approached, he began getting phone calls from the leadership. Take it easy, they told him. First things first. Their priority was to secure power, not to reform the state, and it turned out they were willing to make large compromises to get there.

The nature of those compromises became apparent on May 27, 2012, when Khairat al Shater, the Brotherhood's chief strategist, met with Khaled Meshal, the leader of Hamas, in a café in the InterContinental hotel in Cairo. The conversation was secretly recorded by Egyptian intelligence and later leaked to a newspaper. Meshal had had his differences with the Egyptian Islamists over the years, but ideologically, Hamas was a sister movement to the Brotherhood. Meshal was thrilled by the prospect of Islamist dominance in Egypt, and he'd flown from his base in Qatar to discuss Brotherhood strategy. One item on the agenda was what to do about Beltagy. According to the transcript, the men mostly discussed the presidential election, but at one point, the word Mukhabaraat (literally "intelligence") was mentioned: perhaps the most feared word in Arab countries.

MESHAL: *The brothers in Intelligence complained a lot about the issue of Muhammad Beltagy, he's been criticizing them, more than once.*
SHATER: *We've talked to him, but the degree of his discipline is weak.*
MESHAL: *I tried to get him on the phone, but he didn't pick up, I let it go.*
SHATER: *No, we've talked to him many times, and the Supreme Guide [the Brotherhood's top leader] talked to him, and I talked to him. They [the Intelligence] had told me this, but they . . . one of them*

called him and talked to him. They wanted to open a line with him.
Issues shouldn't be going in a path that messes up everyone. When
you tell him, the Intelligence are upset with you, he replies, "Well so-
and-so talked to me, and sat down with me and met me . . ."

The details of this cozy chat were ambiguous, but the stink of complic-
ity was astounding. Here were the most powerful Islamist leaders in
the Arab world speaking of Egyptian security officials—the very men
who'd specialized in jailing and torturing their people for decades—as
"brothers." Barely fifteen months after the revolution, the Brotherhood
had reached some kind of backroom deal with the Intelligence Ministry
as the price of expanded power. It was also clear that Beltagy was not
going along with it, though he seemed unwilling to confront the Brotherhood leaders directly.

The context for the conversation was an event of tremendous importance, for the Brotherhood and for Egypt: the country's first presidential election. The Brotherhood had promised a year earlier not to run
a candidate, recognizing that pushing for too much power too quickly
would risk a backlash. They had changed their minds in February
2012, shocking and disappointing many of their own members. The
lure of the presidency was too strong. The first round of voting, in a
field of twelve candidates, had taken place a few days before Khairat
Shater and Khaled Meshal sat down together. All the more centrist
candidates were knocked out, including a liberal Islamist who'd left the
Brotherhood and the country's former foreign minister. Only two were
left standing: the Brotherhood's candidate, an engineer named Muhammad Morsi, and Ahmed Shafiq, a former prime minister under
Mubarak. For the liberals, it was a nightmarish choice: the Brotherhood vs. the old regime.

Beltagy was not happy either. He had come close to resigning from
the Brotherhood after the group insisted on running a presidential
candidate. It was a profoundly unwise decision, one he knew would
come back to haunt them. But his greatest fear was that the Interior
Ministry barons would steal the election from Morsi, putting an unre-
pentant Mubarak ally in the president's chair. Shater and the other

Brotherhood leaders were trying (as the Shater-Meshal recording made clear) to forestall this possibility by making deals with the deep state. Beltagy chose a different approach. He reasoned that if the liberals could be persuaded to side publicly with Morsi, the generals would not dare to fake the election. He crafted a pitch for his old friends from Tahrir: with public support from liberals, Morsi would no longer need the reactionary Salafis and would be free to govern as a centrist. It was a leap of faith, no doubt. But Beltagy saw no other way. He shuttled from meeting to meeting for two weeks, securing the help of his leftist friends. Together, they wrote up a list of conditions for their support to Morsi. Most of them were too vague to be meaningful: launching a "national unity project" and forming a "national salvation government" including figures from every political group. Still, the pressure made a difference. A gallery of revolutionary figures, including Wael Ghoneim and the novelist Alaa Aswany, showed up for a press conference with Morsi at the Fairmont Hotel in Cairo, pledging their support in exchange for his agreement to govern by consensus.

Morsi was declared winner of Egypt's presidential election on June 24, by a narrow margin of just over 3 percent. It was an odd moment. This was the country's first democratically elected president in six thousand years of history, but he was virtually unknown to Egyptians. He'd been nominated only after the Brotherhood's first choice, Khairat Shater, was disqualified from running on a legal technicality. The Brotherhood chose Morsi as his replacement because he was safe, an organization man through and through. He looked the part: a bull-headed man of sixty with a helmet of short dark hair, clunky glasses, and almost no neck. He conveyed a mulelike immovability, and little else. Urban Egyptians mocked him from the start for his peasantlike demeanor and his verbal clumsiness. But his flaws ran much deeper than style. He lacked Beltagy's gift for friendship and bridge-building. Even a skilled politician would have struggled to balance Egypt's hostile factions and scheming generals, but Morsi seemed not even to understand the vulnerability of his position. He began invoking the phrase "electoral legitimacy" at every moment of tension. He was Egypt's president, he said, the choice of the people, and no unofficial agreements with liberals, or anyone else, would bind him. This stubbornness seemed to confirm the liberals' worst fears about a hidden Islamist agenda. At the same time, Morsi paid little attention to Egypt's shattered economy, despite a litany of terrifying indicators. Tourism had collapsed after the 2011 revolution, and inflation and unemployment doubled under Morsi's watch. By 2013, fuel shortages and power outages would be worse than ever before. With government debt rising fast, Morsi pleaded for more loans from abroad, scarcely gesturing at reforms to his country's sluggish bureaucracies.

As the autumn of 2012 began, the committee tasked with writing a new constitution became a battleground. The Salafis pushed for a more explicit adherence to sharia, and demanded that the sheikhs of al Azhar, Egypt's Islamic university, be given a role as interpreters. This was terrifying to liberals—the sanctioning of an unelected religious council that could veto or modify legislation. They wanted more guarantees of civic rights and less interference by the military in politics. Beltagy sided with the liberals on this last count, proposing during one meeting to add an additional civilian in the National Defense Council so as to water down the army's control. The army representative in the room, General Mamdouh Shahin, promptly yelled at Beltagy, "If you add one of yours, I will add one of mine!" The military won, and the entire exchange was caught on camera.

In the end, the Brotherhood leadership tried to have it both ways and lost the confidence of a large middle ground of Egyptians. They allowed the Salafis to insert an article defining the principles of Islamic law in ways that frightened and infuriated not just liberals but many ordinary people as well. They also gave in to the army, which kept its dominant role in government and got a new clause allowing military trials of civilians. The Brotherhood's mastermind, Khairat al Shater, was working from a script that was almost a perfect inversion of Beltagy's. Where one man wanted to rein in the military and ally with the liberals, the other was strenuously catering to the generals and the security elite. What Shater didn't understand was that the generals and the *feloul* didn't want his cooperation; they wanted his head. The Supreme Constitutional Court, full of Mubarak-era men, was poised to declare the

whole constitutional process null and void. It would be another set-
back, months of work wasted, a well-aimed blow at Morsi's agenda.

Morsi responded with his most disastrous move yet. On November
22, without warning, he declared his own powers to be above the reach
of the court, as the guardian of the revolution. In theory, this was just a
temporary measure to get the constitution passed, but no one believed that. It looked like Ayatollah Khomeini all over again; the mask,
it seemed, had fallen. The liberals called it a coup d'état. ElBaradei, the
Nobel laureate and liberal icon, accused Morsi of "appointing himself
Egypt's new pharaoh." Within days, mobs began attacking Brotherhood
offices in cities across the country, smashing windows and starting
fires. The identity of these rioters instantly became a subject of fero-
cious debate. Some were probably ordinary protesters who'd got out of
control. But a new group of activists calling itself the Black Bloc had
also appeared. They wore masks, and they made clear that their sole
mission was the toppling of Morsi's government by any means necessary. The Brotherhood started warning about a conspiracy. This time
they were not wrong. It is impossible to know how much coordination
was involved, but there is little doubt that some in the military and the
police were giving quiet encouragement to the rioters, and perhaps
more. The police mostly did little to stop the vandalism. Within a
week of Morsi's constitutional declaration, at least a dozen Brotherhood offices were destroyed. In Tahrir Square, tens of thousands of
people gathered, packing the square and holding up signs that echoed
the chant of 2011: THE PEOPLE DEMAND THE FALL OF THE REGIME.
They began organizing marches to the presidential palace, holding up
signs with ominous slogans written on them: THE LAST WARNING. The
police fired tear gas to keep the crowds back from the palace, but they
seemed unable—or unwilling—to stop them.

Beltagy was paralyzed. He'd had no advance notice of Morsi's decision. His phone was lighting up with calls from old Tahrir allies demanding to know what Morsi was thinking. Beltagy did not know what
to tell them. His instinct had always been to look for middle ground,
but now there was none. One night on a TV interview, he said he was
disappointed with Morsi's lack of transparency. But he seemed angrier

at the liberals. When the host asked Beltagy about the "Brotherhoodiz-ing" of the state, he lashed out: "We don't have access to five crucial state institutions: the judiciary, the military, the police, intelligence, and security. This continues up until now. We are still essentially running the country with Mubarak public servants. And you're telling me that we're failing?" The interviewer shot back: "It's your fault for not remov-ing them." Beltagy's eyes got visibly wider, and he replied: "Okay—you're afraid of me making any changes that would allow me to succeed, but you blame me for not doing that?"

Early in the day on December 5, Beltagy's phone lit up with a famil-iar number: Khaled Abdulhamid, his Socialist friend. Khaled was in the back of a speeding car, on his way to a big protest at the presidential palace. He was troubled by the bloodlust he sensed in the protesters all around him.

"Muhammad, listen, I hear the Brotherhood is sending people down here to the palace, to confront the protesters," he said. "You've got to stop them before it's too late."

Usually the two men slipped into sync when violence was in the air, but this time there was a pause at the other end of the line.

"Why?" Beltagy said. "You've been there for days, why shouldn't the Brotherhood be there too? People are threatening to attack the presi-dent and our people want to defend him. Do you know how many Brotherhood offices have been burned?"

Khaled replied that he didn't like the violence or the ugly slogans on his own side, but he feared it could get worse. "If the Brotherhood comes, there will be blood," he predicted. "It would be blood between the people, between one social group and another, not just police brutality. It's the beginning of the end. Listen, there were tens of thousands of people here yesterday and it was peaceful. No one is going to attack Morsi."

Beltagy wasn't buying it. "We're the biggest political party in the country, and you've already taken over Tahrir. We cannot even go there now," Beltagy said. "Where should we demonstrate? In a bath-room?" The arguments went back and forth for more than ten minutes, and finally Khaled issued a last warning: "This is the worst decision the Brotherhood will ever make."

Twelve hours later, Beltagy—who was outside Cairo at a conference about the constitution—glimpsed the TV in his hotel room. He'd been getting texts all evening but had tried to ignore them. Now he saw the screen, with its red scroll at the bottom *Violent Clashes at the Presidential Palace*. The camera showed a dark boulevard, with thick crowds of young men running back and forth and dark projectiles flying through the air under the yellow glare of streetlights. There were fires burning in the background, and a siren wailed. Two men rushed past, carrying a wounded comrade with blood on his face. Chants alternated in the crowd: "Down with the regime" from one side and "Allahu Akbar" from the other. The camera began showing footage from earlier in the day: Brotherhood men attacking a protest camp, pulling down tents, carrying off street barricades, grabbing people by their shirts and frog-marching them away from the palace. That was how it had begun. Then, after dark, it had turned into a street battle, with stones, then bottles, and then knives and Molotov cocktails. The police fired tear gas but there wasn't much they could do; the crowds were too large. The fighting lasted into the next morning, leaving at least seven people dead and more than six hundred people crippled and burned and bruised.

It was just as Khaled had warned: this was much worse than protesters being killed by the police. This was Egyptians killing each other. It was the first time it had happened on this scale since the 1950s. Beltagy watched it unfold on the screen, the nausea slowly rising in his belly. He wondered if his friend Khaled was safe, not knowing that he too at that moment was watching the same images on a screen. Both men were thinking of their conversation earlier that day, both sensing it would be their last.

Even then, some people said Morsi might have pulled back. Everyone was calling it a national tragedy, and if ever there was a day for conciliation, for large gestures, this was it. Yet when he delivered a televised speech to the nation the following night, Morsi sounded as brittle and intransigent as any ancien régime tyrant. He blamed it all on a "fifth column" and refused to give any ground. He wrapped himself in the flag just as Mubarak had, warning against hired thugs and saboteurs, never acknowledging the depth of the anger he had provoked. In a sense, Morsi had made the same basic error as Mubarak: he had confused his own followers with Egypt. The Brotherhood had never been a majority of the population, but its electoral victories in 2011 and 2012 had fostered a comforting illusion of depth. The group's leaders failed to realize that most of those voters were people with no commitment to the Brotherhood or anyone else. Vast numbers of them were now swinging the other way.

For Beltagy's Socialist friend Khaled Abdulhamid and many other leftists, Morsi had become something much worse than a failure: he was an enemy. No one took much comfort when the street fighting died down. A line had been crossed. Morsi got his constitutional referendum passed in mid-December, but the victory looked Pyrrhic. Egypt was sliding toward a confrontation. It was no longer delusional to speak of a civil war. A new oppositional force had emerged called the National Salvation Front, a mix of liberal figures, the old Mubarak elite, and young protesters, with the tacit support of the military. It was the Brotherhood's nightmare come true. The Front was not interested in changing the constitution or influencing Morsi. They wanted him gone, out of office, erased from Egyptian political life. They were willing to do almost anything to make that happen.

Three months later, Khaled Abdelhamid's first child was born, a daughter. It was a welcome relief from the hell of politics. A few days later, back home from the hospital, he and his wife had a party and invited a group of friends over. They had music playing, people were drinking and toasting his fatherhood, the window was open, letting in the spring night air. His phone rang, vibrating in his pocket, and he took it out. He'd been getting congratulatory calls all day. He looked at the number on the screen and recognized it right away: Beltagy. He stared at it for a moment. He could almost hear the sound of Beltagy's voice, offering his blessings. But the veil was between them now, invisible and absolute. He put the phone back in his pocket. The same number lit up on his phone later that night, and again the next day. He never picked up.

On June 27, 2013, one of Egypt's best-known young poets received an unexpected phone call. Abdul Rahman Yusuf had been famous even before the revolution, and afterward he was instantly recognizable anywhere. He looked like a Hollywood matinee idol from the black-and-white era, with his dark, elegant features and his regal manner. His fame derived partly from his father, Yusuf Qaradawi, a theologian with a vast Islamist following and a reputation in the West as a hate-monger. His son could not have been more different: a clean-shaven aesthete who wore beautifully tailored European suits and rarely ever spoke of religion. His business card identified him as "the Poet" and featured a color image of his face in profile. But behind the narcissism was a remarkably independent and disillusioned thinker. He had been in the first wave of Tahrir revolutionaries, and he was never afraid to criticize the military, the Brotherhood, or his own peers.

The number on his phone now was familiar: Muhammad Beltagy. The two men had known each other since the night of January 25, 2011, when they'd stood together on a stage in the shared euphoria of Tahrir Square's first night. They'd been friendly since then, though Yusuf never hid his dislike of the Brotherhood. But he hadn't heard from Beltagy for months. He'd been dismayed at the way Beltagy had fallen in line with Morsi's endless blunders. He'd become just another Brother-hood figure. And now, after a moment of small talk, Beltagy was rev-ving up his old plea for dialogue and building bridges. Yusuf listened in silence for a few minutes as Beltagy sketched out his hopes: to ar-range a meeting, to try to rebuild the Tahrir alliance. Beltagy clearly hadn't given up. He mentioned that he was reaching out to all his lib-eral friends, even the ones who blocked his calls. It was never too late, there was still time. He went on and on. Finally, Yusuf couldn't hold back any longer.

"Dr. Beltagy, don't you know what's happening?" the poet shouted. "The tanks are in the streets. It's too late. Can't you see?"

It was much too late. The movement known as Tamarod, or rebel-lion, had galvanized a nationwide uprising against the Brotherhood. It was a youth movement and advertised itself constantly as a replay of the 2011 revolution. Tamarod claimed to have gathered twenty-two million signatures calling for a petition demanding Morsi's removal and new elections. But there was a crucial difference from 2011. This movement had the quiet backing of the previous revolution's enemies: the security services, the army, and the old Mubarak elite. The billionaire Naguib Sawiris had donated publicity worth millions. Three days after Beltagy's phone call, on June 30, Tahrir Square was solidly packed with a mass of chanting people that spread to every boulevard around, a starfish-shaped crush of humanity. This big demonstration, which had been in the works for weeks, was billed as the "second revolution," and by most accounts, Tahrir and its environs were fuller that day than they'd been in January 2011. There were vast turnouts in Egypt's other major cities too. All the liberal groups from Tahrir were there, along with Mohamed ElBaradei, the Nobel laureate their standard-bearer. Their slogans this time were all denunciations of the Brotherhood. The old antimilitary rhetoric was gone. When army helicopters flew low over Tahrir, the crowd sent up wild cheers of approval. Protesters posed for pictures with soldiers and policemen guarding the entrances. It was as if their new hatred for Morsi had dissolved all memory of their struggle against military rule. Once again, they chanted, the people and the army were "one hand."

Beltagy did not see any of this. He was across town in the Islamist demonstration at Rabaa al-Adawiya Square, established two days earlier. There, too, rivers of people were crowded into an intersection before a makeshift stage. The chants at Rabaa were for Morsi and for "legitimacy," the Brotherhood's shield against all critics. The Egyptian army's helicopter pilots who flew over Cairo on that day would have seen Egypt's polarized politics inscribed on the city's face: two vast, opposed gatherings, each full of chanting crowds, each utterly self-convinced and suffused with righteous rage.

Yet in a sense, Abdul Rahman Yusuf was wrong. Beltagy did see what was coming. He'd been talking for months about 1954, the year Gamal Abdel Nasser had cracked down and banned the Brotherhood. Beltagy knew the Brotherhood had brought much of this on itself, but he never broke ranks. There was no more talk of leaving the group, no public criticism. He'd been forced to make a choice, just like the liberals who resigned themselves to getting in bed with the military. There was no more room for the Beltagy whose "discipline [was] weak," at least not in public.

One of the only people to whom he confided his doubts now was his seventeen-year-old daughter, Asmaa. When he got back to the house, at midnight or even later, she would be in the living room waiting for him. The rest of the family was usually in bed. The two of them would sit together and she'd ask about Parliament, about the Brotherhood, about the opposition, about strategy. He treated her like an adult. Asmaa had been exceptional since childhood, with her intense curiosity and quiet astuteness. On Twitter, she had been recording her thoughts about the Arab revolutions ever since the very first protests. "I roam the Square, storing in my mind scenes and images in all their details and spontaneity," she wrote in late 2011. "My heart is hanging between Taiz and Bani Walid. My soul hovers over Hama and Deir al Zour." Her commentary has the sentimental impetuosity of an adolescent but the range and sophistication of an educated adult. Writing on the fly, in half-finished sentences, she tosses out questions, writes mash notes to revolutionaries in Yemen and Syria, invokes philosophers, poets, documentary films. She quotes Sufi philosophers and old Arab proverbs. It is the diary of a woman struggling to find her bearings between the comfort of tradition and the lure of new ideas. Asmaa began attending meetings of the new youth parties in 2011, including the Socialists. Like her older brother, Ammar, she disliked the Brotherhood's rigidity and sympathized with more liberal groups. She remained publicly loyal to her father, and only a few of her tweets hint at disagreement with the Brotherhood. In private, during their late-night conversations, she frequently offered him advice, her mother told me. He listened, nodding occasionally, his eyes tired but focused.

By the time of the big rally on June 30, Muhammad Beltagy was no longer coming home at all. He'd had so many death threats that he stayed away most nights. During the rally, he got word from medical colleagues that his clinic office in Shobra al Khaima had been ransacked and torn apart, by police or by thugs, it wasn't clear. That same night, anti-Brotherhood protesters coming from Tahrir began gathering near the group's main headquarters, a six-story dun-colored building in the Muqattam district. Near midnight, they started throwing Molotov cocktails at the upper windows. There were members inside, and they fought back, firing bird shot to scare the attackers away. A street battle broke out in the darkness, but the Brotherhood, outnumbered, could not keep the rioters out. By the next morning, eight men were dead and the building was a smoking ruin. Looters had dragged away everything they could find: papers, rugs, furniture.

The next day, as protesters surged back into Tahrir, a military officer read a statement on state television. Citing the "historic circumstances," the Supreme Council of the Armed Forces was issuing an ultimatum: "If the demands of the people have not been met" after forty-eight hours, the council would announce a "road map" to be "enforced under the military's supervision." The crowd in Tahrir, hearing the broadcast live, erupted in cheers. At the Rabaa sit-in, the news was met with rage and disbelief. That afternoon, the men in the crowd seemed ready for war, many of them carrying makeshift clubs and wearing construction hard hats. Beltagy stood before them onstage, his eyes glowing, and said, "No coup of any kind against legitimacy will pass, except over our dead bodies!" By nightfall, more clashes were breaking out between pro- and anti-Morsi crowds all over Egypt. At least eighteen people were dead by morning.

Once again, Morsi faced a deadline and a choice between concession and defiance. The whole world, it seemed, was pleading with this clumsy, bullish man: the U.S. ambassador, Anne Patterson, was calling and urging him to make a deal with the military. Other diplomats added their voices. Even the leader of Tunisia's Islamist movement, Rached Ghannouchi, had come to Cairo to urge compromise. He was not given a meeting. Late on the night of July 2, Morsi delivered his final speech as president, as rigid and tone-deaf as ever: "Legitimacy is the only way to protect our country and prevent bloodshed, to move to a new phase. Legitimacy is the only thing that guarantees for all of us that there will not be any fighting and conflict, that there will not be bloodshed." As if blood were not already being shed. His pigheadedness amazed even his own ministers, who had been peeling off in droves. The Egyptian cabinet's official Twitter feed issued a stinging critique of Morsi. Twenty-four hours later, when the generals announced that they'd taken over Egypt, the officers of the presidential guard could be seen waving victory flags and cheering on the palace roof. Morsi had never been fully in charge, even in his own house.

The military coup of July 3 arrived with a tableau. Egyptians tuned in to the announcement that night, after hours of anticipation, and saw an officer appear on-screen in a short-sleeved khaki shirt and black beret, his hands firmly clutching a lectern. This was Abdelfattah al Sisi, the commander of the armed forces. As he began speaking, the camera panned slowly backward, and gradually it became clear that he was on a kind of stage, with two groups of men sitting in chairs on either side. On Sisi's left was a Coptic bishop, his long black-and-gold robe emblazoned with a crucifix. Next to him was a prominent sheikh from al Azhar, in black gown and white turban. Behind them was the bearded leader of the ultraconservative Salafi Party, al Nour. To Sisi's right, with a clutch of army and navy officers, was Mohamed ElBaradei. It was all as carefully choreographed as a Renaissance court masque. Sisi was telling Egyptians that he had the backing of leading Muslims and Christian religious authorities, and of the liberals—and by extension, the international community.

The camera then panned slowly back in again, focusing on Sisi himself. This was a face Egyptians did not yet know well, but it was being imprinted, in that very moment, on their collective consciousness. It was a youthful-looking face, clean shaven, with regular but rounded features and even a hint of baby fat. His brown eyes conveyed a boyish simplicity, with no trace of hidden depth or rancor or reserve. You had a strange feeling that he was insulated from the crisis he was talking about, and many people found this reassuring. In a sense it was true: he had spent his entire adult life in the parallel world of the Egyptian army, which operates its own economy, its own social clubs, its own gated communities, and tends to view civilians as unruly sheep. In one leaked recording, Sisi told his fellow officers that the military's relationship with the people was like "the very big brother, the very big father who has a son who is a bit of a failure and does not understand the facts." In some ways Sisi had been running Egypt even before the coup, and even before the revolution itself. As head of military intelligence in 2010, he had secretly warned his fellow officers that Mubarak aimed to install his son Gamal as the next ruler, and that this would lead to vast popular uprisings. When that happened, Sisi said, he believed the military should side with "the people," easing Mubarak out while maintaining a firm grip on power.

One of the things Sisi said in his first postcoup press conference was: "The army was the one to first announce that it was out of politics. It still is, and it will remain away from politics." But the entire nonverbal part of the conference—a serene Sisi surrounded by that reassuring cast of officers and robed dignitaries—conveyed the opposite. Within hours, people were waving posters bearing Sisi's face in Tahrir Square. Egypt needed a savior, and it was not going to be one of the costumed men sitting in chairs on either side of the stage.

From that day forward, Beltagy was marooned at Rabaa, along with every other recognizable member of the Brotherhood: members of Parliament, bearded sheikhs, the Supreme Guide himself. No one doubted that they would be hauled off to jail the moment they walked beyond the borders of Rabaa Square. So they stayed there, along with tens of thousands of followers, in what had once been an intersection in eastern Cairo. For those who'd known the place beforehand, it now was almost unrecognizable. The crowds and the atmosphere of chaos spread for blocks in every direction from the Rabaa mosque. If you went there by taxi, the driver would sometimes refuse to take you, or if he did, he'd drop you off blocks away. You had to walk to the rows of metal barricades the protesters had set up, where multiple lines of young men were doing pat-downs, just as they had during the glory days of Tahrir in 2011. When you got closer to the center, near the mosque, the crowd got thicker, obscuring the streets and buildings and pushing you along with it. Soon you were picking your way among families sprawled on mats, old men squatting, children running from tent to tent, vendors selling watermelon or roasted corn. Sheets and blankets had been hung from ropes to wall off women's areas and makeshift clinics, turning the whole square and the blocks around it into a maze where you quickly lost your bearings. The only way to get oriented was to look for the main stage, where huge loudspeakers were constantly blasting out speeches or songs or prayers.

The sit-in was a strange blend of carnival and apocalyptic cult meeting. You sensed that it couldn't last, that people could not live in such a dense crush of anger and sweat and sewage for very long, and it only got worse when the Ramadan fast started a few days after the coup. You would arrive at midday and it would be more than a hundred degrees there, the July sun beating down fiercely on the tents. Thousands of people lay sprawled all over the place trying to sleep, most of them on nothing more than a plastic mat over hard pavement. There were almost no bathrooms, no showers, no air-conditioned rooms to escape to. The smell was stifling, a vile cocktail of rotting food and mud and unwashed bodies. During those long afternoons, a miserable torpor settled over the place, with most people too weak from lack of food and water to move. Children howled, and women in black robes and head scarves winced in the heat, their faces red, muttering prayers. It was like stumbling onto a prison camp. The day dragged on for ages, and when at last the shadows lengthened and the sun touched the horizon, it was as if a painful blister had been lanced. The call to evening prayer sounded on the speakers. People stirred back to life. The air cooled a bit, the sky slowly tinted to a deep, merciful blue. Young men began rolling out carts full of plastic-wrapped plates of food: dates, rice, stewed beans. People spread blankets for the *iftar*, the ritual breaking of the fast. The stage lit up, a great bank of floodlights illuminating its metal scaffoldings and the banners that hung on them. The speeches began soon after sundown and went on almost until dawn.

When I first saw Beltagy on that stage, I was amazed. His usual smile had tightened, so that it almost resembled a grimace. In a ragged voice, he led the crowd in a chant: *Our blood and souls, we sacrifice for you, Islam.* Standing next to him was Safwat Hegazy, a notoriously aggressive ideologue. Beltagy's language had become darker and more devout: he spoke about reliving the days of the Prophet, about standing up to the tanks with bodies and blood. He'd already spoken onstage so often that he'd become one of the symbols of the protest, which was being broadcast almost continuously on al Jazeera. Watching him, it was hard to believe he had ever been an outlier in the Brotherhood. Now he was its standard-bearer.

Afterward, I found him in an outbuilding behind the mosque, and he agreed to talk. He had dark circles under his eyes, and he slumped a bit in his chair. I asked him about his liberal friends and whether he was in touch with any of them. He sighed. "It was a terrible shock," he said. "So many friends we used to deal with now take the coup as a given. Many show sympathy to the arrests, the killings, the imprisonments. They aren't taking any stance against the main crime—the military coup. Some even defend it." As he went on, the old Beltagy slowly reappeared. He said Morsi had made huge mistakes. He said the Brotherhood had not tried hard enough to reach out to liberals. But something new and troubling emerged: he began sketching paranoid theories, saying that the United States and Israel had deliberately undermined Morsi and had helped plot the coup. He seemed utterly deluded about the reality the Brotherhood was facing. The Rabaa protest, he said, would win over the Egyptian public and defeat the coup. There was no other way. Any compromise with the "coup government" was impossible. I looked across the room and saw Beltagy's wife and his daughter, Asmaa, waiting for him. I felt like putting away my notebook and telling him: This is madness. Instead I shook his hand and said good night.

Other people did try. Several of Beltagy's young ex-Brotherhood friends came to Rabaa to reason with him. Their message was mostly the same. *Dr. Beltagy, the presidency is lost. Just cut a deal. Rabaa has built a lot of pressure: use it to get what you can. There could be new elections, the Brotherhood would still have a role. You have nothing to gain by staying here.* Beltagy listened with his tight smile and refused to budge. One of these visitors told me that he felt Beltagy knew he was making the wrong decision. "I was surprised," the younger man said, "because I thought of Beltagy as someone who only went with what he really believed, that he understood the art of what is possible. But I think he had reached a point where he felt they had gone too far and couldn't go home; they would all be arrested. And even then, they never imagined things would get as bad as they did." Even Beltagy's aging mother showed up one night. She said during an interview months later that she had urged him to "slow things down." He smiled and replied, "Mother, what can I do? I can't close my eyes to what is happening."

Over the next several weeks, the atmosphere at Rabaa grew darker and more fatalist. When I first got there, you could still find men holding up incongruous signs: LIBERALS FOR MORSI. CHRISTIANS FOR MORSI. ACTORS FOR MORSI. They still had hopes of drawing the rest of Egypt to their cause. You occasionally glimpsed a woman without a hijab in the crowd, or a few long-haired leftists making common cause. By late July, that was gone. Almost two hundred protesters had been gunned down by the police in a string of separate protests over that month. The liberals of Egypt applauded, and many of them called for stronger measures. The Islamists sensed that they'd been cast out. The prospect of death hung in the air, and people talked about it all the time on the stage, the same words recurring like threats: *blood, martyrdom, corpses, souls, sacrifice.* There were tirades onstage about the "evil ones" who tried to "ban religion from our lives." The crowd would chant in response: "Islamic, Islamic, Egypt is an Islamic state!"

One night, wandering among the tents, I found a group of long-bearded Salafis sitting together, and they invited me to join them for tea. The leader of the biggest Salafi political party had endorsed the coup, but these men—like much of the party's rank and file—could not have felt more differently. "Many of the youth now say, 'No more ballot boxes,'" one of them told me. "We used to believe in the caliphate. The international community said we should go with ballot boxes, so we followed that path. But then they flip the ballot boxes over on us. So forget it. If ballot boxes don't bring righteousness, we will all go back to demanding a caliphate." Another man piped up: "It has been a tough test, but it has had benefits—now we know who our true friends are. The liberals, the Christian leaders, they stood with the old regime. It was painful to see some Muslims going against us at first, but they have now seen their mistake and returned to us. The Islamic path is clear."

In early August, not long before the end, I found myself on a dark, empty street a block or two outside the edge of the sit-in. It was late, close to midnight. Next to me was a thirty-four-year-old doctor named Ali Mashad, who'd left the Brotherhood a couple years earlier. We were sitting in chairs from a café that had closed hours earlier. Ali glanced over occasionally at the protest, glowing hivelike in the distance. "This is not the Brotherhood I know," he said, flicking an ash from his cigarette. "They are talking the language of the Salafis, because that is the language of the street. This is the Brotherhood's pragmatism: they say what each one wants to hear. They are oppressed, yes. But it's their own fault. They are creating an Islamic state, right here. It's their Paris Commune. I think this is the end of the Brotherhood. The 2011 revolution was the beginning of their end. And now you are creating a new monster, Islamic anarchists. It will be decentralized. The youth are losing confidence in democracy. We had a real chance to remake our society on a better basis on January 25, to achieve reconciliation between Christians and Muslims, Islamists, secularists. We failed. Our elite, they carry the past with them. Our history is repeating itself."

He was quiet for a long time, and we both gazed at the lights of the sit-in. His voice had been almost mocking at first, but when he resumed talking he seemed to be fighting back tears. "My heart is with the ordinary people there, who will be killed," he said. "I have spent so much of my life with them. But my mind refuses to support their ideas. The people went out to protest on June 30 because they lost their belief in democracy. The people at Rabaa have lost their belief too. Where are we going? Oligarchy? Theocracy? I am confused. I never before wanted to leave Egypt. Now I am thinking I have no place here."

Early on the morning of August 14, 2013, Asmaa Beltagy poured water onto her hands from a small plastic bottle and began washing her face and forearms. She would have used a faucet for the ritual prayer ablution, but there was almost no water left at Rabaa. When she was done, she poured water gently onto her mother's face. They were in one of the mosque outbuildings, at the center of the sit-in. Her mother, Sana, was so anxious she could barely stand. The gunshots were getting more frequent, and they could smell the tear gas. They thought it was just another skirmish on the edges of the protest; there had been several in the previous weeks. They were wrong. The Interior Ministry had begun massing its forces well before dawn. There were armored personnel carriers, bulldozers, hundreds of armed riot police and soldiers in gas masks. There were snipers on the roofs of all the higher buildings surrounding the Rabaa. The plan to clear the square for good was under way. The trucks began broadcasting a prerecorded warning just after 6:00 a.m., telling protesters to leave. But no one heard it except those at the very edges. The police began shooting within minutes, rubber bullets at first, then live fire. No one could get out. The younger men started building fortifications out of wood and furniture, and tearing up chunks of pavement to throw at the attackers. The government would later claim that the protesters fired the first shots, and they claimed to have recovered fifteen handguns (from a sit-in with perhaps thirty thousand people). They provided no evidence.

Asmaa stayed with her mother for an hour, comforting her and leading a group of women in prayers. Her father was in a meeting with Brotherhood leaders. The gunfire got louder and louder as the bulldozers crashed through the hand-built rock walls on the southern side of the square, then rolled forward over a line of parked cars. Snipers were shooting anyone who moved between buildings. By 8:30, the mosque was full of dead and dying people. Asmaa told her mother she was going to the field hospital to help. Her mother said it was too dangerous, but Asmaa said she could not stand doing nothing while people were dying, and finally she left. She found her way to the field hospital, near the mosque, and asked what she could do that would be useful. A doctor told her the best thing would be to help pile up rocks for protesters to throw at the armored vehicles.

A few minutes later, as she was tossing rocks onto the pile, a sniper's bullet passed through her chest, knocking her to the ground. The men nearby quickly picked her up and carried her into the clinic. Someone took a cell phone video of her lying on a gurney, covered by a blue cloth. A doctor in blue scrubs fiddles with her IV drip. Her brother Ammar is standing by the bed, his face contorted with anguish. The camera moves in close, and you see beads of sweat on her pale face. She winces in pain at one point and moves her head back and forth. After that she gazes upward, her big green eyes almost luminous. She seems fully conscious but distant, as if contemplating something terribly sad. "Oh, God," she says, several times, in a faint voice.

She died moments later. There was a lull in the assault at midday, and Ammar Beltagy and his brother Anas carried their sister's body out of the field clinic, hoping to take her to a morgue. But as they walked out, a volley of loud gunfire jolted them, forcing them to drop her body on the ground. The police were now firing directly into the hospital. Ammar and Anas pressed their cheeks into the pavement next to Asmaa as the APCs got closer to them. The gunfire was so loud and intense they both felt sure they would die, Ammar later told me. They could hear the screams of dying men lying on the pavement nearby. A few brave hospital workers ran through the gunfire to help them. One video taken around this time shows a doctor crouching down to pick up a wounded man, then carrying him a few feet, until another round of gunshots rings out: the doctor stops short, struck in the head by a bullet, and he and his patient both fall to the ground.

There were now hundreds of dead bodies littering the square. The bulldozers and APCs rolled over them as they advanced, leaving crushed and shredded human remains on the pavement. The soldiers were firing at anyone in their way. In other videos taken by survivors, you can see men being shot as they lie flat on the ground, struggling to stay under the line of fire. You can hear the constant barking sound of gunfire, and an eerie electronic buzz emitted by the APCs as they advance. No one knows how many people died at Rabaa that day, but an investigation by Human Rights Watch confirmed at least 817 dead and estimated a total of well over a thousand. Another 87, at least—this is the Egyptian government figure—died at the smaller sit-in at Nahda Square. Small numbers of protesters fired back with guns and Molotov cocktails in both squares, killing 10 officers. It was the single bloodiest day in modern Egyptian history. Two days later, 120 more protesters were gunned down, and it did not stop there.

Muhammad Beltagy was in the mosque when he heard about his

daughter's death. Soon afterward, he gave a nine-minute interview to a Brotherhood cameraman. In the clip, he is standing, surrounded by young men with handkerchiefs on their necks to ward off tear gas. His face is sweaty and creased with exhaustion. He looks directly into the camera. "What happened in the past hours, beginning at 6:00 a.m., this massacre, is a war to eradicate the masses," he says. "Sisi knows his coup will fail. He is trying to dirty the hands of the military so he's not the only one to face a criminal trial. He has started a civil war." He goes on, his voice rising to a ragged shout, his arms waving in the air for emphasis. It seems clear that Beltagy believed he would reach people and win them over, that Egyptians would recoil in horror from the killings. Only in the final moments of the clip does he talk about his own loss. "My daughter sacrificed her soul," he says. His voice seems to crack for a split second but he recovers and finishes his sentence. "She along with her sisters, sacrificed for no material interest or power, but only because we want this people to live in dignity." The man standing behind Beltagy, who has held his composure throughout, breaks into a sob.

But most Egyptians did not recoil. Many welcomed the massacre. They accepted the version broadcast on state-run channels that day: the Islamists started the violence, and they were to blame. The government minimized the death toll and declared that everything had been done to reduce casualties. TV stations played and replayed the same clips of protesters throwing rocks and brandishing what looked like weapons. When video footage documenting the scale of the killings spread, the official press dismissed it as fake. Asmaa Beltagy, some stations said, had not really been killed. Regime supporters began circulating stories on Facebook and Twitter that her death was a ruse, that she'd been seen alive in Cairo.

A week later, in hiding, Beltagy posted a letter to Asmaa on his official Facebook page, addressing her as "my beloved daughter and dignified teacher." He spoke about her precocity and independence. He said he regretted not spending more time with her while he could. He described a dream he'd had before she died in which she wore a wedding dress, a dream that now seemed prophetic. "It caused me severe pain not to be at your last farewell and see you for the last time; not to kiss your forehead; and not to be honored to lead your funeral prayer. I swear to God, my darling, I was not afraid for my life or of an unjust prison, but I wanted to carry the message you gave your soul for, to complete the revolution, to win and achieve its objectives."

Soon afterward, just before the police captured him in a dawn raid on a farm warehouse in Giza, he recorded one more statement. It appears to have been filmed in a small room, with a drawn curtain behind him and the hum of a loud fan in the background. In it, he counters the regime's version of the massacre, saying the police falsified death certificates to minimize the toll. He denies that the Brotherhood stocked weapons at the sit-in and warns that the label of terrorism was being used to justify murder. Finally, he pauses, removing his clunky black reading glasses, and looks directly into the camera. His face is contorted with emotion. "I swear to God," he says, "the Brotherhood did not sacrifice our souls and our offspring for mere personal interests. I would imagine our souls are worth more than that. And I beg the Egyptian people not to listen to those trying to categorize us as terrorists, at a time when the military coup itself is drowned in blood. Don't listen, don't allow yourselves to be silenced in the midst of these massacres. Again, I swear we did not make these sacrifices for any other reason than the pursuit of happiness, freedom, and dignity."

His plea was not heard. In the world outside that cramped hideaway, Egypt had entered a frenzy of hero worship. People felt their society was on the brink of an abyss, and they were seized by some collective impulse to bow down before a god for salvation. Men came out on the streets to salute Sisi, and women shrieked and ululated when his motorcade passed. In late July, when he went on national television again to ask Egyptians to give him a "mandate" to confront terrorism, the streets were packed. Posters of him in black beret and uniform sold in the tens of thousands, and his framed picture appeared in restaurants and offices. One female columnist, Ghada al Sherif, wrote a column titled "Sisi, you just need to wink," declaring that if the general wanted wives or concubines, she was available. Everyone compared him to Nasser, Egypt's last Great Man. An unsigned editorial appeared in *al Ahram*, Egypt's state newspaper, under the headline "Catch the al-Sisi Mania":

> *He stands straight and tall, impeccably attired and starched from head to toe. His freshly washed countenance and youthful zeal shield a Herculean strength and nerves of steel. He wears the feathers of a dove but has the piercing eyes of a hawk. During our thousand days of darkness, dozens of potential leaders pranced and boasted, to no avail . . . Abdel-Fattah Al-Sisi's name lit up the darkness. He was called upon at a supreme moment in history; a kind of mysterious rendez-vous with destiny . . . What the West cannot comprehend is the warm affinity between people and army in Egypt, which has endured for centuries. Gamal Abdel-Nasser is a recent example, even when he ruled with the firm grip of a military dictator. Whatever else is going on in the rest of this vast universe, this much is certain—Al-Sisi has captured the imagination of all Egyptians, if not all the world. He popped out of nowhere—almost— and his secret ingredient was hope. Napoleon Bonaparte once said "a leader deals with hope," and the brand of hope that Al-Sisi deals, breathed new life into our withering, perishing dreams . . . Therefore, for those who raise an eyebrow at the portraits, flags, pins, pictures, chocolates, cups and other forms of Al-Sisi mania that fill the streets of Egypt, it is only a fraction of the love and appreciation we feel for this strong yet modest, soft-spoken, sincere and compassionate leader . . .*

Even if Sisi had wanted to escape the crown, it seemed impossible. Decades earlier, Gamal Abdel Nasser had written, "I do not know why I always imagine that in this region, there is a role wandering aimlessly about in search of an actor to play it." Nothing had changed since the 1950s, or so it seemed: the people wanted their Big Man, and they would have him.

This was the lens through which people saw the Rabaa massacre. They had found a savior, and therefore whatever he did was right. The Brotherhood was a terrorist group, a cancer on Egypt, and the general had given them what they deserved. If anything, they said, he'd been too merciful, had waited too long to clear out Rabaa. This wasn't just the line you heard from jingoistic taxi drivers; the liberals and the columnists were fully on board. Intellectuals, diplomats, people who'd spent years in the West—they'd all shake their heads and tell you it had to be done. "You don't understand these people," they'd say. "We were on the verge of an Islamist takeover, just like Iran in '79. We should all be grateful to Sisi for having the backbone to strike them down." Any Egyptian who expressed doubts became suspect, a possible collaborator. The regime newspapers went into a xenophobic frenzy, saying the Western human rights groups, and even Obama himself, were fomenting Islamist plots to destroy Egypt. The young leaders of the 2011 revolution were not spared. Within months, some of its best-known figures, such as Ahmed Maher and Alaa Abdelfattah, would be in prison, accused of speaking out against a government that was even less tolerant of dissent than Mubarak's had been. A small group of Egyptian liberals protested these injustices and the return of military rule. Others tried to have it both ways, including Mohamed ElBaradei. He had blessed Sisi's coup and then accepted a role as an interim vice president in the new regime shortly afterward. But immediately after the Rabaa massacre, ElBaradei resigned, saying he could not "bear the responsibility for a single drop of blood" shed there, and moved back to Vienna, where he had lived for years prior to the 2011 uprising.

One of Beltagy's former political allies, a political scientist with Arab nationalist views, was now calling for even harsher measures against the Brotherhood. I was curious and went to see him in his downtown office. He was a smallish man named Gamal Zahran, with close-cut white hair and brown-tinted sunglasses that he wore even indoors. He had been elected to Parliament with Beltagy's help in 2005. Now he had a gigantic poster of Nasser on the door of his office. We chatted a bit about politics, and then I reminded Zahran of his friendship with Beltagy. He put down his pen, and his face grew rigid. "Never," he said. "I was his colleague but never his friend, I never went to his house." I told him Beltagy's children remembered seeing him around the house so often in 2005 that they assumed he must be an uncle. He waved his hand and shouted that Beltagy was a terrorist and a liar, and deserved to be executed. "Each member of the Brotherhood is assigned a role, it

was the same with him," he said. "They show flowing emotions in public, but they have no real feelings. They hide their terrorism. I was one
of those calling for using violence against the sit-in from the very first.
Anyway, it wasn't a sit-in, it was terrorism. What happened there is
their punishment. We hold them responsible for it. And those who talk
of reconciliation are just a fifth column, or traitors." He went on in that
vein for a while. Before leaving, I asked him if he had any more political ambitions since leaving the Parliament. "No," he said, "I just want
to remain the conscience of the revolution."

It was as if the hatred of the two sides had become a kind of reflec-
tor oven, the opposed metal surfaces beaming back and forth a mutual
frenzy of madness and contempt. It was not confined to Egypt: in the
Gulf, columnists relished the Brotherhood's fall and hailed Sisi as
their favorite son. The Saudi and Emirati governments had pledged $8
billion in aid within days of the coup in July, and Kuwait soon added
$4 billion. Egypt would burn through those sums in a matter of months,
its economy still in free fall despite Sisi's pledges of restoration.

Six weeks after the coup, Egypt's Gulf sponsors greeted the Rabaa
massacre with discreet silence. But Turkey's Islamist prime minister,
Recep Tayyip Erdoğan, lashed out angrily. He saw the coup and its
aftermath as a threat to his own party and his vision for the Middle
East. He cut off all support to Egypt and called for criminal trials for
those who ordered the Rabaa dispersal. He blasted Europe and the
West for failing to denounce the coup, and in a typically confused gesture, he also accused Israel of plotting it. Egypt responded by signaling
that it would endorse, for the first time, recognition of the Armenian
genocide carried out by Turkey in 1915. After Asmaa Beltagy's killing,
Erdoğan co-opted her in this rhetorical battle. He appeared on Turkish
state television as Beltagy's letter to his daughter was read out loud,
translated into Turkish, with the text also appearing in subtitles on the
screen. A sentimental Islamic hymn played in the background. Half-
way through, Turkish viewers watched in amazement as their prime
minister—who had not deigned to mourn for the young people killed
when his own police force cleared Gezi Park in Istanbul earlier that
summer—lowered his head, his face clenched with emotion, and began

dabbing tears from his cheeks with a handkerchief. Soon afterward, the Turkish press reported that other gestures were on the way: a street, a school, and a park were to be renamed in honor of Asmaa Beltagy.

One morning in late September 2013, hundreds of men crowded into a conference room in the Gonen hotel in Istanbul, a bland white tower just off a highway near the airport. Some wore business suits, some Egyptian-style galabiyas, and some wore the austere white dishdashas of the Gulf. They were there to attend a meeting of Brotherhood members and their Islamist allies. As the meeting began, a man in a white Gulf-style headdress stood up at a lectern and began assailing what he called a global war against Islam. He said the time for peaceful resistance was over: they must strike back violently at the criminal infidel regime now in power in Egypt. He urged specific steps: burning police stations and trains, targeting regime thugs and officers.

Almost instantly, several men in the audience got up from their seats and began to protest. One of these men told me he urged all the attendees to leave the room, and many of them did. They stormed into the lobby, their faces tight with anger and embarrassment. They said the Brotherhood could not associate itself with this kind of talk: "Violence is a red line." Others argued with them, saying the Brotherhood must defend itself and Egypt. Perhaps some violence was permissible, but not killing. The conference dissolved in acrimony, with hotel staff struggling to tamp down the shouting. But it did not end there. A few days later, cell phone videos begin appearing online, showing the remainder of the meeting, held by a much smaller group. The videos show bearded men sitting at a table or standing at a microphone, delivering furious tirades against the crimes of Abdelfattah al Sisi in high Islamic style. The camera cannot conceal the fact that they are no longer in a hotel. The horizon tilts and sways behind them. Occasionally a diving gull or a patch of gray seawater is visible, along with the minarets of Istanbul, perhaps a half mile away. They were on board a rented ferry, bobbing on the Sea of Marmara. They'd been banned from the city by the Turkish authorities.

That furtive and meandering boat trip might as well be an emblem of the Muslim Brotherhood in exile. Its members were still filtering out of Egypt, fearing jail or worse. The richest ones were able to bribe airport officials and fly directly from Cairo. The unluckier ones made long, miserable car trips, fleeing south into Sudan or west into Libya, begging for visas or travel permits, most of them making their way eventually to the two places in the Arab world that had pro-Brotherhood rulers: Turkey and Qatar. Even then, they kept wandering from hotel to hotel, constantly repeating among themselves the same arguments about violence and restraint. They were a supremely hierarchical organization whose head had been cut off: all the senior leaders in Egypt and much of the midlevel rank and file were in jail, soon to be condemned to long prison terms. Those who'd escaped were all traumatized. Almost overnight they had gone from the summit of power to the status of a terrorist group. I met at least a dozen Brotherhood members who told me they'd lost thirty or forty good friends in a single day at Rabaa. Most of them felt obliged to keep silent in fear of losing their visas. But for some, it was exactly the opposite: they survived as paid mouthpieces. The ones in Qatar had often been allowed into the country via agreements with al Jazeera that kept them appearing on-screen day after day as "experts" on Egypt's political crisis. They knew they were valued only as pawns of Qatar's old disputes with its Gulf neighbors. They would repeat the points they knew they were expected to make: that there were vast demonstrations every day in Egypt, that Sisi had no support and would soon be overthrown. None of it was true.

The Brotherhood churned out its own propaganda too. It maintained a media operations room in Istanbul, and its leaders periodically issued august-sounding statements on Facebook, responding to events in Egypt, disowning the claims of rogue members or spies, always insisting firmly that the group did not practice or condone violence and would never do so. But behind closed doors, a different message emerged. In January 2014, a group of senior Brotherhood leaders met in Istanbul with some of their Islamist allies. This time, a list of proposed "resistance" tactics to be used was discussed and agreed on, including vandalizing and burning police cars. It was all written up in a memo to be sent to Brotherhood members in Egypt. According to one man who was in the room, some participants urged harsher methods, including the targeted killings of regime thugs and officers. At one point, the senior Brotherhood member in the meeting said, "If you want to do something, do it, but don't tell us about it." Within a few weeks, burning police cars began showing up in cell phone videos uploaded onto Facebook by young men with ties to the Brotherhood.

It was sporadic at first, the attacks minor. It was easy enough for Brotherhood officials to dismiss it as the work of rogues, or even regime ploys aimed at tarnishing the group. But over the course of the following year, the Brotherhood's attitude toward violence seemed to slowly shift. The leadership had always denounced the jihadi insurgency in the Sinai Peninsula, where hundreds of Egyptian soldiers and policemen were being killed. Now, young men linked to the Brotherhood began asking why they were condemned to inaction while the Sinai jihadis landed real blows against Sisi's regime. Gradually, the violence spread beyond the Sinai. In late 2014, there was a series of small bombings on banks, businesses, and bus stations, often doing damage but hurting no one. In early 2015, the bombings intensified, with new groups going public for the first time to claim responsibility, groups with names like the Popular Resistance Movement and Revolutionary Punishment. No one could prove these groups were linked to the Brotherhood or its Islamist allies, but the Brotherhood itself was hinting at that possibility. Its members were more and more willing to promote violence as a form of resistance. You could hear incitements to murder on TV channels affiliated with the Brotherhood. Young men began advertising on Facebook or Twitter that they'd renounced their commitment to pacifism. In the spring of 2015, one young Brotherhood member living in exile, a man who'd always maintained an absolute opposition to violence of any kind, told me he'd changed his mind. "If it's less than murder, I don't consider it violence," he said. Burning police cars or vandalizing government buildings, beating and injuring officers and thugs who were guilty of murder—all this fell within the category of resistance to the regime, he said. I asked him how he had made this decision, and he said it was more or less the Brotherhood view. But there wasn't really a Brotherhood doctrine anymore. There were platitudes that no one really believed, and there were hints, whispers, the constant insinuation that you could be guided by your own gut feeling, as long as your heart was in the right place. I began to believe that Ali Mashad had been right on that night, when we sat together in the darkness just outside Rabaa Square. The Brotherhood was slowly disintegrating, bereft of a vision or a plan. Some of its members were being drawn to places like Syria and Libya, where no one would hold them back and their desire for revenge could be satisfied.

Muhammad Beltagy, meanwhile, was in solitary confinement in Egypt's most notorious prison, accused of incitement to murder. He was given little access to his lawyer, and his family rarely got to see him, so it was difficult to know whether he had any regrets. But some of the Brotherhood's leaders in exile eventually produced an internal document outlining the worst mistakes the group had made. They wrote that the Brotherhood should have taken a more "revolutionary" position starting in late 2011, instead of trying to court the military council. It should have tried harder to build bridges with liberals. It should never have run a presidential candidate, and it should have been less doctrinaire all along. After I read this, I asked one of the authors if they had been thinking of Beltagy. "Yes," he said. "Dr. Beltagy's criticisms were accurate all along. Unfortunately, he was not listened to."

6

— In the Caliph's Shadow (Yemen, Syria) —

One of the first great takeaways of the Arab Spring in 2011 was the idea that it would destroy Al Qaeda. A nonviolent movement had achieved in eighteen days what decades of jihadi violence had failed to. Arab youth had staked their claim to a democratic future in Tahrir Square, with the whole world watching and applauding. Surely this would drain the swamp of radical Islam. Liberals were not the only ones who felt this way. Some of the most prominent jihadi ideologues seemed troubled. Ayman Zawahiri, Al Qaeda's number two man, responded to the first Arab Spring protests by issuing a long series of defensive online tirades. He declared that the uprisings, despite their peaceful appearance, had been made possible by the September 11 terrorist attacks. He delivered shrill warnings to Arab youth to beware the false allure of secular democracy. Young people glanced at these missives and laughed. For the first time, Al Qaeda's leaders seemed visibly anxious about losing touch with the Arab masses. The jihadi movement was sinking into the background, its spokesmen merging with Mubarak and

Ben Ali and all the other old men whose time was over. You could almost hear the suicide bombers unsnapping their belts and walking away.

Or so it seemed at first. Then the wind shifted again. It didn't take long for the protesters' nonviolent ethos to flicker out in the battle zones of Libya, Syria, and Yemen. Under the convenient cover of street protests—where they could travel without being recognized—the jihadis were suddenly watching the collapse of the state in all three countries. This was an opportunity they'd never had before: to seize territory and govern it themselves, in accordance with the sharia principles they'd been promoting for decades.

This rallying cry was an ancient one, and had welled up during many earlier periods of turbulence in the Arab world. The idea of an Islamic state was rooted in the community founded in seventh-century Arabia by the Prophet Muhammad. Muhammad embodied the fusion of politics and religion: he was both the messenger of God and a shrewd ruler. That dual role itself had origins in the culture of the desert-dwelling Arab Bedouin. They saw life as a journey through a wasteland in which one could easily go astray and die. To survive, it was essential to band together in a caravan under the leadership of a guide who knew the right paths, or roads. The Islamic words *sunna* (normative custom), *sira* (exemplary behavior), and *sharia* (religious law) are all derived from roots related to roads and desert travel. Muhammad's followers saw him as nothing less than their vehicle of salvation: the man who would bind together the *Umma*, the Islamic community, and guide it to its destination. The first part of this equation was as important as the second, because scattering and dispersing in the desert meant going astray and perishing. "Satan is with the individual," one eighth-century caliph is said to have remarked. Only a rightly guided leader could keep the caravan intact: without him, later Muslims came to believe, they would have no path to salvation, and would die as infidels.

After Muhammad's death in A.D. 632, his successors assumed the same august responsibilities for the community of Muslims, at least in theory. They came to be known as *khalifa*, the word for deputy or successor. They saw themselves as God's deputy or, in a later formulation, God's shadow on earth. There was relatively little dissension over the first four caliphs—Abu Bakr, Omar, Uthman, and Ali—who came to be known as the "rightly guided ones." After that, as the Muslim community grew through conquest and became more diverse, the caliphate suffered a slow dilution. Disagreements over succession led to breakaway sects, the most prominent of which would become the Shiites. The seat of the caliphate migrated over the centuries from Arabia to Damascus to Baghdad and finally to Istanbul, losing touch with its tribal roots. Some caliphs became mere puppet figures, providing Islamic window dressing for the military man who held the reins of power. Even at times when he did rule, the caliph—or sultan, in a later guise—was no longer a vehicle of salvation. Most Muslims acknowledged his role as the titular leader of the faith, but tended to look to Islamic law and its guardians, the ulema, or scholars, for religious legitimacy and guidance. These scholars emerged gradually over the centuries, largely independent of government. They were seen as the people's defenders, often with a subtly oppositional relationship with the ruler. They were a bit like a local priesthood and school board and historical society all wrapped into one. They stood for *taqlid*, adherence to a rich and varied body of law that had grown over time, providing a bulwark against the whims of the sultans.

All of this collapsed when the Ottoman Empire was defeated at the end of World War I. The last remnant of the caliphate was gone, and the Ottomans had already domesticated the ulema into state functionaries. Under the pressure of British and French colonialists who ruled Egypt and Syria in the 1920s and '30s, sharia was being abandoned or spliced selectively into secular codes of law. The Muslim community had lost its path to salvation, or so many people believed. The question was how to get it back. Some Islamic reformists and ideologues argued that the only way forward was to capture the state and use it to re-Islamize society by force. This idea's most radical theorists, like the Egyptian Sayyid Qutb, declared that twentieth-century Arab leaders were no longer Muslims at all and could therefore be lawfully killed in the service of a purifying jihad. Yet even for militant Islamists who accepted Qutb's view, like Osama bin Laden, it was risky to move too quickly. Imposing Islam from the top down, rather than building it from the bottom up as the ulema had, could alienate people and discredit the very ideas the jihadis hoped to promote. This was especially true when sharia was stripped down to a populist cartoon, shorn of its ancient *taqlid* and nuance: head choppings in the public square. The Taliban gave the world a grisly foretaste of this kind of Islamic rule in Afghanistan in the 1990s, and it did not end well. Osama bin Laden and his deputy, Zawahiri, worried that declaring an Islamic state prematurely in the Arab world would go just as badly.

But the young jihadis of 2011 were in love with the idea of bringing back the caliphate, and they did not want to wait. After the conquest of Jaar, Al Qaeda's leader in Yemen declared a smaller variation on the idea: an Islamic emirate. The group rebuilt water, sewage, and electrical lines, and sought to increase the staffing of schools and hospitals. Al Qaeda also developed a media campaign to advertise its achievements, with correspondents interviewing smiling villagers who declared they'd never seen the town work so well. They may have meant it. Apart from their engineering achievements, Al Qaeda eliminated the area's rampant banditry and resolved a number of legal disputes that had festered for years, according to some local people interviewed after the jihadis were forced out. The more difficult issue was *hudud*, the Islamic canonical punishments. Here, Al Qaeda took an uncharacteristically gentle approach, at least at first. The leader of the Yemen branch, writing about the experience a year later to another jihadi in Morocco, put it like this: "You have to take a gradual approach with them when it comes to religious practices. You can't beat people for drinking alcohol when they don't even know the basics of how to pray. We have to first stop the great sins, and then move gradually to the lesser and lesser ones . . . Try to avoid enforcing Islamic punishments as much as possible, unless you are forced to do so."

Many Yemenis appreciated this restraint and seem to have welcomed the new emirate. But gradually the jihadis' clemency drained away under the pressure of war. By June 2012, the protocaliphate was gone, its soldiers killed or pushed back into the desert by Yemeni troops and paid tribal militias (with an assist from American advisers and drones). It had been a failure in any conventional sense. But it taught valuable lessons. The Yemeni experience made clear that local people and tribes who remained neutral were bound to become enemies in time. To preempt that, the leaders of Al Qaeda would have to adopt a more brutal approach: to demand absolute loyalty and terrify bystanders into obedience.

This made perfect sense to the leaders of Al Qaeda's Iraqi branch, who had been relying for years on an ingenious manifesto called "The Management of Savagery." Published online in 2004, it was billed as a field guide for the establishment of an Islamic state. Its author was an anonymous jihadi writing under the pen name Abu Bakr Naji. He argued that political transitions like the one under way in Iraq after the American invasion of 2003 presented jihadis with the perfect opportunity to weaken enemy states through what he called a "power of vexation and exhaustion." The goal was to carve out areas of "savagery," or lawlessness, which can then be transformed—once the enemy is expelled—into the nucleus of a new caliphate. Naji's tract was unusual in its emphasis on the need for extreme violence in jihad. "One who previously engaged in jihad knows that it is naught but violence, crudeness, terrorism, frightening [others], and massacring—I am talking about jihad and fighting, not about Islam and one should not confuse them," he wrote.

In the summer of 2011, sensing an extraordinary opportunity, the Iraqi group sent its first team of fighters to Syria. At around the same time, it began capitalizing on dramatic new openings in Iraq. The last American troops withdrew at the end of 2011, and President Obama made it perfectly clear that he was washing his hands of the place. This was welcome news to Iraq's Shiite prime minister, Nouri al Maliki, who began rounding up Sunni officials high and low. A new wave of sectarian killings soon followed. This was manna to his Shiite political base. But the systematic firing of competent Sunni commanders was hollowing out Iraq's military and security services. You could almost hear the jihadis laughing: the Pax Americana was being unraveled, day by day. Sunnis now found themselves pushed into the arms of Abu Bakr al Baghdadi, the leader of Al Qaeda's Iraqi branch. Who else, they asked, would protect them from Maliki and his Shiite thugs? In early 2013, Baghdadi's group changed its name to the Islamic State of Iraq and the Levant (the old term for greater Syria, including Lebanon, Jordan, and Palestine). That name alone helped to establish its status and appeal to the men who were streaming into Syria from across the Arab world, looking for the *dawla* that had failed them in their own countries.

At that time, Baghdadi was still an almost unknown figure in the West. To his men he had an aura of sanctity and ruthlessness that was immensely appealing. He had a doctorate in Islamic studies from Baghdad University and could wield Koranic verse with stunning grace. His calm manner and expressionless dark eyes shielded an almost unparalleled ferocity toward those who did not share his views. "Fighting them is more of a priority than fighting the Americans," he would say of wayward Islamists. Baghdadi's most brazen move was to publicly reject the authority of Al Qaeda itself. In mid-2013, he refused an order from Ayman Zawahiri to return to Iraq. This was a shocking act of insubordination in a culture that prized strict obedience to one's emir. He also rejected the older generation's entire approach to jihad. Baghdadi saw extreme violence as a necessary tool, and he was focused single-mindedly on establishing a caliphate. In early February 2014, after weeks of bloody combat between the jihadi factions, global Al Qaeda's leadership issued a statement formally disowning ISIS, as the group was now known in the West. That stark announcement of divorce made news around the world. Some analysts saw it as a serious miscalculation by Baghdadi. It was hard to imagine that a young commander could survive being excommunicated by Al Qaeda's reigning global leader.

What those observers did not know was that thousands of young men were slipping across the Turkish border into Syria, inspired by the dream of a restored caliphate. These zealous migrants—including hundreds of eager volunteers for suicide missions—were turning ISIS into the most powerful jihadi group in history. By mid-June they would accomplish one of the most extraordinary surprise attacks of all time, surging across the Syrian border to conquer a vast swath of northern and western Iraq. The Iraqi army melted away before them, and even in Baghdad people feared for their lives. It was the first time a terrorist group had gained control over such a vast area. Beyond the landgrab, ISIS achieved a psychic blitzkrieg, a ripping of the collective mental map. Their conquests seemed to lay bare a world where the old states were melting down and being replaced by fierce new entities that abided by different rules. The leaders of the American military acknowledged—and President Obama repeated—that they'd seriously underestimated ISIS.

Yet in some ways, the battlefield images that flooded across the screens of the world were less striking than a video released by ISIS on July 14, 2014. This was not the usual stuff of ISIS propaganda, the beheadings and firing squads and exploding cars. This film begins with a still shot: the calm sanctuary of the Grand Mosque in the Iraqi city of Mosul. People are visible sitting and standing near the pulpit. There is a soft clutter of voices, which soon dims to an awed silence. A man in a heavy black robe and black turban slowly ascends the steps to the pulpit. He reaches the top step and turns to face the audience, his body framed by a thick marble column inlaid with faded blue-and-white tilework. He has impenetrable dark eyes and a thick black beard fringed with gray. Touching one hand to his lower chest, he speaks the traditional Islamic greeting into a microphone on a stand: "Peace be upon you, and His mercy and His blessings." He does not seem to be looking out at the men ranged before him, but inward, as if contemplating some immensely solemn burden. He gathers his robe and sits down. His face, in profile to the camera, is a mask of quiet severity. He waits, eyes closed, until the call to prayer is over and then rises to stand at the microphone. He looks out at the audience and seems to acknowledge them fully for the first time. A scroll at the bottom of the screen reveals that this is the Caliph Ibrahim, the Commander of the Faithful. The caliphate, he declares, is "an obligation upon the Muslims—an obligation that has been lost for centuries and absent from the reality of the world, and so many Muslims were ignorant of it. The Muslims sin by losing it, and they must always seek to establish it, and they have done so, and all praise is due to God."

Listening to this speech, you knew instantly that most mainstream Muslims would deplore it as a faux-medieval drama cooked up by a frustrated actor. But that did not matter. Baghdadi spoke with such eloquence and conviction that even those who loathed his message were moved and troubled by its power. He seemed to speak from a place of deep humility and reverence. He used no notes. You sensed that this was a moment he had been working toward for many, many years. "I have been plagued with this great matter, plagued with this responsibility, and it is a heavy responsibility," he said of his elevation as caliph. "I was placed as your caretaker, and I am not better than you. So if you find me to be just, then help me, and if you find me to be unjust, then advise me and make me right, and obey me as I obey God through you. If I disobey Him, there can be no obedience to me from you. I do not promise you, as the kings and rulers promise their followers, luxury, security, and relaxation; instead, I promise you what God promised to His faithful worshippers." He did not need to add that his caliphate was modeled on the earliest days of Islam—in fact, on the very words of the first sermon that the first caliph, Abu Bakr, had given—not on some latter-day Ottoman sultan. He aimed to guide the Muslim community to salvation, just as the Prophet Muhammad and his first successors had.

Baghdadi's message was electrifying not only to ISIS members. It also energized a legion of mostly young sympathizers around the world, some of them converts from other religions. Many of them now began moving beyond the stage of Internet daydreams and forming plans to immigrate to the Islamic state. ISIS had a small army of propagandists, informants, and smugglers who would help these online disciples make the journey. One of them was a woman who would soon become the court poet of ISIS. She called herself Ahlam al Nasr, or Dreams of Victory. She'd grown up in Syria, and when the caliphate was declared, in late June 2014, she was living with her family in the Gulf. After her first attempt to run away from home and join ISIS failed—she didn't say how—she poured out her anguish in a prose poem:

The state of one longing for the Caliphate's rule but physically removed from it is like that of a fish being hung by its fins over the surface of the sea: it sees but cannot reach it. The sun burns it with a heat that sucks the life out of it. Oh Lord, have mercy on me.

By the time Ahlam succeeded in immigrating to Raqqa a few months later in the autumn of 2014, she was already a celebrity there. She had just published a volume of poems online called *The Blaze of Truth*, and it became a tremendous hit among the Islamic state's sympathizers. Soon after arriving, she wrote a prose poem describing her own journey to the Islamic state, providing would-be migrants with a reassuringly detailed (if not entirely accurate) account of what to expect. Like all her poems, it conveys a wild, almost abject sincerity. It is the work of a young woman who seems to have lived most of her life behind veils and closed doors, and has poured her spirit through the tiny keyhole allowed to her. In the poem, she describes her anxious ride across the border and her arrival in Raqqa in a state of rapture. Raqqa is in fact a dusty, run-down provincial town, with rows of drab cinder-block houses and very little greenery, but Ahlam makes it sound like heaven. The gun-toting holy warriors are always smiling, she notes, and they stop their cars at intersections for all pedestrians—not just women. Her eagerness never flags as she is led through the new state's police headquarters and media operations center. A gun shop elicits wild enthusiasm. "How fantastic! It is called 'the Glory of Jihad.'" she writes. "I purchased some items and held a dagger in my hand. Those accompanying me gave me a sonic bomb, a dagger, and a machine gun as well as the ISIS flag." She relates encounters with taxi drivers, children, and a gas station attendant who confesses sheepishly that he's been smoking. Ahlam's guides lecture him, but let him off with a polite warning, and even give him a tip.

This was propaganda, but to some people it rang true, especially if they had lived through the twin hells of regime rule in Raqqa and the criminal chaos that followed it. I met a twenty-nine-year-old construction worker from Raqqa who went home in the summer of 2014 at his parents' request after living in Turkey for a year. He was suspicious of ISIS at first, he told me, but that began to change after his visit to a local mosque for Friday prayer. He was used to government-appointed imams giving bland and dutiful sermons, "messages from the regime," as he put it. This time, he listened in amazement as an ISIS leader stood up and spoke about the life of Muhammad and the importance of justice. "The hair on my arms stood up," he told me. The difference from the old days was like "earth and sky." At the same time, he was noticing all the ways ISIS was trying to change everyday life in Raqqa. Crime had disappeared. In a society where the rich often treated peasants like slaves, ISIS commanders "treated ordinary workers as they treat fellow jihadis," he said. "They eat with us, pray with us. They will not start eating until you have started. They are very straight people." This was true of the foreigners as well as the Arabs. Once, he said, his father accidentally struck a Chinese jihadi with his car. He got out of the car, and to his amazement, the Chinese man began apologizing, in broken Arabic, for having gotten in the way. He then asked politely if the father could give him a ride to the hospital to get his leg treated. All these experiences created a sense of patriotism the construction worker had never felt before. "The flag was flying over our city with 'There is no god but God' written on it," he told me. "You have this feeling, we have our own state. It is small, but it is so important. You have a feeling of true belonging."

This sense of belonging was enhanced by ISIS's media campaign of confrontation with the West, which reached its height with the video-taped beheading of the American journalist James Foley in August 2014. That atrocity and the others that followed amplified ISIS's reputation as a global byword for evil, and galvanized Western public opinion in favor of the American-led bombing campaign that had begun earlier that month. Yet the more they were demonized in the West, the stronger they seemed to their followers. The group's victims were only a fraction of those killed by Bashar al Assad's regime over three years of war, but ISIS's mastery of Internet gore captured the imagination. Their zest for killing seemed monstrous, almost apocalyptic. That perception tallied perfectly with ISIS's own millenarian obsession with the End of Days. By the end of 2014, the ISIS propaganda machine was releasing some ninety thousand messages a day on Twitter, Facebook, YouTube, and other media.

At the same time, ISIS was sending very different messages to a smaller group of supporters. Its surrogates began posting ads for petroleum engineers, offering to pay as much as $10,000 per month. Unlike every jihadi group that preceded it, ISIS was making millions of dollars a month in a range of industries: oil and gas, cement, wheat and other crops, even the illicit and lucrative trade in human organs, which were harvested and transported on ice over the Turkish border. They were willing to adapt their xenophobic principles when money was involved. ISIS may not have been a full-fledged state, but it had gone far beyond the brief experiment in jihadi self-rule in southern Yemen three years earlier.

One morning in mid-January 2015, a small, furtive-looking man in a black hooded parka stood alone on the Turkish side of the Akçakale border crossing with Syria. The weather was sunny and cold, and there was almost no one in sight. The man glanced around uneasily and finally approached a Turkish street sweeper in a blue jumpsuit. "I want to cross to the other side," he said. "What can I do?" The street sweeper demanded seventy-five Turkish liras and pointed to a small hole in the fence not far from the main gate. The man paid him but hesitated. He had come a long way and was now barely ten yards from his destination: the dusty brown hills of northern Syria, where the Islamic state began. "What about the guards?" he said. "No problem," the street sweeper replied. "Just go." The man walked toward the hole in the gate. He bent down and squeezed through. On the other side, he began to run. One of the Turkish guards saw him and shouted. He did not stop.

The newcomer's name was Abu Ali. He had another name and another life, but like most migrants to the Islamic state, he had cast it off. He wanted to be born again. In early 2015, ISIS was at the height of its power and was still attracting thousands of eager new disciples every month from all over the world. The American-led coalition had been bombing Islamic state targets for months, without dislodging it from any of its terrain. If anything, it seemed to grow stronger. Some American military officers and analysts were saying they believed it could survive for years or even decades. ISIS regularly rolled out gruesome videos of public beheadings and executions, and trumpeted its practice of selling captured non-Muslim women into sex slavery. All this ferocity only seemed to amplify its appeal to young and frustrated Muslims.

But now some of the true believers were discovering that life in the Islamic state was not quite the paradise they had imagined. A new narrative—of disillusionment, of horror, of black comedy—was slowly leaking out from the inside. Abu Ali would become one of its voices.

I met him in the late summer of 2015 in Urfa, a Turkish town near the border. It was about three months after he'd escaped from ISIS, with the help of smugglers and a network of sympathetic activists. We spent the day sitting in an outdoor café in a public park, with Turkish families strolling around under the trees. The smell of sweet tobacco drifted by, and we could hear the squeals of children playing in a water fountain not far away. His handlers were still nervous about surveillance by Turkish intelligence agents, and they got up occasionally to walk the park perimeter and see if we were being watched. They knew he would probably be tried and jailed if he were extradited to Jordan, the country whose passport he held.

Abu Ali was a far cry from the archetypal young jihadi: short and bald, with a delicately cut chin and nervous brown eyes. He was thirty-eight years old, and after a lifetime smoking and drinking, he knew he wasn't cut out to be a fighter. He told me he'd joined ISIS in the hopes of getting a desk job and making himself into a good Muslim. He'd been born in Kuwait, but he'd spent most of his life in Aleppo, the old trading hub in northern Syria. His life there had been a kind of parable of old regime Arab corruption. He worked for his father, who made a good living as an expediter—helping Syrians navigate the maze of government bribes required to buy a car. Abu Ali helped out with the paperwork. "I'd get up about nine a.m., go to the office, drink coffee and sign some papers for about two hours, and then go home," he told me. "It was corrupt but it was okay with me." He also went to bars and clubs and partied several nights a week, despite his wife's constant haranguing. She was infertile, and the absence of children made their days especially empty.

By 2012, Abu Ali's profligate life began tilting toward despair. His father's government work had stopped after the rebel Free Syrian Army entered Aleppo. He was living off handouts from other family members abroad. He'd held out some hope after the Syrian revolution started in 2011, but now he felt everything was going to hell. He'd gone to religious school as a kid in Kuwait, and as the war closed in on Aleppo in 2012 he sought refuge in Islamic piety (though he couldn't bring himself to give up booze or cigarettes). One of his wife's brothers was an officer in the Syrian military, and one day he told her that her brother was an infidel. That made her furious, and it got back to her family. One of her other brothers—a tailor—confronted Abu Ali, and after a shouting match, Abu Ali declared that his wife was divorced. In Islamic law, that's all it takes. She moved out. After that, Abu Ali felt he had nothing left to lose. He bought a plane ticket to Istanbul, and from there took a bus south to Urfa. Then it was a half-hour trip by minibus to the Syrian border. "My heart was pounding and pounding the whole trip," he told me. "I hesitated a bit. But I told myself, it's the devil trying to change my mind. Don't listen. Just go."

Abu Ali's heart was pounding even louder as he sneaked through the border fence later that sunny January morning and bolted into ISIS territory. After about one hundred yards he saw a group of ISIS men with long beards and guns, sitting in chairs by a building. He stopped short. "Why are you running?" one of them asked. "I am running to you!" he said, between gasps. He gestured backward toward the Turkish guards at the gate. The ISIS man looked at him and smiled. "Relax," he said. "They are our friends."

Abu Ali's arrival must have struck the ISIS men as almost comically unlikely. Most migrants to the Islamic state work with smugglers and are shepherded from place to place by a clandestine network. Abu Ali came alone and totally unprepared. Still, they welcomed him warmly and seemed delighted when he said he was Jordanian. "We want Arabs to join us, not just all these foreigners," one of them said. After an hour or so, a car appeared, and another ISIS man drove Abu Ali to a reception house not far away. It was a large one-story building with a garden out back, and about a dozen other new arrivals who were getting acclimated. "It was like an airport," Abu Ali told me. "I saw Americans, English, French, people from other countries—there was only one Syrian."

For the next five days, he slept on a mattress and talked endlessly with the other migrants, who mostly spoke English. The ISIS officials told them they were investigating their backgrounds. The emir in charge was Syrian, a very short, friendly man who had lost one of his legs in battle and hobbled around on an artificial one. He once caught Abu Ali smoking and gave him a stern lecture, but otherwise he was always smiling. "Whatever you asked, they'd say 'no problem,'" Abu Ali said. "I told them I don't want to fight, just an administration job," he said. "They said 'no problem, but you must do the religious and military training like everybody else. You never know when you might need it.' I said fine."

There were chickens in the garden out back, and the emir insisted that only the Americans and Europeans be allowed to slaughter them. It was training for killing infidels, he said. That was a little odd, but it didn't bother Abu Ali. One thing did, though. The emir mentioned in passing that the Free Syrian Army's fighters were infidels. The other volunteers took it in stride, but Abu Ali, who has a constitutional inability not to speak his mind, asked what he meant. "Let's not talk about this now," the emir said. "We'll discuss it after the sharia course." Abu Ali persisted. "I have seen FSA fighters praying. They fast at Ramadan. Doesn't that mean they're Muslims?" The emir looked impatient. "Like I said, we'll talk about it later," he said. "You *really* need a religion course."

At the end of five days, it was time for the new recruits to leave. Abu Ali got into a minibus with about fifteen others and they were driven to Raqqa, the Islamic state's capital, about an hour away. They spent a day there in another guesthouse, and then a bus drove them westward for several hours, until the roads turned into dirt tracks and they climbed into the Bel'as mountains, a dry, craggy range of dun-colored peaks to the east of the city of Homs. It was very cold and there was snow on the ground. The men got off the bus and walked along a path toward a group of caves in the mountain slope. Other buses were arriving nearby. This was where the sharia training would take place, they were told. The caves were dark and damp, but there were gas-fueled generators and electric lights on the walls. The men slept on thin pallets, shivering under their blankets. There were about three hundred men in all. Most were of Arab descent, but they came from all over—including one British convert to Islam who said he had worked at the London Stock Exchange and had his nine-year-old son with him. For the next two weeks, all of them would be awakened before dawn. They'd perform the dawn prayer and then go outside for running and push-ups before the sharia lessons began at first light. The lessons were very basic, focusing on the difference between Muslims and non-Muslims, and the requirement to fight infidels and apostates. Many of the recruits knew no Arabic, and some were illiterate. At breakfast they'd be given a few bits of white cheese—"it was cubes, like that *vache qui rit* stuff," Abu Ali said—some stale bread, and water. Later in the day, it was beans and bread. In the evening, after prayers, the recruits would gather inside the cave for announcements and news updates, often broadcast with a laptop and projector against the cave wall.

One night the emir in charge of the training course, a bald Syrian with pale skin who had been a history teacher in Homs in his previous life, said there was a special event in store. Once the men were all seated on the cave floor, the emir turned on the projector and a video flickered on the wall: an Arab man in an orange jumpsuit in a cage. Flames licked toward the cage, following a trail of gasoline, and engulfed the man. A voice-over intoned that this was the Jordanian pilot Moaz al Kasasbeh, who had been captured after his plane crashed. His grotesque execution by fire was seizing the world's attention at that very moment, and even some jihadis were denouncing it as an immoral act. The men in the cave were also shocked, but they stayed quiet. The emir stood up and explained that this pilot had dropped bombs on Muslims, and his execution by fire was a just retribution under Islamic law.

Abu Ali soon sensed dozens of eyes turning in his direction. He was the only Jordanian there, and they all knew it. He hadn't said anything, but his horror at the video must have been visible on his face. The emir also stared at him. Then the emir muttered something and laughed derisively, and some of the recruits followed suit. This was clearly some sort of loyalty test. Abu Ali felt their eyes on him, and he began to shake. He'd been taught as a child that burning a man to death was forbidden in Islam. The images had sickened him. He held steady for a minute or so, and then he heard himself say, "May God help me." Almost immediately, two ISIS guards took him by the arms and led him out of the cave. The emir followed later. He sat down on the rocks with Abu Ali and asked him why he had spoken those words. Did he question what ISIS had done? Abu Ali said no. He had spoken out only because people were provoking him. The emir seemed satisfied. "At the beginning of this course you were a *kafir* [an unbeliever]," he said. "Now you are becoming a Muslim."

Abu Ali was intensely relieved. He'd escaped punishment. But from that moment on, he told me, "I began to suspect everything around me." ISIS was not the utopia he'd imagined.

When the two-week sharia course was over, most of the men were transported to another group of damp mountain caves a few miles away. They now started the military-training class. It followed a similar routine: up at dawn for prayers and a few scraps of cheese and bread, followed by some live-fire exercises with AK-47s and rocket-propelled grenades. There was also a lot of running. Abu Ali, with his smoker's lungs, would just sit down on the rocks when he got tired. The trainers shouted at him, and he would hold up his hand and shout back, "I'm doing administration, not combat." He was already getting a reputation as a laggard. On the last day of the course, the men were summoned from their cave in the morning and asked to stand in line. The emir stood in front of them and told them to raise their right hands. He then recited an oath of loyalty and asked them all to repeat it. It required them to obey the *wali al amr*, the ruler of the age, in all he commanded, unless his commandments were unjust. As soon as the oath was over, the men were split up into groups. Abu Ali found himself standing with about three dozen other men near a bus. A Syrian commander in battle fatigues told them they were going to the front lines in Iraq. Abu Ali pushed his way to the front. "Sir, I don't want to go to the front line," he told the man. "They said I could do administration in Raqqa." The commander looked at him, stone-faced. "You swore an oath," he said. "You must listen and obey now. The penalty could be death." Abu Ali stood for a moment, registering the shock. "Right, I guess I'll go to Iraq," he said, and walked toward the bus.

About ten bumpy hours later, Abu Ali arrived in Mosul, Iraq's third-largest city. He scarcely saw any of it, because they were shepherded into another guesthouse, where they spent the night. The next day the men were herded onto a truck with a canvas covering in back and driven several hours across a barren landscape of desert. They stopped at an abandoned oil facility and the men were split up. Abu Ali and a few others continued on to Falluja. The roads were so bad and the driver so erratic that one of the men with him broke an arm. They then crossed the Euphrates River in boats, and after another day of travel they arrived in Garma, a village just west of Baghdad near the front line. Abu Ali and twelve other men were led to a former Iraqi army officer in civilian dress. They could hear warplanes soaring overhead, and every now and then the earth shook as a bomb exploded. With almost no formalities, the commander pointed to a large earth berm about four hundred yards away. "The Iraqi army is on the other side of that berm," he said. "You will capture the berm tomorrow morning."

Once again, Abu Ali's reactions got the better of him. "How the hell are we going to capture that berm?" he said. "It's twelve of us against the Iraqi army." The officer looked surprised at this breach of ISIS protocol. "Allah is with you," he said. "You will be victorious." A few hours later, they were given a more detailed briefing. They would attack shortly after 3:00 a.m. The squad leader, another Iraqi, suggested that Abu Ali wear a suicide belt into battle. He refused outright. "Why don't you wear it?" he said. "You want to go to paradise more than I do." The leader was not amused. He told Abu Ali to man a Dushka, a Russian-made heavy machine gun. Abu Ali replied that he had no idea how to use a Dushka. As it turned out, another man came forward just before the attack and said he knew how to fire a Dushka. Abu Ali, exhausted and terrified, nearly wept with relief. He was assigned to the medical team.

For the next few hours, Abu Ali and another recruit dragged wounded men from the battlefield. It was terrifying work. They could hear and feel bullets whizzing past them in the predawn darkness, and some of the men they dragged—there were no stretchers—were screaming in pain. They had to leave many others behind. At one point, the commander told him, "If your brother on the field is too badly injured and can't come back, give him a bomb. He can explode himself when the Iraqi army comes this way." The battle went on for two more days, until it was clear that the assault was failing. Dozens of ISIS fighters had been killed, and the commanders seemed to put little value on retrieving their bodies or even rescuing wounded men. Many were left to die. On the morning of the third day, Abu Ali and a new friend named Abu Hassan walked together into the headquarters in Garma and confronted the Iraqi commander. "We don't want to fight anymore. You are leaving dead and wounded men behind. The Prophet Muhammad, peace be upon Him, did not force men to fight against their will." The commander seemed disgusted but unsure what to do. Finally he sent the two men to the rear.

Abu Ali knew he was taking a risk by refusing to fight, but the alternative, he felt, was almost certain death. He expected a punishment. Instead, to his surprise, he found himself almost forgotten. He and Abu Hassan were left for days in an abandoned house in Garma. They got along well. Abu Hassan was a former thief who had joined ISIS in the hopes of making some money. As it turned out, ISIS paid him a monthly salary of $150 at first, and then stopped. For his part, Abu Ali told me he had repeatedly been promised a salary for months, and finally was paid a grand total of $50.

The two conscientious objectors were in luck: there was electricity in the house and, even better, a television. They spent hours watching news updates and movies. They knew this was strictly forbidden by ISIS, so they kept the windows shut. This made it almost unbearably hot and stuffy inside, but it was better than boredom. At one point *Rambo* came on. "I wish Rambo would join us here," Abu Ali said. "We really need him." That drew a long chuckle from Abu Hassan. Later they watched music videos by Elissa, the Lebanese pop singer. A woman showing her body and singing—this was *very* forbidden. After a day or so, a fellow ISIS fighter from Kurdistan stopped by the house and caught them with the TV on. He gave them a stern lecture and they promised to reform. After he left, they waited about five minutes. Abu Hassan looked at Abu Ali, who nodded, and he turned the TV back on. It was a news show with a woman presenter. Suddenly the door burst open. It was the Kurdish fighter, who had waited just outside to ambush them. He pointed his AK-47 at the TV and fired. Abu Ali jumped backward as the TV blew apart, shattered glass and bits of plastic spraying across the room. "Hey, man, we're your brothers, calm down!" Abu Ali shouted. "We committed a sin but we won't do it again!" The Kurd glared at them and stomped out.

The next day Abu Ali was transferred to another guesthouse, in Falluja, not far away, which was under ISIS control. This one was crowded with men. Not long afterward he was amazed to hear the sound of two girls giggling in the next room. Another fighter told him the girls were Yazidis who'd been captured in northern Iraq eight months earlier, when ISIS overran the area and sold hundreds of Yazidi women and girls into sex slavery. They were thirteen and fourteen years old, the man said. They'd been offered to the governor of Falluja, who didn't want them, so they were being kept here for the moment. Abu Ali had heard about the Yazidi sex slaves, though he'd never encountered any himself. The men called them *sabaya*. They were mostly rewards for officers or men who'd done well on the front—not for delinquents like Abu Ali. Over the next few hours he heard the girls laughing, and once he heard them sobbing. He assumed it was because they missed their families. Later that day, a shouting match erupted among the dozen or so men in Abu Ali's guesthouse. All of them wanted the *sabaya*. It went on for a half hour or so, getting increasingly heated.

Then a man in fatigues burst in. He looked like a commander. He asked where the *sabaya* were, and one of the men pointed to the door of the next room. He marched in without a word. Two loud shots rang out. The man in fatigues walked out again. Abu Ali, sitting in a chair by the door, stared up at him, frozen. "What did you do?" he said. The man seemed unruffled. "Those girls were causing trouble between the brothers, so I dealt with them," he said. And he walked out.

Abu Ali was not the only ISIS member who was sickened by what he saw. The initial euphoria had worn off for many of the migrants. Some of them complained about unnecessary cruelty, some about favoritism and hypocrisy in the ranks. Many others simply had not reckoned on the rigors of life in a terrorist army. A few of them, amazingly, complained that ISIS was not radical enough—that it was bending its principles for political reasons. There are no reliable numbers, but by early 2015 one anti-ISIS rebel group in northern Syria began hearing so many stories about people desperate to escape that they organized a smuggling network to bring them out. I met one defector who was as different from Abu Ali as anyone could be: twenty-two years old, well built, recklessly brave, with years of combat experience behind him. He went by the nom de guerre Abu Abdullah. He said he had taken part in the conquest of Raqqa, the ISIS capital, and later served in the group's intelligence wing, helping to plant bombs and sniff out traitors, some of whom were later executed.

Abu Abdullah's disillusionment began, he told me, in the late summer of 2014. A tribe in eastern Syria called the al-Shaitat had rebelled against ISIS, and in the ensuing battles, close to a thousand of them were massacred. Abu Abdullah knew little about it, but he was assigned to do security for a convoy of dump trucks that were en route to the town of Slouk, not far from where the battle took place. Outside the town is a deep natural gorge known as al-Houta. It is an unearthly place, a steep slope leading down to a dark hole hundreds of feet deep. As the trucks arrived at the edge of the gorge, they tilted their beds backward, and Abu Abdullah was horrified to see the corpses of women and children tumbling out. It was not just a few. There were dozens of them. Many had been shot in the head. The little bodies rolled down the slope of the gorge, shedding bloody scarves and shoes as they went, like garbage flooding into a bin. Abu Abdullah was not a reflective man, from what I could tell. He was a bullheaded kid who had joined ISIS because he thought they were the best shot to liberate his hometown. But "at moments like that, you doubt," he told me.

He kept fighting for ISIS another six months. The disappointments accumulated. A corrupt commander evaded punishment through connections with high-ranking ISIS figures. When Abu Abdullah tried to report the violations, it was he who went to jail, not the commander. Once he knew he wanted to defect, in the spring of 2015, he rode back to the al-Houta gorge one afternoon on his motorcycle. After checking to make sure no one was around, he climbed down a ways and shot a film with his cell phone. It is a haunting video. In the golden afternoon light, the gorge looks a bit like part of the Grand Canyon, with layered sedimentary rocks in varying tones of rusty brown and umber. The camera pans upward, showing the fading blue sky and a buttelike silhouette, and then down toward the black hole at the bottom. You can see corpses strewn at various places on the way down. Some are very close to the camera, and some have rolled down toward the pit. The film unfolds in silence, apart from the occasional grinding of Abu Abdullah's shoes on the stones and sand. It goes on for more than five minutes, and at a certain point you begin to wonder why he is continuing to film the same motionless scene for so long. Then it dawns: the camera is mimicking his own preoccupation. This is a place he cannot forget.

For Abu Ali, marooned in his guesthouse in Falluja in the spring of 2015, the disillusionment with ISIS was not just a matter of extreme violence or of his own laziness. Once TV was no longer an option, he filled his days by reading. ISIS, it turns out, stocks its guesthouses with works by the medieval Islamic theologians Ibn Taymiyya and Ibn Qayyim al-Jawziyya. These two thinkers are touchstones for the modern jihadi movement, in part because they urged rebellion against the nominally Muslim Mongols of their time. But their effect, in Abu Ali's case, was not quite what ISIS intended. "When I read these books, I saw where they get their worst ideas," he told me. "Ibn Taymiyya says that a man who believes, fasts, and prays is not a Muslim unless he also curses and fights the ruler. And those who don't recognize that he's an infidel are also infidels. I realized this means my mother and father are both infidels, and their marriage is not legitimate. So we're all bastards."

After two weeks of idleness in Falluja, Abu Ali was packed onto a bus bound for Syria with other recruits who had refused to fight. They followed the same route in reverse, from Ramadi to Mosul and across the Syrian desert. It was a relief to get away from the air strikes of Iraq, the anxiety of knowing a bomb could fall at any moment. But the men on board knew they were likely to be punished. Arriving back in Raqqa, they were taken to a soccer stadium. This was Point 11, a notorious ISIS prison and security center. Abu Ali and the other twenty-seven men with him had their rifles taken away and were put into a former locker room in the stadium basement. They stayed there for a day, and were then blindfolded and driven by bus to another holding center. Many were terrified and thought they were going to be executed. But instead a man arrived the next day and addressed them: "Brothers, do not say, 'I will not fight anymore.' Just say, 'I prefer to fight in Syria.' You will be given one more chance."

All the men agreed, and later that day, Abu Ali was driven to his first new assignment: prison guard at Point 11. The three weeks he spent there made him more sure than ever that he could not stomach the violence of life in the Islamic state. He often heard the screams of prisoners being tortured. He heard a Tunisian commander shoot two men to death, only because they wanted to return to their home countries. Abu Ali used his cell phone to shoot a three-minute video in the basement of Point 11. It is painful to watch: a gaunt old man with white hair and a long white beard lies on the floor of what looks like a locker room, while ISIS soldiers kick and beat him savagely. The old man begs for mercy. Eventually, the soldiers drag him by his arms into a dark room, and the clip ends.

By this time, Abu Ali had been with ISIS for three months. He had seen many men die, and had been lucky to survive. But somehow he had not lost his willingness to flout ISIS expectations. After three weeks at Point 11, he was bused north, to another battle zone not far from Aleppo. He got close enough to the front line that he could hear the warplanes shrieking overhead and feel the ground shaking after the bombs struck. It was like Iraq all over again. He was terrified. His new commander was Syrian, a strong-looking man about twenty years old. Abu Ali couldn't help himself. "Why do I have to fight?" he asked. "They told me I could be in administration. I'm not young like you, I'm thirty-eight years old. My knees are bad. I can barely run." The man looked at him impatiently. "If you don't want to fight, why did you come?" he said. "You swore an oath." But he let him stay in the rear for a day. Abu Ali found himself wishing a stray bullet would hit him in the arm, just enough injury to get him a desk job. The next day he came up with more excuses. He said he'd been an alcoholic before joining ISIS and had a nerve disease as a result. He was passed from commander to commander. All of them knew he was lying, but eventually they got so sick of dealing with him that they gave in. A Tunisian commander gave him a withering look and a document that exempted him from battle on medical grounds. "We really don't need people like you," he said.

A few days later, Abu Ali found himself alone in a house in the town of Manbij, not far from the front. There was an Internet café next door, and to his delight, he was able to access the wireless signal. Soon after he did so, he heard the chime of a WhatsApp message on his phone. He looked at it and his heart leapt: it was his wife. She had seen that he was online. She had written an old expression that they both liked: "If you love something, let it go. If it doesn't come back, it wasn't meant for you. But if it does, it will be yours forever." After reading it, Abu Ali hesitated for a minute or two before answering. He found himself shaking with emotion. There was another chime. She had written: "What's the matter? Don't you know me?" He wrote back teasingly: "No, you must have the wrong number." But almost instantly he began writing again, asking how she was, and where. He apologized for his mistakes. He told her he wanted to come back.

As he recalled that moment, months later, Abu Ali told me, "The second I saw her first message I started hating them all. I said to myself: What an idiot I've been! What have I done?" It was then, he said, that he knew he had to get out. He had heard a rumor that one of his comrades in the Iraq battle, a man from Morocco, had escaped to Turkey. He sent him a WhatsApp message. The Moroccan wrote back quickly. He said he was in Istanbul. He gave the name and number of a man he said could help. Abu Ali sent a message to that man, who wrote back and told him to wait for instructions. Two days later, the man wrote again: *Go to Raqqa.* Equipped with his sick-leave document, Abu Ali got on a civilian bus early the next morning. He was wearing an Afghan-style cloak that identified him as a member of ISIS, and no one gave him any trouble. When he got to Raqqa, he went straight to an Internet café and stayed there for hours. He had no idea what he would do if he had to stay overnight. Finally a message appeared on his phone: "Go to Tal Abyad, right now." A second message gave him the name of an Internet café and a time. He went to the main bus depot in Raqqa, where it was easy enough to find a bus heading north to Tal Abyad, near the Turkish border. At the last checkpoint, an ISIS soldier eyed him suspiciously and asked why he was going to the border. Abu Ali pulled out his documents and started to explain. It turned out the soldier, who looked about fifteen years old, was illiterate. He let him pass.

By the time he arrived in Tal Abyad it was 9:00 p.m., well past dark. He found an Internet café and went inside to wait for the next message. As he looked around, it became clear that everyone in the café was ISIS: long beards, AK-47s on the shoulder, Afghan robes. Abu Ali felt himself shaking. He tried not to look at anyone, but one man was eyeing him suspiciously. The meeting time came and went. The café would soon be closing. He said to himself, That's it, I'm done for. Just before eleven o'clock, two motorcycles pulled up outside, and one of the riders shouted through the café door at Abu Ali: "The food's ready, sorry we're late." Abu Ali got up to go. As he did so, the ISIS man who'd been staring at him in the café stepped forward. "Where are you from?" he said. Abu Ali replied in an Aleppo accent—he figured a local by himself was less suspicious than a foreigner: "I'm sorry, I'm late, I have to go." He walked out the door and got on the back of one of the motorcycles, scarcely breathing. But the bike took off down the road and no one followed. The next day, after a sleepless night in a nearby house, the men who'd rescued him from the café accompanied him to a remote stretch on the border.

The men were paid smugglers working for a network called Thuwar Raqqa, Revolutionaries of Raqqa. The network had started helping people escape from ISIS only a few months earlier. Thuwar Raqqa was a small fighting group, about twelve hundred men in all, allied with both the Free Syrian Army and the dominant Kurdish paramilitary group in northern Syria. The network's members were all from Raqqa and the surrounding area, and they had lots of informants and allies in the areas ruled by the Islamic state. They thought of themselves as a kind of government in exile and were already sketching out plans for the reconquest of their home city. I met two of these men in Turkey. They were both quiet and watchful, and seemed to speak only as much as was necessary. They were extraordinarily brave men, who regularly risked their lives in ISIS territory. Several of their companions in Thuwar Raqqa had been beheaded by ISIS, accused—correctly—of spying.

These were the same two men who greeted Abu Ali as he crawled through a hole in the border fence to freedom on the night of May 25, 2015, just over four months after he'd gone in. He lived for the next three months under their protection, in a rented apartment near the border. "These are my friends," Abu Ali told me when I met him in Urfa. "They saved me."

But someone else had saved him too. After a few weeks, his handlers gave permission for him to take a bus north to Antalya, the resort town where his former wife and her family were living. He waited until 3:00 a.m. and walked to the house (she had told him where to go via WhatsApp). When he was just below her window, he typed into his phone: "I'm here." A few minutes later she slipped out. They faced each other in the darkness and embraced for a long time. He could feel her sobbing against his chest. They walked to a public park nearby and sat down on a bench. They talked for about an hour. "I forgive you," she said finally. "But don't fuck up again." Dawn was about to break. He walked her back to the house, and she said she would persuade her brothers to let them get married again. He gave her a last kiss, and she went inside.

When I met him, Abu Ali was making plans to head back to Antalya to rejoin his wife. He aimed to make some money working as a dishwasher, get remarried, and then—he hoped—he and his wife would join the tide of refugees heading on boats to Greece and then onward to northern Europe. The Arab world was falling apart, he said, and he saw no future there.

He told me he'd learned a lot during his time with ISIS. "I still love the idea of an Islamic state," he said. "But I've realized, I can't live in it. The long beards, the harshness, the no smoking—I just can't do it." He'd already reverted to some of his old habits, he said. He was looking forward to life in Antalya, which he'd been told was a "party town." At the same time, he knew he was something of a misfit in the outside world. He carried a stigma. As we spoke, he gazed wistfully around at the Turkish families wandering through the park around us.

"I envy ordinary civilians," Abu Ali said. "Even poor people—I envy them. Because in the eyes of the world, I'm a terrorist."

Before he got up to go, I asked Abu Ali what he expected in the months and years to come. Would ISIS last? What about the Assad regime? Who could fill the vacuum if they vanished? He paused for a little while and stared down at the table between us.

"I think this war is never going to end," he said. "The regime may end, ISIS may end. But the war? Never."

7

— Reconciliation (Tunisia) —

By the time the old man reached the stage, there was a turbulent sea of strobe lights and fireworks and drifting colored smoke in the dark esplanade of Kasbah Square. It looked as if half the population of Tunis was out there. The young MC had to bellow into his microphone to break through the chanting. "Let us welcome the leader of the Islamic movement, the leader of Ennahda, Sheikh Rached Ghannouchi!" Instantly, the chants changed into deep roars of approval. The old man stepped forward, the spotlight illuminating his tall, gaunt figure and dark suit, and began doing his trademark wave, a slow, mechanical motion. It was as familiar to this crowd as the gestures of their own parents. So was his voice, a dry, nasal instrument that one Tunisian comedian had compared to a car that won't start. Rached Ghannouchi had been guiding the Tunisian Islamic movement for more than three decades, longer than most of this crowd had been alive. His long face, with its peaked brows and downward-sloping eyes, gave him the look of a benevolent crocodile. "This is the largest crowd Tunis has ever seen!" Ghannouchi said as he took the microphone. "This vast crowd is proof that the revolution has not died. It's a revolution all over again." The crowd roared approvingly at the sound of his voice. They began to chant: *Loyal, loyal, to the blood of the martyrs!*

It was the night of August 3, 2013. Ghannouchi smiled uneasily as he gazed out at the crowd: he knew the enthusiasm was laced with anger. His Ennahda-led government was under attack, and this was their moment for a show of force. It had been nine days since the left-wing politician Mohamed Brahmi had been gunned down in front of his house by assassins on a motorbike, and Tunis was on fire. Demonstrations had started before the body was cold, big crowds gathering every day to accuse the Islamists of murder and to demand they resign. *Ghannouchi is a killer!* they chanted. *Egypt has a hero named Sisi, where is ours? No reconciliation, No compromise!* They were following the same script as in Cairo, where the Brotherhood had been overthrown a month earlier. The Tunisian secularists had adopted the same names: Tamarod, the National Salvation Council. They were begging the army for a coup. Dozens of them resigned from Parliament. *Our blood is red, theirs is black*, was one of the phrases you heard. As if they were preparing alibis for a murder not yet committed. There was tear gas in the streets almost every day, and the police seemed unable to control the crowds. Tunis, some said, was on the brink of civil war, the last domino of the Arab winter.

It was hard for outsiders to take it all in. Tunisia had been the cradle of the 2011 uprisings, and in many ways the most hopeful. This was a small, pacific country that seemed—on the map—to hover in the Mediterranean between Africa and Europe. It had none of the gunpowder of its neighbors: no sectarian rifts, no tribal strife, no violent insurgencies, no oil. The army was weak and apolitical. Walking down Bourguiba Avenue in Tunis, with its parallel rows of pollarded ficus trees, its umbrella-sheltered espresso bars, its cathedral, and its century-old theater, you could easily imagine you were in southern France or Italy. Like those countries, Tunisia had strong labor unions, run by Communists. It even had potty-mouthed comedians and topless beaches. Tunisians were more literate than most of their Arab neighbors, and mostly healthier: the state had followed the European model there too, investing in education and state-sponsored health care instead of defense.

Tunisians had risen up against a dictator they believed was imperiling this legacy. It was their good luck that Zine El Abidine Ben Ali, for all his corruption and misrule, was not nearly as brutal as most other Arab autocrats, and he did not have the army behind him. The protests came boiling out of the Tunisian *bled* in December 2010, and soon the trademark Arab Spring line emerged for the first time: *ash sha'ab ureed isqaat an nizam*, the people want the fall of the regime. (This being Tunisia, it was mostly voiced instead with a single French word: "*Dégage!*") President Ben Ali fled the country with his inner circle on January 14, 2011, barely two days after the demonstrations reached the capital. A new civilian government emerged almost immediately, and within another six weeks, the protesters had secured further victories, banishing more tainted regime figures. Unlike so many other Arab countries, Tunisia still had a few veteran politicians who were relatively untainted and acceptable (more or less) to all. A former stalwart of the postcolonial era presided over a bloodless transition and paved the way, in the autumn of 2011, for elections that were deemed free and fair. The revolution's first year ended well.

The descent started soon after the elections, in October 2011. Ghannouchi's party won more than 41 percent of the new Parliament, enough to form a government. It was well organized, and it was the mildest and most democratic Islamist party in history. Their vision of Turkish-style Islamism and an entrepreneurial economy—a more liberal version of the Muslim Brotherhood in Egypt—appealed to many swing voters who were willing to try something new and had some sympathy for the Islamists' mistreatment by the old regime. But like any political party, Ennahda was reluctant to alienate its ideological base, which included many harder-line Islamists. They thought they could control them. As in Egypt, it worked the other way around: their radical cousins dragged them down.

The trouble started with a Salafi group called Ansar Sharia, or supporters of Islamic law. It had first appeared on the scene in 2011, one of several seemingly unrelated groups by the same name in different Arab countries. At least one of them was a front group for Al Qaeda, which was trying to rebrand itself to suit the age of populist revolution. The Tunisian version presented itself as a peaceful and independent organization, at least at first. But like the others, it was committed to building an Islamic state, and its tactics grew progressively more militant. The leaders of Ansar Sharia saw Ennahda as a convenient umbrella under which it could launch a cultural jihad. In 2012, Ansar Sharia held rallies all over the country and brought Salafi speakers from the Gulf. They demanded sharia law, and they organized boycotts and threats when Tunisian TV stations or newspapers aired "un-Islamic" material. They were behind the mob that stormed the U.S. embassy in Tunis in September. Even then, when the danger should have been obvious, Ennahda failed to crack down.

When jihadis with ties to Ansar Sharia assassinated two leftist politicians in 2013—one in February, one in July—it didn't matter who pulled the trigger. Ennahda took the blame. In a sense, they deserved it, and Rached Ghannouchi knew it. They had let it happen. Their mistakes had allowed a furious anti-Islamist movement to form, as in Egypt. And as in Egypt, it was threatening to destroy them.

Ghannouchi knew all this as he addressed the crowd on that August night in 2013. He had already made up his mind that the only way to avoid the Egyptian fiasco was with radical change. He had shared his decision with a few top confidants just before going onstage: the Islamist movement could survive only by giving up everything it had won at the polls. Tonight he planned to give the crowd a warning of what lay ahead. He knew it would not be easy. After a few minutes of familiar applause lines, he paused and shifted his tone. "We call for national reconciliation in this country," he said. "We want Tunis to reconcile with itself, to reconcile with its people." The crowd did not respond. This was not what they were expecting. They had come here to bare their teeth against the coup makers. They wanted words of defiance, not of compromise. They had all seen the footage of Rabaa Square in Cairo, and some of them seemed to be consciously parroting the slogans there. Ghannouchi retreated a bit, threw them some more red meat. "We will never accept a coup in this country!" he thundered. The crowd was with him again, the flags waving, the cheers lasting on and on. But a few minutes later, he tacked back away from them again. He hinted that the years of dictatorship had not been all bad, that the years after independence had brought achievements. And again he spoke of reconciliation and unity. "National unity is the highest goal, and we will need to make sacrifices for this unity," he said. "Tunis is older than Ennahda, Tunis is older than all of us." Now part of the crowd was openly booing the father figure who had led their movement for decades. This was unheard of at an Ennahda rally. "Listen to me a little more," Ghannouchi said, struggling to penetrate the din. There were chants in the back of the crowd: *Death to the coup makers.* "Listen to me . . ." He had lost them. It would take almost a full minute before his young aides, bellowing patriotic chants for the crowd to follow, had regained control.

As his speech came to an end, Ghannouchi was thinking about the enormity of the task he faced. He was convinced that the only way to avoid civil war was for Ennahda to resign from the government and agree to new elections—elections it was likely to lose. But it was clear that his own people did not want to concede anything. Perhaps he couldn't blame them; the slogans on the other side of town were just as bad. The secularists thought they owned the street, and they wanted blood. Ghannouchi didn't only need to convince his own people. He also needed a partner on the other side, someone with the power and the will to disarm. He wasn't sure there was one.

On that same evening, Beji Caid Essebsi was perched on a couch in his elegant Tunis villa, watching the news of both rallies on TV. He was the country's last remaining elder statesman, and he looked the part. At eighty-six, he had the stoical air of an admiral standing erect on a sinking ship, with his pale, collapsing jowls, perennially pursed lips, and eyes that seemed to be fixed disapprovingly in the middle distance. He was a rigid secularist and had spent his entire career in the service of Tunisia's great postwar modernizer, the dictator Habib Bourguiba.

Essebsi was the last living link to that era—now seen through a thick cloud of nostalgia. He had inherited the mantle of the country's new anti-Islamist movement, and many of the protesters were calling for him to take power, like General Sisi in Egypt. Part of him would have loved to. He hated the Islamists. They seemed determined to ruin everything he'd achieved. He wanted to snap his fingers and banish them forever from his beloved Tunis. But he knew it couldn't be done. There were too many, and the Tunisian army was far too weak to pull off a coup.

The phone rang, and he recognized the number: Nabil Karwi, the owner of Nessma, Tunisia's biggest TV station. The words began pouring out of the receiver, rapid-fire. Even on the phone, Karwi emanated the verve of a born impresario and adman. You could almost see him through the telephone: a small man with a big voice, strutting back and forth as he talked, unable to sit down, his eyes gleaming behind rimless designer glasses, one hand reaching up to stroke his coiled, slicked-back hair. Essebsi was used to hearing Karwi's bright ideas. The two of them had been partners for almost two years now. It was in the wood-paneled penthouse office of Karwi's TV station that they'd hatched the plans for Nidaa Tounes, the anti-Islamist political party that was now rallying all the opposition to its side. Karwi had been the prime mover back then. He'd been vilified by the Islamists for his station's liberal programs and threatened with death. He'd been forced to flee to Paris, and even there he'd been attacked. On his return, he recruited Essebsi to help him fight back. In that first meeting, in early 2012, he had told Essebsi, "You and I are like two men in a bar on a highway in an old American movie. The Hells Angels are coming, and we can wait for them to kill us, or we can go out and fight." (Karwi loved repeating this story, and he recited his conversations with Essebsi for me line by line, like an audio play.) Essebsi began appearing regularly on Nessma, fulminating against the Islamists and reminding Tunisians of the great legacy that was being destroyed. It struck a nerve. Many Tunisians feared that the Islamists they'd voted into power in 2011 were turning Tunisia into Afghanistan. They turned to Essebsi as a savior, liberal youth and old regime cronies alike. Karwi used to say he saw the new party as Noah's ark: we have Noah, now all we need is to get the animals on board.

"Si Beji," Karwi was saying—everyone used the term of deep respect with Essebsi—"I've got people coming into my office all day, saying, *Kill them, destroy them, the Islamists have got to go.* And look, I hate them as much as anyone does. But let's be realistic: Do we have the army or the police behind us, the way they did in Egypt? Do we have millions of dollars to bring people to Tunis? I think we should calm down a bit and think. If we do this full tilt, the Islamists will fight back. They will call for holy war, and then no one can stop it. The country will be destroyed."

Essebsi listened. When he spoke, his cold staccato formed a sharp contrast with Karwi's flowing monologue. "It's true," he said. "So what do you propose?"

Karwi shot back: "You must meet Ghannouchi. Go on TV and throw down the glove. He can't refuse."

Ten days later, Ghannouchi was on a private plane bound for Paris. The meeting was set to take place in the Hotel Bristol, just across from the Élysée Palace. Essebsi had to be in Paris for medical checkups, but meeting outside the country made sense anyway. They wanted strict secrecy. No one in either of the two political camps could know, because both sides were dead set against any gesture of rapprochement. Apart from the two men, only a handful of intimates were told. Karwi had recruited his billionaire friend Slim Riyahi to approach Ghannouchi and arrange the flight to Paris, and the hotel. The Islamist leader brought only one aide with him.

They met on the following morning, a Thursday, in a cavernous hotel suite with ocher walls and a view of the Eiffel Tower. Ghannouchi walked in looking almost clerical: black suit, white shirt, no tie. Essebsi wore his usual blue suit and tie. The two men shook hands, and Essebsi asked him about the trip from Tunis. Riyahi and Karwi helped to break the ice with some small talk, and then they arranged chairs around a coffee table and sat down. There were only four of them. Ghannouchi had held his aide back, and only after a half hour of talk did he ask if it was all right for him to come in. He'd been warned about Essebsi's Gallic preoccupation with protocol, his insistence on gestures of respect. That was all right with him. Ghannouchi had never worn his ego on his sleeve. He played the long game.

The two men had met before, but this summer morning in Paris was the first time they really took the measure of each other. They could scarcely have been more different. Essebsi was the embodiment of the old political elite in Tunis, the heir of a family that had been close to the Ottoman beys for generations. His pale skin hinted at his non-Arab origins. Like many of the Tunisian elite, he was part Turkish and part European. One of his great-great-grandfathers had been an Italian boy, kidnapped by corsairs from a Sardinian beach at the age of about ten and pressed into service in the *maison beylicale*. That first Caid Essebsi—the name came from his official role as tobacco master in the palace—passed on his status to his descendants. The family had preserved a quasi-aristocratic standing, marrying into the tiny circle of power and wealth in the capital. Beji's own father had died when he was young, and after attending Tunisia's best schools, Beji was sent to France to study law. It was there, in 1950, that he encountered Bourguiba, then the exiled leader of the Tunisian anticolonialist movement, who became a substitute father and lifelong inspiration. Years later, Essebsi described in a reverent memoir how Bourguiba took him on their first day together to the Place de la Sorbonne to pay homage at the stone statue of Auguste Comte, France's great advocate of science and the "religion of humanity." The message was unmistakable: Tunisia's future lay with a rigorous secularism. France would remain the beacon for all development, even if French colonialism at home was the enemy. It went without saying that Bourguiba's vision was entirely de haut en bas. Building the state came first, and democracy, perhaps, in a distant future. Essebsi still breathed this air of austerity and high purpose, as if he too expected someday to be memorialized in stone in a Paris square.

Ghannouchi had come from the far end of the Arab social world. He was the son of a farmer in Tunisia's remote southeast, a village with no electricity or paved roads, and did not ride in a car until he was fifteen. He and his nine brothers and sisters worked in the fields every day and then gathered for a simple meal of couscous and broth. They ate meat only a few times a year. During the long winter nights, the family would sit together for hours weaving baskets from palm leaves, to help supplement their income. They would sip hot tea and sing hymns about the Prophet Muhammad to keep up their spirits and stay awake. Ghannouchi's father was one of a few villagers who had memorized the Koran, and that gave him a certain status in a place where Islam was the fulcrum of daily life. His son Rached might never have left the village if not for an older brother who got a job that paid enough for his schooling. He went to the local branch of Zaytouna, an ancient network of Arabic-language schools that included a strong Islamic component (and was later abolished by Bourguiba). When he made his first trip to Tunis, at the age of eighteen, he was amazed by its French-style cafés and boulevards, its women dressed in revealing European clothes. He became, he later wrote, "a stranger in my own country." He formed an aspiration to speak for all the other villagers who found themselves exiled at home.

These two opposed life trajectories now faced each other in Paris above the clinking of teacups and the soft hum of the air-conditioning. Essebsi started first, as they all knew he would. "Clearly, we are in a very big crisis," he said. "The situation could not be more serious, and you cannot handle this by yourself." He began reviewing the previous two and a half years, since Ennahda had first formed a government after winning the elections of 2011. He enumerated a long list of mistakes, starting with the Salafi preachers who'd been allowed to come to the country, often greeted like heroes at the airport. The extremists of Ansar Sharia had been left to do as they pleased, flying the black flag in public rallies and building training camps in the desert. Members of Parliament had openly espoused the jihad in Syria, including members of Ennahda's own guidance bureau. The party had done nothing to stop this. Then, in September 2012, had come the attack on the U.S. embassy in Tunis, a preventable catastrophe. "It is very clear that you do not know how to manage the state, you have no experience," Essebsi said at one point. He went on to the mismanagement of the economy: Ghannouchi had poor relations with the French, an essential trading partner. He had done little to shore up the ailing tourism industry.

Through it all, Ghannouchi just kept nodding his head, saying, now and then, "You're right." Karwi remembers being amazed by the man's patience. Not once did he speak up or try to interrupt. Finally, after forty-five minutes, Essebsi had exhausted himself. The lecture was over. The men sipped their tea in silence for a moment.

Then Ghannouchi began. "I believe that the most important thing now is to save the republic and its institutions, to make sure we do not go to civil war," he said. "We must find a path of reconciliation that will guide us through this period." He went on to talk about his own mistakes. His movement had been in opposition, and mostly in exile, for decades; they had much to learn about governing. He was willing to see Ennahda step down, though it would take a lot of work to persuade people inside the party. He was also willing to make significant concessions on the constitution. He even hinted that he saw no obstacle to Essebsi himself becoming president. After outlining all this, he asked Essebsi whether he'd be willing to go on TV and calm his followers, to urge patience and compromise. Essebsi politely demurred. "The pressure right now is on you," he said. "I cannot simply take it away. But let us continue to meet, and we may find ways to manage the situation." Ghannouchi agreed. Karwi then asked the men to pose for a photograph. Slim Riyahi, the businessman, stood between them. He is smiling for the picture, but the other two look sternly into the camera. They signed a joint press release about the meeting, then shook hands and said goodbye.

They made it public three days later, a Sunday. In Tunisia's small political world it was, as Karwi put it, a "media bomb." Instantly both Ghannouchi and Essebsi were the subject of furious criticism within their parties. When Ennahda's Shoura council—the main deliberative body—met the next day, more than 100 of the 120-odd people present voted their disapproval of what he'd done. Ghannouchi gave a speech asking the members to let him try a policy of conciliation. If it failed, he said, he would take full responsibility and resign. Some members wanted another vote to expressly forbid him from holding any further meetings with Essebsi, but they were voted down. As the meeting broke up, Ghannouchi sensed that he was taking a risk. He wasn't yet sure whether he could trust Essebsi. But he got his first inklings of success a few days later. On August 23, on the eve of a big opposition rally, Essebsi announced that he would not attend. The rally fizzled, and the message was clear to everyone: Beji wants to lower the temperature. He was giving Ghannouchi what he'd asked for in Paris after all.

It was hard to say whether the policy of détente would succeed. Protests smoldered on, even as Tunisia's business and professional elite began holding an endless round of talkathons. They were led by four groups: the big labor union, known as the UGTT; the lawyers' and business leaders' councils; and a human rights group. They began coordinating with the main political parties and drew up plans to resume a "national dialogue" that had collapsed earlier that year. But there were plenty of leftists who still held Ennahda responsible for Brahmi's assassination and wanted revenge.

On the morning of October 5, Ghannouchi walked into the Palais des Congrès, a huge banquet hall used for public functions in downtown Tunis. He did not know it, but he was walking into an ambush. The entire political class was there, clustered by a bank of TV cameras: the leaders of the "quartet" running the national dialogue and the heads of all the parties. That much was expected. But instead of a discussion, he was being presented with a fait accompli. A "road map" for the national dialogue had been prepared for all parties to sign, and it included the demand that the Ennahda-led government relinquish all power to a caretaker authority. This was a huge concession, one his party was not yet prepared for. He sensed right away that many in that room were expecting him to refuse. They wanted the event to turn into a public denunciation of Ennahda and its leader. As he waited his turn to sign, Ghannouchi later told me, he felt "a mountain on my shoulder." His party's Shoura council had already voted overwhelmingly that they would join the national dialogue only on condition that Ennahda not be forced from power. He now had to weigh his own judgment against the party he represented. He signed, in full view of millions of Tunisians.

Then came the most difficult moment in his political life. He got into a car with his aides, and they drove straight to Gammarth, a Tunis suburb on the coast. The party's entire Shoura council was waiting for him in the conference room of a hotel. A murmur of angry voices was audible as he walked in and took his seat. One by one, members unleashed their fury. More than sixty spoke against the decision to sign. Some said it was treason against the movement and a betrayal of those who had died defending it. One of Ghannouchi's advisers told me he had never seen him facing this much anger.

Finally it was Ghannouchi's turn to speak. He acknowledged the anger and said he felt it was a bitter moment for him and for the Islamic movement. But he then said he believed that signing the road map was necessary in order to save Tunisia from civil war. It was a moment when the movement's interests had to be weighed against the country's, and the country's interests were higher. He concluded with these words: "If you want to go to a confrontation, go. But I will not be part of it." Once again, he was threatening to resign. It was his trump card. Ghannouchi had the status of a philosopher-king in the movement, and they knew they would be crippled without him. After three hours of discussion, the council agreed reluctantly to let the signature stand.

Much of Tunisia was now asking: What is Ghannouchi's game? How did he get the strength to go against his own party? And to win? You could say he'd been scared into compromise by the coup in Egypt. Everyone had. By October, even the fiercest Tunisian secularists had to admit that the "hero" of Egypt looked a little tarnished. The massacre at Rabaa had shocked everyone, and the gathering insurgency in Egypt's Sinai Peninsula—billed as retaliation—was bearing out the worst fears.

But Ghannouchi's signature on that document wasn't just about fear. It was the product of a half century of political and intellectual evolution. He was an Islamist, but in a vastly different sense from the leaders of the Muslim Brotherhood, whose education consisted mostly of rereading the Koran in prison. Ghannouchi escaped the narrow mental world of his village as a young man. He lived abroad for decades, reading widely in three languages and constantly weaving new strands into the fabric of political Islam. In a sense, he was the opposite of Sayyid Qutb, the notorious Egyptian radical whose work helped shape the leaders of both the Muslim Brotherhood and Al Qaeda. Qutb traveled to the United States in 1948 and spent almost two years there, but he never breached the wall of his own deep resentments and anxieties. Qutb's famously hysterical description of a church dance in Greeley, Colorado, has become a touchstone for analysts of radical Islam: he recoiled from the "animal instincts" on display, the sacrilegious mingling of unmarried men and women. Everything he saw strengthened his own convictions about Western materialism and Muslim superiority. He learned nothing in his two-year journey, apart from some facts and figures on American industrial output. In his later writings, he cast America as the torchbearer of a diabolical Western effort to separate the sacred and the secular, one that had begun centuries earlier with the Enlightenment. Only through violent jihad, he concluded, could this modern-day barbarism be defeated.

Ghannouchi had read Qutb as a young man, and sympathized with his desire to reclaim a lost Islamic heritage. But he soon rejected Qutb's apocalyptic certainty. Ghannouchi's own exposure to the West started much earlier and went much deeper. In his twenties, he spent time bumming around Europe, working as a grape picker in rural France, washing dishes in a restaurant, watching left-wing protests in Paris in 1968. He read Marx, Freud, and Sartre, and debated their ideas with the high school students to whom he taught philosophy back in Tunis. A few years later, after committing himself to political Islam, he was humbled by the courage of left-wing Tunisian activists who risked their lives in street protests and suffered torture in jail. His own Islamist peers abhorred the dictatorship but did nothing about it. He decided to make common cause with the leftists and the trade unions. This was an unusually pragmatic gesture at a time when many Islamists still considered Socialists to be infidels, as bad as or even worse than the dictators. At the end of the 1970s, Ghannouchi briefly found inspiration in the Iranian revolution, which seemed to offer a model for melding faith and politics. He helped found the movement that would become Ennahda, articulating a democratic Islamism that would later be copied by the Egyptian Brotherhood.

There were flickers of success, especially after the senescent Bourguiba was pushed aside in 1987 by his former prime minister, Zine El Abidine Ben Ali. But after a few gestures of openness, Ben Ali soon proved himself more brutal and far more corrupt than his predecessor. A crackdown on the Islamists left hundreds in prison, and most of the leadership fled abroad. By the decade's end, Ghannouchi was living in London, along with much of the group's leadership. An exile community of Islamists formed—Pakistanis, Palestinians, Egyptians, Jordanians— and began comparing notes. They watched in dismay as the Algerian elections of 1991 spiraled into a murderous civil war. It was a time of hard questions. "We had to ask ourselves, why have we failed?" one of Ghannouchi's closest advisers told me. "Is the Islamic movement a force for unity or a force for division? We talked endlessly about this. And we decided we had to make changes. Ennahda doesn't say this, but most of our members don't accept women not wearing veils. And Tunisian leftists do not accept openly religious people. Some of us felt the society would have to overcome these divisions before any progress could be made."

These debates were still under way when Bouazizi set himself on fire in December 2010. Nothing had been resolved; no one was prepared. Ghannouchi returned to Tunis with no playbook in hand. It was not until three years later that he was forced to face head-on the dilemma that had preoccupied the Islamists in London: how to reach an accommodation with political enemies without losing their own base. The national dialogue that began in the autumn of 2013 was long overdue.

It was also painful, as they'd known it would be. "People did not like each other," I was told by a lawyer who played a prominent role. "They all had a great need to talk, to yell at each other, to get the feelings out. Sometimes one man would talk for thirty or forty minutes straight." He smiled wearily at the memory. "But he needed to say it." The dialogue meetings were arranged by the leaders of four pillars of Tunisian society, known as the Quartet: the federation of trade unions, known as the UGTT; the employers institute; the Tunisian human rights league; and the lawyers' syndicate. Houcine Abassi, the secretary general of the UGTT, played the role of referee. He was a short, compactly built man with a dour expression stamped on his face and a reputation for honesty and fairness. One of the ground rules of the talks was that no one could smoke—it was intended to limit the marathon meetings—but an exception was made for the chain-smoking Abassi, whose mediating role was essential.

It was the Quartet itself—not the political bosses—that was ultimately awarded the Nobel Peace Prize in 2015 for its efforts to ease the Tunisian political crisis and avert civil war. But the national dialogue's heart and soul was the ongoing conversation between Essebsi and Ghannouchi. They were present during almost all the meetings, which sometimes went on until dawn. They also continued having their own one-on-one meetings. These remained mostly secret, because Tunisia's pundits and party bosses were still paranoid about a "deal" being made behind their backs. They met once every two weeks or so, alternating between Essebsi's upscale villa in the Sukra district and Ghannouchi's more austere apartment in Nahli. They had a new go-between, a mutual friend named Ali ben Nsib who sat in and sometimes took part. The mood at their meetings slowly shifted, Nsib told me. An initial tone of polite *froideur* gave way to ease and some laughter. They discovered that they had some things in common, despite their vastly different life stories. For all his secularism, Essebsi knew the Koran well, and often quoted it. Both men had been traumatized as boys by encounters with the French military, at almost exactly the same age. Essebsi had witnessed a demonstration in April 1938 in Tunis, when French police opened fire on protesters and killed twenty-two. Ghannouchi had a similar experience in 1952, when he saw the bodies of four *fallaga* rebels in the marketplace of his town. French soldiers had shot them and stood guard to prevent locals from burying them, a deliberate outrage to Muslim sensibility. Memories like those helped form a bond. Essebsi began to feel that his Islamist counterpart was a Tunisian patriot. And Ghannouchi recognized that Essebsi had—like him—grown uncomfortable with Bourguiba's autocratic ways long before the Ben Ali era began. Another piece of common ground came from economics. Essebsi led a party dominated by free-market businessmen, and Ghannouchi—like most of his peers in the Egyptian Muslim Brotherhood—was all for business-friendly policies. Some of the leftists in Tunisia's labor unions saw this early, lamenting that the Islamists and Nidaa Tounes could form a right-wing alliance to privatize Tunisia's state enterprises and do the bidding of the IMF.

Apart from all this, both of them sensed the irony of their geriatric dominance after a revolution supposedly defined by youth. During one chat, the eighty-six-year-old Essebsi said something about his return to politics after such a long absence, and Ghannouchi cracked: "We all thought you'd already been filed away in the national archives." Essebsi shot back: "Yes. They found you in a different archive."

They were edging toward each other, sideways, like two ancient crabs. Their parties followed suit, slowly and reluctantly. Two months of hard negotiation over a caretaker prime minister finally bore fruit in December. That decision allowed Ennahda to formally cede power, and the tension in the dialogue sessions eased from that moment onward. The next turning point came in mid-January, when Parliament was debating an article in the draft constitution mandating an age ceiling of seventy-five for presidential candidates. This would exclude Essebsi, whose hunger for the presidency was no secret. Most of Ennahda's members opposed any change, and their rivals insisted on it. Ghannouchi knew that his relationship with Essebsi—and everything that flowed from it—depended on breaking the deadlock. He convened an emergency 6:30 a.m. meeting of Ennahda's twelve-member executive bureau on the day of the vote, and once again laid all his political weight on the line. Again, the hard-liners complained and leveled bitter accusations, and then buckled. This was "a red carpet for Essebsi to reach the presidency," Ghannouchi later put it. As soon as the meeting broke up, his aides telephoned Essebsi to let him know. Ali ben Nsib was with the old man when he got the word. "He was genuinely moved," he said. "This was the moment when their relationship became one of real mutual trust."

At midnight on January 26, 2014, 204 out of 217 Parliament members voted to pass the new constitution. No one could quite believe it. Shouts of joy filled the vast opera-style deputies' chamber, with its limestone columns and velvet-seated balconies. Old Islamist firebrands hugged their rivals across the aisle, tears streaming from their eyes. In the hallway outside, people picked up legislators and heaved them into the air, singing the national anthem. "Our blood and souls we sacrifice for you, our flag!" they chanted. "With the blood of the martyrs, we have succeeded!" Women ululated, and people broke into ecstatic call-and-response songs. The parties spilled out into the streets and in homes across the city, almost until dawn. The feeling was universal: the worst of the crisis was over. Civil war had been averted. But the days afterward brought a more somber recognition. The reconciliation was only a signed document. The elections were still to come, and they had the power to knock down everything that the two old men had built.

In theory, the personal rapport between Ghannouchi and Essebsi would now extend to their respective political parties and the popular base each one stood for. But Essebsi's party, Nidaa Tounes, was a very unstable mix of leftists, opportunistic businessmen, and old regime figures. The ink on the constitution was scarcely dry before the first fissures and power struggles began appearing in the early months of 2014, making it more apparent than ever that without the unifying figure of Bejbouj, as the faithful called him, the party was nothing. One sour old Tunisian pundit described it to me as "a sick lion guiding a pack of errant wolves." Even Essebsi, for all the hero worship he drew, was valued mostly as a link to the past. He'd never been a major figure in his own time. To most of his new followers, he was a stand-in for the country's one acknowledged father figure, Bourguiba. No one understood this better than Karwi, who had helped build him up. "We built this party on three things," he told me, as he puffed a cigar and patted the heavy wooden table in his office where the party was first conceived. "First, fear and hatred of Islamists; next, nostalgia; a single charismatic figure; and of course, greed for power. It wasn't a political party. It was just a way to get rid of the Islamists. Once people thought that was done, things began to come apart."

This awareness drifted uneasily over Tunisian politics through the spring and summer, when people could still daydream and pretend that all was well, congratulate themselves for avoiding the horror shows under way in Syria and Libya and Egypt. They had many things to be grateful for: Tunisia was a relative oasis of peace and liberty. Dozens of new newspapers and websites had appeared after the revolution, and some critics and comedians were pillorying the Ennahda-allied president in ways that would have been unthinkable under Ben Ali. Some young journalists were producing investigative civic journalism at a higher level than anything available elsewhere in the Arab world, critiquing the new government's performance on subjects ranging from garbage collection to counterterrorism. The country's tourism industry had suffered, but it still brought in money. Tunisia's close ties with Europe seemed likely to sustain a higher standard of living than some of its larger neighbors, despite its lack of oil.

Still, the tenuousness of the political compromise became unavoidable once the election campaign got under way in the fall. One afternoon in October, I was waiting in line outside a sports arena in the city of Sousse, an hour southeast of the capital. Someone with a TV camera was filming the crush of people pressing up against the narrow doors, where the crowd got so large you wondered if there was any room left inside. Once we got through and beyond the cameras, the entry hall was almost empty. The same cheap tactics were on display near the stage, a hundred yards onward. There was a din of whistling and cheering and Pharrell Williams's "Happy" blasting from huge black speakers up at the front. There were red banners and flags waving everywhere, and party members were screaming like Beatles fans in 1964. They looked like a bused-in crowd. Two huge TV cameras on swivel arms were sweeping over the audience, and the giant video screens up front showed the results simultaneously: a giddy roller-coaster view of the pumped-up crowd. What you didn't see on the screens was the empty back half of the room. I made my way to the front, where a woman with a clipboard shouted into my ear and led me to a seat in the media section, underneath a giant poster of Habib Bourguiba. After a few minutes, the Nidaa Tounes parliamentary candidates for Sousse began delivering their speeches. They were a mix of local boosterism, anger at the Islamists, and hero worship. Each one ended with the same refrain: "Long live Nidaa, long live Tunis, long live Beji Caid Essebsi." I tried chatting with a campaign volunteer, a slick-looking young business-man in a dark suit, but when I asked him what Nidaa Tounes stood for, he told me he'd introduce me to one of the candidates. "We want Tunisia to succeed," he said into my ear.

When the stump speeches were over, the music stopped, the lights dimmed, and a film flickered into life on the two big screens. The familiar figure of Bourguiba appeared in black and white, moving in the jerky sped-up rhythm of old newsreels. We watched him attending parades, meeting women's rights activists, visiting the United States. "It was an era of golden innovation," the scroll on the bottom of the screen declared. This went on for twenty-five minutes. Then the screen went black, and an enormous, forbidding photograph of Bourguiba's face appeared, cast in shades of gray. It loomed over the crowd for a moment, phantomlike. A scratchy voice emerged from the speakers, and the lips on the photograph began to jiggle up and down implausibly, as if squeezed by invisible hands. The great man was delivering his message of Tunisian secularism from beyond the grave, with the help of Photoshop. At last he stopped, and the macabre portrait faded slowly into blackness again.

It was then that the entourage emerged from a back corner of the stage. For a moment, you almost thought they'd brought Bourguiba back to life for a final speech. Essebsi walked briskly onto the stage, lips pursed, eyes somber, as the Tunisian national anthem began blasting from the speakers and the crowd bolted upright, all at once. Once the song was over, Essebsi put out his hand for silence. His face conveyed a cold impatience. "Habib Bourguiba's vision is the vision of Nidaa, and of the Tunisian people," he said. "The state Bourguiba created will return." It was as if he were only a warm-up speaker, readying the crowd for his dead mentor. He went on to talk about the importance of this election, of the need to get everyone out to vote. Then he said something that amazed me: "We will succeed, we must succeed, or else Tunisia will see a new Dark Ages." I thought I'd misunderstood, but he repeated the line a few minutes later. This felt like desperation. I thought of Karwi's formula: hatred, fear, nostalgia. Would that really bring people to the polls? And then, after only about fifteen minutes, the speech was over, and people began bolting for the exits. Essebsi was almost eighty-eight years old, and his brevity was understandable. But if this was the best his party could do, it did not bode well for the secularist heirs of Habib Bourguiba.

The contrast with Ennahda's get-out-the-vote efforts was staggering. The Islamists sent out teams of well-dressed young people to knock on doors in cities and towns across Tunisia. The party had selected a theme that highlighted their confidence: It doesn't matter if we win or lose, because a fair election is a victory for us all. They repeated it like a catechism. They did the same with terrorism, their great Achilles' heel. Everyone had blamed them for the black flags and the assassinations of 2013, so Ghannouchi and his lieutenants made sure the new talking points reached every single candidate: terrorism is the nation's biggest threat. At one rally I attended in central Tunis, virtually every speaker hailed the counterterrorism forces as the "heroes of the nation." They were assembled on a stage that had been curated like a museum display of Tunisian diversity. Two of the women seated on the platform wore no hijab. Ghannouchi mounted the stage in a shower of applause and gently patted the head of a little boy who was standing by the podium, camera-ready. One of the speakers released a white dove that fluttered up over the crowd. Ghannouchi spoke last. There had been a counter-terrorist raid a day or two earlier in which an officer had been killed, and Ghannouchi spoke emotionally of this man, mentioning his name and calling him a martyr for all Tunisians to be proud of.

It was hard to know how much all this political theater mattered outside the party faithful. Early one morning, I drove three hours south from Tunis to Sidi Bouzid, where the protests started in December 2010. The road from the capital passes from the relative grandeur of an old colonial town to a dusty backwater of half-deserted villages and brown fields lined with cacti. Here and there, smoke rises from the horizon. Old women stand by wooden shacks on the roadside, selling loaves of Berber bread for the equivalent of about 10 cents apiece. It is almost meaningless to speak of unemployment in southern Tunisia; the formal economy scarcely exists. Many people depend on smuggling from the Algerian or Libyan borders to get by. Phosphate mining was once the region's main industry, accounting for more than half the country's total GDP. By 2014 it was at a standstill, and protests over joblessness were spreading. This kind of discontent could prove far more dangerous than the Islamic slogans that provoke so much fear in the West. It has happened before: the mining towns of the south erupted in protest over corrupt hiring practices in 2008, and that upwelling—brutally repressed by the Ben Ali government—helped plant the seeds for the broader protests that began almost three years later.

Sidi Bouzid is a small, seedy farming town with square cinder-block houses and semi-arid plains extending around it in every direction. It is a world away from the Gallic boulevards of Tunisia's coastal cities. Near the gatehouse of the governor's office, where Mohamed Bouazizi burned himself to death in 2010, a huge billboard with his smiling face on it now towers overhead. The town has received some government largesse since 2011, thanks to its role as the birthplace of the revolution. But the unemployment rate is still high, and crowds of young men hang around all day in cafés, watching sports on TV and smoking. It was quiet on election day in 2014, with only small lines forming at polling stations. I spoke to dozens of them as they waited to enter, and most told me more or less the same thing: they were voting for Beji, but not because they really liked or trusted him. The Islamists had failed, they said, and needed to be sent a message. Both parties were untrustworthy, and it was better to keep them both in check. In a café near the center of town, I met a wiry thirty-year-old with green eyes named Basem Abdulli, who was staring up at a television with a few friends. He had been in the same café on the morning Bouazizi died, he told me. "We heard someone had set himself on fire, so we all went to see. We found his cart in the street. We asked what had happened. The police came and told us all to go home. Some more people showed up, from Gafsa. We started stoning the police. It started from there." After that, he said, the protests were mostly at night. They'd burn tires and block roads. He was arrested once and taken to jail, where the police beat him badly and left him with a head injury. He turned sideways and showed me the scar: a brownish ridge above his ear. "Now we have no jobs, no benefits," he went on. "We feel we were punished for making this revolution."

I asked him about the election, and he told me he was voting for a small, independent party. He knew they had no chance of winning more than a seat or two, but he didn't care. "I have not given up hope," he said. "There are some good people. Maybe they can make a difference." Two little boys were standing nearby, listening to us and watching. They looked about eight years old. One of them spoke up: "If I were old enough, I would vote." The other shook his head. "I wouldn't vote, no way," he said. "They are all corrupt."

A few days later, when the preliminary electoral results were announced, Ennahda held a celebration at their downtown headquarters. They had lost decisively: 27.79 percent of the vote, compared with 37.5 percent for Nidaa Tounes. But they maintained this was good news. A successful election was a victory for all Tunisians. It was a pose, of course. But the confidence was genuine. They knew they were being punished for the mistakes of the past three years, but they also knew they were likely to inherit the country eventually. Anyone with two eyes could see that they were Tunisia's strongest and most unified political force. And the Islamists knew that their rivals might not find it any easier to govern than they had.

In the days that followed, Ennahda's leaders disappeared from view. They were holding a conclave, where another punishing internal battle was under way. It was not really about assigning blame for the loss of Parliament, as the rumors suggested. It was about the presidential election, scheduled for late November. Ghannouchi had already persuaded the party not to run a candidate. This had been a relatively easy affair; all you had to do was point to Cairo, where the Brotherhood's fatal decision to seek the presidency had helped to destroy it. Now, Ghannouchi and his top advisers were asking for another concession. They wanted the party to remain neutral in the presidential race. In effect, this would mean endorsing Essebsi over his chief rival, Moncef Marzouki, who had been Ennahda's loyal ally for the preceding three years. Ghannouchi's logic was impeccable: Beji was likely to win anyway. And even if he didn't, Marzouki would have very little power against a Parliament dominated by Essebsi's party. Better for Ennahda to back the winning horse and have some influence. More than that: Ghannouchi said Ennahda should join Nidaa in a coalition government.

To Ghannouchi's critics, this was pure betrayal. To throw one's own ally under the bus in favor of a man who would just as soon toss them all in jail—or worse? Some of them also argued for a second principle: you need an opposition to keep the government honest. This was the more natural role of Ennahda, they said. Ghannouchi countered that Tunisia was still too fragile for that kind of divided government. Only a unified government could undertake the difficult reforms that were necessary to grow the economy, like cutting back on state subsidies for oil and food. "I told them that we had to put the interests of the country over those of the party," he told me afterward. "It was a bitter moment. We had to balance our principles against the new reality. That way, we could preserve the country and its institutions—and we can return to power later." In the end, he won out again, but many in the movement were angry. Hamad Jebali, Ennahda's first prime minister, announced his withdrawal from the party. Others said they were reconsidering their membership.

Throughout this period, Ghannouchi and Essebsi continued to meet, discussing ways to steer their movements into a working relationship. On December 1, the project was on the point of foundering. As they stood together in Essebsi's living room after dinner, with the winter darkness pressing in from the garden doors, Essebsi explained that he'd been unable to broker a deal on the position of parliamentary president. The coalition depended on that appointment. If he couldn't do it by the next day, the deadline would pass, and their plans for a joint government would collapse. Ghannouchi nodded, his face looking dour.

"Sheikh Rached, have confidence in me," Essebsi said.

"I have confidence in you," came the reply.

"We are brothers," Essebsi said.

"Yes, we are brothers." They embraced, an awkward hug between two reserved old men.

The next day, Essebsi persuaded his party to extend the opening session, giving him time to secure the joint appointment that allowed the coalition to succeed. It was the first vote of the new Parliament, and the two main parties—ostensibly bitter enemies—had voted in sync.

In the weeks that followed, Ghannouchi returned the favor, moving beyond his party's official position of neutrality. He hinted broadly in television interviews that his preferred candidate in the presidential runoff was Essebsi. In private, he made clear that he hoped others in the party would follow his lead. Most of them did not, but in the end it didn't matter: the momentum was with Beji. When the results were announced, Ghannouchi went straight to the house to congratulate him. Essebsi ribbed him a little, saying the tally suggested that many of Ennahda's members had voted for his opponent. Ghannouchi smiled. "I voted for you," he said. Essebsi took his hand. "Sometimes one vote is worth a thousand," he replied.

In January 2015, two weeks after Essebsi took the oath as Tunisia's next president, his younger brother Kamel died. A public funeral service was planned, but on the evening before, the family gathered in private at Essebsi's home in Tunis. After leaving them alone for a decent interval, the chief of the presidential guard knocked on the door and discreetly urged the president to return to the palace. Night was falling. Essebsi brushed him off, saying he was waiting for one more guest. A full hour passed. At last a black car pulled up in the darkness outside the house. A man emerged from the backseat: Ghannouchi. He strode up to the group, and as he offered his condolences, Essebsi embraced him. "He wanted to send a message, to the presidential guard and everyone else," a friend of Essebsi's told me. "He was letting them know that he regards Rached Ghannouchi as a member of his family."

Ghannouchi was now a landmark in the history of the Islamist movement. He had not stopped at making common cause with a rigorously secularist old regime figure. His liberal Islam was, in some respects, to the left of many Arab liberals. In early 2015, he told a French interviewer that homosexuality was a private matter and should not be criminalized. He said he had no desire to Islamize Europe, and he advised French authorities to set up their own Islamic schools, to make sure that Muslims there kept their faith within the bounds of secular republican ideology and steered clear of the Salafi doctrines imported from Saudi Arabia and the Gulf. At home, he gave full assent to a crackdown on the radical mosques that had been indoctrinating Tunisian youth in a jihadi mind-set. Ghannouchi had always been a reviled figure to jihadi ideologues, but now some said he was worse than an infidel. He was reaching the top of their wanted list. It was an achievement of sorts, but it carried the seeds of a new danger.

On March 18, three gunmen dressed in military uniforms attacked the Bardo Museum in Tunis and took hostages. Within hours, twenty-one people were dead, mostly European tourists, and about fifty were injured. The killers were jihadis loosely affiliated with Al Qaeda's North African branch, and had trained in Libya. The killings marked a break with the past in several ways. Less than two years earlier, leading jihadis had declared that Tunisia was a place of *da'wa*—religious outreach and consolidation—not jihad. They believed the Ennahda electoral victory gave them a sanctuary in which to grow and develop. That moment had clearly passed. Tunisia was now a target, a state run by infidels, including Ennahda. The bloodshed was splashed all over newspapers in Europe and the United States, prompting frantic speculation that Tunisia was sinking into the arc of chaos stretching from Libya to Yemen. In a sense, that perception was more damaging than the attack itself. Two months afterward, as I wandered through the winding, cloacal halls of the Tunis medina, I saw scarcely a single tourist. Merchant after merchant told me mournfully that all the cruise ships had canceled their stops in the Tunis port. It was shaping up to be the worst summer season they'd ever had, they said. Half an hour south, in the holiday town of Hammamat, I found the long avenue of beachside hotels almost empty. A few local people sipped colored fruit drinks under the umbrellas. It would get worse.

Some conservatives inside the party felt Ghannouchi had given up too much. One of the movement's conservative standard-bearers, a sixty-two-year-old businessman named Habib Ellouze, told me that Ghannouchi's concessions were alienating many people. "They feel the Islamic identity is weakening, that we are becoming just an ordinary political party," he said. "If this continues, some members will leave the party, and perhaps they will form their own organization." It is not just a question of faith. Many Ennahda members were tortured in jail, and they believe Ghannouchi is tamping down calls for a more thorough accounting of the old regime's human rights abuses. Some of those abuses, after all, were committed while Essebsi served as interior minister in the 1960s; he retained a powerful role in Parliament during the early Ben Ali era. These tensions inside the party have led to repeated calls for Ennahda to separate its political party from the broader social movement. That could dilute Ghannouchi's influence, allowing conservatives to establish a separate base and shatter the ruling coalition.

Even if the equilibrium holds, it is hard to say what kind of legacy will be granted to Tunisia's two grand old men. The idea that they achieved a historic synthesis, a reweaving of the country's Islamic and Western ancestries, is an appealing one. And in many ways, Tunisia did seem to have pulled back from the crater's edge in mid-2015. The coalition government was coalescing and planning reforms, albeit slowly. Most of the Islamists seemed to have come around to the belief in compromise and reconciliation. Leftists spoke optimistically about a working relationship with the people they'd once hoped to eradicate. But the greatest dangers and the greatest opportunities lay beyond the country's borders. Five years after the death of Mohamed Bouazizi, most Tunisians still hoped that their small country could be a model, spreading its dream of reconciliation across a region troubled by war and tyranny. They also knew the same winds could blow in reverse and smash everything they had built.

— Epilogue —

One morning in the summer of 2015, I woke early to the sound of my cell phone. A voice called my name—jubilant at first—and then began an anxious monologue, interrupted by what sounded like thunder. "God help us, Mr. Robert. The sky is raining bombs on us. Yemenis are dying. The Saudis are killing us by air, and Ali Abdullah Saleh is killing us by land. They are all criminals."

It was Saeed, the Yemeni who had led the forty-year rebellion against the Sheikh of Ja'ashin. I had never heard him sound so frightened. He was still living in the tent that had been his home since the start of the revolution, but now the bombs were falling in the Taiz foothills, he said. It sounded close. Yemen had been under Saudi bombardment for months, and the country was almost entirely cut off from the world. Food and water were getting scarce, Saeed said. The native cheerfulness that had held firm through four decades of war and revolution was starting to fray. I wanted to tell him something encouraging, but I couldn't think what to say.

It was the same with many of my Arab friends in 2015. The whole region seemed to be sinking into a dismayingly familiar chaos, with dictators (or would-be dictators) and jihadi groups killing and yet somehow sustaining each other in a weird symbiosis. Yemen had once been the Arab world's exception and stepchild. Now it was becoming almost typical: a failed state where new divisions formed all the time, like a pane of glass shattering into ever-smaller shards. The only thing being democratized was violence.

Saeed told me he no longer understood his own country. The revolution's one achievement seemed to be getting rid of Ali Abdullah Saleh, yet now the wily old man was back, and in league with his own devils. Saleh still had the billions he'd stolen as president. He had the support of the Huthis, the northern rebels he'd fought against as president. It was as if the worst nightmares of the Tahrir Square protests had come to life: the dictator and the zealots in a cynical pact for power. The Huthis, of course, claimed the revolution's mantle as their own.

Saeed had watched in amazement throughout 2014 as this strange alliance marched southward like a many-armed monster, taking one Yemeni province after another. In September of that year they conquered Sanaa, the capital. The Huthi movement's teenage soldiers wandered the streets, spraying the sky with bullets, setting up checkpoints wherever they liked. The nominal president, Abdu Rabbu Mansour Hadi, was granted a puppet's role for a few months and then fled, first to Aden and then to Riyadh, the Saudi capital. No one would miss him.

Saeed had called me one day in early 2015 and told me that the city of Taiz, where he lived, had become an independent republic. I had heard the same kind of thing in Libya, in Syria, in Iraq: it was as if the whole region was devolving back to city-states. Saeed sounded proud. The city had refused to side with either party in a stupid war. It would survive on its own. But none of these proud declarations lasted long. The Huthis were soon at the gates of Taiz. The country was polarizing in their wake, with money flowing in from outside: Iran backed the Huthis, and Saudi Arabia paid the tribes to fight on the other side.

Then in late March 2015, the Saudis upped the ante. They declared war on the Huthis, dropping thousands of American-made bombs onto the Arab world's poorest country. They swore they would continue until President Hadi was restored to power. Gigantic explosions lit up Yemen's cities by night, and daylight revealed medieval stone towers—one of them a UNESCO Heritage site—reduced to rubble. Hundreds of civilians were killed. The bombing did not stop the Huthis, who continued their march across Yemen.

Saeed told me there had been huge explosions on the edge of Taiz. He wanted to see his wife but was afraid to travel to Ja'ashin, he said, for fear of the bombs.

"Mr. Robert, I don't know if we will speak again," he said, as one of our conversations came to an end. "Please pass my word to the world: Do not forget us."

Those words sound melodramatic on paper. They were becoming oddly commonplace. "Can I ask a favor?" an Egyptian friend wrote to me on Facebook around the same time. "If you do not hear from me again tomorrow, can you send word to my friends? It will mean I am arrested or dead."

In Egypt, Muhammad Beltagy was beyond anyone's help. After a long show trial, he was sentenced to death in May 2015, along with dozens of other Muslim Brotherhood leaders. Egypt's former president, Muhammad Morsi, was one of them. The accusations against them were a wild brew of conspiracy theory, involving a prison break plotted by Hamas and Hezbollah. Beltagy's family had not seen him in months. He had grown a long beard in prison, and he now resembled the cartoon zealot the Egyptian authorities had labeled him. He'd been tortured, he told the judge. He had long since made clear that he was prepared for martyrdom and did not expect to survive. Once, when the charges against him were read out loud, he and his fellow defendants—crowded into a wire cage, like animals—burst into helpless laughter. You wondered what was going on in their minds. But you could not hear them: after the initial hearings, they were kept behind a soundproof plexiglass wall.

When the death sentence was affirmed by Egypt's rubber-stamp

Grand Mufti, the chief judge delivered an ode to President Sisi that scarcely touched on the legal accusations. The presidency of Morsi had been a "black night," the judge said, followed by "the dawn of human conscience" in the form of Sisi's coup. "All Egyptians came out, all over Egypt, demanding the building of a strong and cohesive Egyptian society that does not exclude any of its sons and currents, and ends the state of conflict and division."

Outside the courtroom, the judge's fantasy was getting harder to maintain. The insurgency in Egypt's Sinai Peninsula was growing fiercer. At least two thousand soldiers and police had been killed in the preceding two years. Each bombing led to indiscriminate government raids that left civilians dead, deepening resentment and fueling jihadi recruitment efforts. The violence was creeping from the desert into the heart of Egypt. In late June 2015, Egypt's most senior prosecutor was killed in a car bombing in Cairo. Afterward, Sisi visited a group of Egyptian judges and browbeat them, on camera, for taking so long with the Brotherhood trials. "Revenge for his murder is upon you," Sisi says in the video clip, as the cowed judges listen silently. "We haven't interfered in your work for the past two years . . . All the Egyptian people are saying, and I am saying, *We must implement the law!*" The judges nod obediently.

The Brotherhood's exiled leadership denounced the jihadi violence, but it was hard to avoid the sense that their voices no longer mattered. Egypt's Islamists were taking sides in a conflict that was beginning to look like war. In late May 2015, 159 Muslim scholars from twenty countries issued an open letter declaring all those who collaborate with Sisi's regime to be murderers and calling for them to be punished as such. The Brotherhood publicly endorsed the letter the next day, and within two months more than six hundred thousand people had signed their approval online. More and more young Brotherhood members were openly demanding violence against the state.

Some Brotherhood members went off to the jihad in Syria, but there was a much nearer option: Libya. ISIS had founded a ministate there, too, in the middle of a civil war so fragmented and mercurial that it defied all efforts to distill a larger meaning. Jalal Ragai, the Libyan militia leader I'd befriended in 2011, was another regular voice on my telephone, in a series of calls that documented his own country's descent into chaos. Like Saeed, Jalal had been an optimist who always insisted that the revolution would triumph. He had acted on that belief, handing over the prisoners in his basement to the state, or what passed for it. This was back in 2012. He had since come to regret it.

"We wanted them to have a trial," Jalal told me. "We wanted justice. We brought the prisoners to the military prosecutor in Tripoli, and we gave him everything. All the videotapes you saw, plus the confessions we videotaped, and signed confessions, and military documents, and even all the ID papers. Boxes and boxes of it. The case was all there, one hundred percent." Nasser Salhoba, whose brother had been murdered, watched uneasily as the killer was marched into a Tripoli jail cell guarded by militia fighters.

For a while, it seemed as if Jalal's gamble would pay off. After the killing of American ambassador Chris Stevens in Benghazi in 2012, a popular movement to disband all the Libyan militias gained strength. Huge crowds of protesters overran the barracks of the Benghazi militia whose members were responsible for Stevens's death, chanting "No, no to the brigades" and "The blood we shed for freedom shall not go in vain!" The gunmen fled. But not for long. Within six months, the civilian resistance faltered, and Islamist militias bullied the Parliament into passing legislation that favored them. The government was irrelevant after that.

Libya's internecine militia battles soon grew fiercer. Jalal was in the middle of it: he was shot and almost killed by fighters from the Qa'qa' brigade, an outfit notorious for its involvement in arms smuggling and drug dealing. He spent months in bed recovering from the bullet wounds, and eventually flew to Germany for more surgery on his shattered legs. When he got back to Libya, in late 2013, the country was well on its way to civil war. Two camps had formed, each with a cast of international sponsors, each touting a crew of lawmakers from Libya's collapsed congress. Jalal took the side of what he called the "revolution-ary" camp, because the other side included some of Qaddafi's former generals. That made him an ally of the Islamists, for whom he had no sympathy. But like for many Libyans, his loyalty was mostly a matter of local politics.

By midsummer of 2014, a battle for control of Tripoli had left the country's main airport in ruins, its control tower toppled and the runways pocked with craters. Around that time Jalal got a text message from an acquaintance who worked in the military police building. This was where Jalal's old prisoners were being kept, including Marwan, who had killed Nasser Salhoba's brother. Jalal asked his friend if anyone was guarding them. The friend wrote back that the prisoners had all been released. Not only that, they'd been given guns and uniforms, and they were fighting for one of the militias. Jalal asked about the boxes of documents and videotapes, everything he had so painstakingly gathered to document the crimes committed by Qaddafi and his men. "Forget it," his friend wrote. "Everything is gone."

Libya was not the only place where militias had replaced the state. You could say the same about Iraq, where armed groups loyal to Iran now did much of the hardest fighting, and the national army was better known for running away. Even in Bashar al Assad's Syria, the regime was turning into a shell. Assad was still in charge, but he was utterly dependent on a diverse and toxic mix of volunteer warriors and "popular" militias, some of them manned by criminals. Not all of them were Syrian. A whole Shiite counter-jihad had formed—with fighters coming from Lebanon, Bahrain, even Afghanistan—under the supervision of Iran, Assad's patron. The commander of the Iranian Revolutionary Guard's Quds Force, Qassim Soleimani, was regularly photographed supervising troops in Syria. As Russian planes began bombarding the rebels in the fall of 2015, some Muslim clerics seemed almost to welcome the news, calling for a jihad against Russia that recalled the glory days of the anti-Soviet war in Afghanistan in the 1980s.

In the regime bastion of Jableh, on the Syrian coast, Aliaa Ali watched the Alawi funeral processions come and go throughout 2015. She seemed to spend much of her time in an Internet bubble of Assad loyalists who shared nostalgic photos and memories of their old secular Syria, along with tirades against the hypocrisy and terrorism of the West. She started learning Russian. Her Facebook posts hinted at a sense of frustration and encirclement, often hidden under cheerful self-help maxims: "A free spirit cannot thrive in still waters." "We shall overcome."

Across the border in Turkey, her former friend Noura Kanafani was living in an eerily parallel world of aggrievement and isolation. She had retreated further into private life and had a second baby in the summer of 2015. On Facebook, she posted her own greeting-card mottoes about getting through hard times, along with occasional photographs of children mutilated or burned beyond recognition by the Assad regime's barrel bombs.

One night in the summer of 2015, I went to see Noura's aunt Maha and cousin Mihyar at their home in Antakya, near the border with Syria. It was Ramadan, the Muslim holy month. After we finished the ritual breaking of the fast, an argument broke out about the opposition's many mistakes since 2011. "We can no longer speak of a revolution," one guest said, a former rebel from Latakia. "We are the ones who destroyed it." He laid out a long and sorry list of charges, starting with the Syrian rebels' failure to adhere to a nonviolent ethic. The revolution's mantle, he said, had been claimed early on by self-important exiles who bickered over the future of a country they hadn't seen for years. It was tainted further by the childish proxy battles of Qatar and Saudi Arabia, which funded rival opposition spokesmen. The Syrian National Council had been succeeded by the Syrian National Coalition, among a cluster of other front groups. The acronyms proliferated along with the conferences in five-star hotel ballrooms in Cairo or Istanbul or the Gulf. All this served only to erode the exiles' influence inside Syria, where jihadist groups were gradually destroying or displacing everyone else.

"What is left of the original revolution?" the guest from Latakia said. "Nothing. The opposition has failed totally, and we should honestly admit that if we want to make any progress."

Mihyar would have none of it. "I consider the revolution my mother," he said. "I will not speak ill of my mother, even if it is true that she did some bad things when she was young. These are things that can be discussed only later, after we have defeated Bashar." The struggle against the regime, in other words, was all that mattered, never mind who was carrying it on. He said he was confident the spirit of the revolution in its original form would prevail. This was a little hard to swallow. I asked Mihyar whether it was realistic to expect the nonviolent opposition—now mostly moribund—to prevail over the jihadis *and* the regime. "God willing, yes," he said.

But the dreams of Mihyar and his fellow revolutionaries were starting to collide with other dreams, and not just those of ISIS. Days earlier, at a crossing point on the Turkey-Syria border, I had spoken to refugees fleeing the fighting. I had expected them to talk about the horrors of life in the caliphate. Instead, several told me they were much more worried about the Kurds, whose fighters had forced ISIS from an important border town and now seemed poised to expand their own territory. The hard reality of ethnic difference trumped ideology. These shop owners and construction workers—all of them Arabs—were willing to live in a place where music was forbidden and children watched beheadings in public squares. They were not willing to live in a reborn Kurdistan. Some veterans of the nonviolent protest movement went further, saying they would rather join ISIS and fight in its ranks than see the Kurds carve out their own state on Arab land.

Many of those fleeing Syria stopped only briefly in Turkey before continuing northward. By the late summer of 2015, the exodus of migrants toward Europe had grown so large that even ISIS became alarmed about it and began issuing warnings not to go to the land of unbelief. It was too late. Tens of thousands of families were making their way along the same route, on rickety boats to Greece and onward to Macedonia, Serbia, Hungary, Austria, and Germany. I met a thirty-one-year-old teacher from the Syrian city of Deir al Zour who was on his way north, and when I warned him about the dangers of the cross-ing, he laughed incredulously. "You do not know what we have been living in Syria," he said. "We left because we see no future in our home-land at all. You have a choice: to fight with one of the parties, or get arrested or killed. Or you get out."

Even in Tunisia, where Rached Ghannouchi and Beji Caid Essebsi continued their pas de deux, the sounds of war were getting closer. In late June 2015, a lone gunman slipped into a beach resort in the Tuni-sian coastal town of Sousse and murdered thirty-eight Western tour-ists. ISIS claimed credit. This second atrocity, coming after the March attack on the Bardo Museum, meant that the Tunisian tourism indus-try was effectively dead, probably for years to come. Essebsi went be-yond the usual martial rhetoric in response to the attack, declaring that another massacre would cause the country to "collapse." The prospects for Tunisia's economic revival were dimming. And more jihadist vio-lence, people said, might endanger the entente between Tunisia's two grand old men.

ISIS had become the great menace of a new age, and not just in the Arab world. It was capable of inspiring people as far away as France or even California to murder in the name of God. The massacres in Paris and San Bernardino in the fall of 2015 forced a new reckoning in Europe and America. Terrorism now seemed to lurk everywhere, like a spore that could drift unseen until it transformed a harmless subur-banite into a merciless killer at a holiday party. Every attack deepened the fear, fueling greater suspicion of the masses of Arab and Muslim migrants struggling to escape northward to Europe, and fiercer divi-sions about how to handle them.

For some Arab journalists and men of letters, the spectacle of young people flocking to join ISIS seemed to signal the end of Arab civiliza-tion. An old order was ending, they said, and there was nothing to re-place it but madness. One of the more hard-nosed columnists in the pan-Arab press, Jihad al Khazen, disavowed his Arab identity in a cri de coeur published in March 2015. He asked—without a hint of face-tiousness—if the End of Days was at hand, and declared that he "would not be surprised if the Antichrist emerged from among us tomorrow."

And what about the protesters who had kicked off the Arab Spring? They had scattered in many different directions. Most had given up on politics. A few brave ones were in jail for defying the authorities. Many were very depressed.

One of them, a thirty-five-year-old Egyptian named Ahmed Darrawi, disappeared in mid-2013. His friends and relatives made efforts to find him but came up with nothing. Ahmed had been a member of the vanguard known as the Coalition of Revolutionary Youth, and had been one of the rebellion's more powerful spokesmen. He'd lived in Tahrir through all eighteen days of the revolt and found his life transformed by it. In the months afterward, he neglected his marketing job and his bourgeois life in a posh Cairo suburb. He ran for Parliament as an independent in the elections of 2011. His campaign posters show a smiling young man in a suit, clean shaven, under the banner SECURITY AND DIGNITY. He lost, but he continued speaking and writing about how to fulfill the revolution's goals.

Ahmed's friends and relatives told me he became depressed in the later months of 2012, as divisions hardened between Egypt's political camps. In December of that year, after the bloody street battles between pro- and anti-Morsi demonstrators at the presidential palace, Ahmed's brother Haythem called him. "It's over, the revolution's finished," he recalls Ahmed telling him. "When you see the people who were together in Tahrir killing each other, there's no point anymore." Ahmed grew progressively more withdrawn. Just after the coup that overthrew Morsi, in July 2013, he vanished.

A few months later, in the early winter of 2013, Ahmed posted a video on Twitter. The clip shows a dozen young men around a campfire in the woods of northwestern Syria, singing songs and hunching against the cold. You can hear the wind shuddering in the microphone, and you can see, in the blurred darkness around the fire, the men leaning toward it for warmth, blankets wrapped around their bodies. Someone pours hot coffee from a silver pot that has been heating on the coals. Cigarette ends glow orange and then fade out. The blue light of a cell phone is visible for a moment. The men's eyes gleam as they sing, raggedly but in unison:

How beautiful is the sound of guns echoing in the desert
We don't part from our grenades
The moon and stars are our witnesses
And the wilderness sings of our glory

This was Ahmed's brigade, the Lions of the Caliphate. Several of them were Egyptian veterans of Tahrir Square, like him. They had just pledged their loyalty to ISIS a month or two earlier. Ahmed had a new name: Abu Mouaz al Masri. He was the unit's military commander. In one photograph that emerged later, he is wearing an Afghan-style pakol hat and black galabiya, with a Glock pistol in one hand and a Kalashnikov balanced on the other shoulder. Behind him is a battered pickup truck, and the legs of two men can be seen in the back, standing by a mounted 14.5 mm machine gun. He stares directly into the camera with an expression of cold certainty. A few months later, in the early spring of 2014, Ahmed wrote on Twitter: "Some wonder about all this love and belonging to the Islamic state. My brothers, it's an old lost dream since the fall of the caliphate. And we will make it come true and pass it on, even if only through our mutilated bodies, to a new generation." It was one of his very last postings. Later that spring, Haythem Darrawi received a phone call from an ISIS spokesman congratulating him on his brother's martyrdom. Ahmed had carried out a suicide bombing in Iraq.

Ahmed kept a kind of journal on Twitter in the months before his death, and his entries suggest that he had transferred all the hope he'd once invested in democracy onto the idea of a rigid Islamic utopia, to be established by force of arms. "I found justice in jihad, and dignity and bravery in leaving my old life forever," he wrote at one point. "It's as if I wasn't alive before joining the call, and hadn't tasted what good, sweet living can be until I joined the jihad."

The protesters of 2011 had dreamed of building new countries that would confer genuine citizenship and something more: *karama*, dignity, the rallying cry of all the uprisings. When that dream failed them, many gave way to apathy or despair, or even nostalgia for the old regimes they had assailed. But some ran headlong into the seventh century in search of the same prize. They wanted something they had heard about and imagined all their lives but never really known: a *dawla* that would not melt into air beneath their feet, a place they could call their own, a state that shielded its subjects from humiliation and despair.

— Time Line —
The Arab Uprisings and
Their Aftermath

2010

June 6: Khaled Saeed is beaten to death in Alexandria by Egyptian police. Within days, Google executive Wael Ghoneim launches "We are all Khaled Saeed" on Facebook. Mohamed ElBaradei visits Saeed's family and leads a rally against police abuse in Alexandria. There are concurrent protests in Tahrir Square.

June–September: In Yemen, Ja'ashin peasants establish a protest camp in central Sanaa, in what will later become Change Square.

November: Egyptian parliamentary elections prompt widespread charges of fraud.

December 17: Mohamed Bouazizi sets himself on fire in Sidi Bouzid, Tunisia. Protests start and spread across Tunisia.

2011

January 14: Tunisia's president, Zine El Abidine Ben Ali, capitulates in the face of rising protests and flees the country with his inner circle.

January 25: Egyptian protests start.

January 27: The first large-scale protests in Yemen take place.

January 28: Egypt's "Friday of Anger." Protesters battle police and win control of Tahrir Square in Cairo. Similar battles in other cities across Egypt.

February 11: Egypt's president, Hosni Mubarak, steps down. The Supreme Council of the Armed Forces takes power, promising a transition to civilian authority.

February 14: Protests start in Bahrain.

February 15: Libya's first large-scale protests occur in the eastern city of Benghazi. A police crackdown leads to violent confrontations across Libya.

February 20: Qaddafi's military and police withdraw from Benghazi after intense street fighting. Rebels assert control in most of eastern Libya.

February 27: Libya's National Transitional Council is formed. Two weeks later, France recognizes it as Libya's legitimate government; other countries follow.

March 14: Saudi Arabia sends armored columns into Bahrain. Security forces crush the uprising, carrying out mass arrests within a few days. Bahrain's king declares martial law. The monument in Pearl Square, the uprising's heart, is razed.

March 15: Demonstrations start in Syria, triggered by police mistreatment of teenagers arrested in the southern town of Daraa for writing antigovernment graffiti. Protests spread quickly and are met with mass arrests and shootings.

March 17: The United Nations Security Council authorizes military action in Libya. Air strikes begin immediately, with NATO in command.

March 18: Gunmen aligned with Yemen's government open fire on protesters in the capital, killing at least fifty-two and prompting top military officers to defect. President Ali Abdullah Saleh signals soon afterward that he may step down before the year's end. Much of the country falls out of the government's control.

March 19: Egypt's first postrevolutionary vote, on a constitutional referendum that could lead to early elections, ends in triumph for the Muslim Brotherhood and hints at rising polarization between Islamist and secularist camps.

March 26: Jihadis capture the town of Jaar, in southern Yemen. With the government in collapse, the jihadis gradually extend their control over other towns in the south.

June 3: The Yemeni president Ali Abdullah Saleh is seriously injured by a bombing in the mosque of his compound. He is flown to Saudi Arabia for treatment, leaving the country rudderless.

July–August: In Syria, defecting officers form the Free Syrian Army. Opposition groups form the Syrian National Council, based in Turkey. Nonviolent protests gradually give way to armed struggle. Foreign fighters begin to enter Syria.

August 18: President Obama declares that "the time has come for President Assad to step aside." This is widely understood as a promise of support for the Syrian president's overthrow, and will later be cited by critics of American inaction.

August 20: Libyan rebels begin an assault on Tripoli. Within days Muammar Qaddafi and his followers flee. The civil war is effectively over.

October 20: Muammar al Qaddafi, Libya's ruler for forty-two years, is captured and killed by rebels while trying to flee from the coastal city of Sirte.

October 23: Tunisia holds parliamentary elections, the first to take place since the uprising. Ennahda, the Islamist party led by Rached Ghannouchi, wins a plurality and subsequently forms a coalition government.

November: There are more protests and violence in Egypt after the ruling military council moves to ensure it will play a dominant role even after civilian government is elected.

November 23: After months of evasive maneuvering, the Yemeni president Ali Abdullah Saleh flies to Riyadh, Saudi Arabia, to sign a transition document brokered by Arab and American diplomats. He is given immunity from prosecution in exchange for stepping down.

November 28: Egyptian parliamentary elections start, continuing through January. The Islamists ultimately win a majority of seats, with the Muslim Brotherhood's party taking about 47 percent and the Islamist Nour Party taking about 24 percent.

2012

January: Fighting intensifies in Syria. The Assad regime launches large-scale artillery assaults, destroying many civilian homes in the Damascus suburbs, the city of Homs, and other areas.

April 1: In Egypt, the Muslim Brotherhood decides to run a candidate in the upcoming presidential elections, reversing an earlier pledge and elevating fears among secularists.

April: The death toll in Syria reaches ten thousand, according to civilian monitors and the United Nations.

June: The United Nations declares a state of civil war in Syria. Jihadi groups become more active and visible in the armed opposition, including the Nusra Front, Al Qaeda's branch in Syria.

June: Muhammad Morsi of the Muslim Brotherhood is elected president of Egypt, narrowly defeating an ally of former president Hosni Mubarak.

July 7: Libya has its first parliamentary elections postrevolution. Non-Islamists win a plurality of seats. Optimism runs high, despite the continued presence of armed militias.

July 18: A bomb kills eight top Syrian regime officials during a closed-door meeting, including the defense minister and President Bashar Assad's brother-in-law. No plausible claims of responsibility emerge; the bombing remains a mystery.

July–August: Fighting intensifies in the Syrian city of Aleppo, a center of trade and one of the oldest continually inhabited sites on earth; within a year large parts of the city will be reduced to rubble.

August: Kurdish forces in northern Syria gain effective control over an enclave near the Turkish border.

September: U.S. Ambassador to Libya J. Christopher Stevens is killed in an attack on an American compound in Benghazi following violent protests over an American video seen as insulting to Islam. Angry crowds drive out Ansar Sharia, the Islamist militia that helped organize the attack. Libya's interim head of state vows to disband all illegal militias.

November: The Egyptian president Muhammad Morsi issues a decree temporarily granting himself broad powers above any court as the guardian of the revolution. Large-scale protests begin.

December: The U.S. State Department designates the Nusra Front a terrorist group, amid increasing alarm over jihadi activity in Syria.

2013

March 6: Syrian rebels capture the eastern city of Raqqa, the first regional capital to fall under their control.

May: As government authority frays in Libya, Islamist militias in Tripoli threaten lawmakers, effectively forcing Parliament to pass a law that bars their rivals from office.

June 5: Syrian rebels are routed from the town of Qusayr by Hezbollah forces fighting on behalf of the Assad regime. The victory illustrates the regime's growing dependence on Iran and Hezbollah, its Lebanese Shiite proxy.

June: The death toll in Syria reaches one hundred thousand.

June 30: There are huge protests across Egypt against President Muhammad Morsi. A pro-Islamist sit-in begins in Rabaa Square in Cairo.

July 3: The Egyptian military deposes President Muhammad Morsi and puts him under arrest in an unknown location. Islamist protests expand and confrontations with police begin, with dozens shot and killed. The orchestrator of the coup, General Abdelfattah al Sisi, is Egypt's de facto leader; many hail him as a hero.

July 25: In Tunis, Mohamed Brahmi is assassinated, making him the second opposition leader to be killed in five months. Protests against the Islamist-led government intensify. Starting in August, Ennahda's leader, Rached Ghannouchi, begins meeting with the opposition leader, Beji Caid Essebsi.

August 14: Egyptian security forces clear the two main Islamist protest encampments, killing about a thousand people and arresting thousands more. Within weeks, most of the Muslim Brotherhood leadership is jailed, including Muhammad Beltagy and the group's Supreme Guide, Muhammad Badie. Others go into hiding or escape abroad. Jihadi insurgency in Egypt's Sinai Peninsula gathers strength.

August 21: Rockets containing sarin gas strike an opposition-controlled area near Damascus, killing more than a thousand people. Most analysts agree that the regime launched the attack, the deadliest use of chemical weapons since the Iran-Iraq War. President Obama, who had previously declared chemical weapons use to be a "red line," weighs military intervention, but ultimately decides on a diplomatic solution in which Syria pledges to destroy its chemical weapons stockpile.

September 28: The Tunisian crisis eases as the Islamist Ennahda movement agrees to cede power to an independent caretaker government. Dialogue on a new constitution begins.

October: In Syria, the Islamic State of Iraq and the Levant (known as ISIL or ISIS) consolidates control over the city of Raqqa and begins administering a radical version of Islamic law in what will become its capital.

November: Amid rising lawlessness in Libya, nine people are killed in clashes between the military and Islamist militia fighters in Benghazi.

December: Conflict intensifies between ISIS and other jihadi groups, including the Nusra Front, Al Qaeda's official branch in Syria.

2014

January 26: Tunisia's lawmakers approve a new constitution, prompting nationwide celebrations.

February 3: After months of internecine fighting in Syria, Al Qaeda formally disavows any connection with ISIS.

May: In Libya, the renegade general Khalifa Haftar launches a military assault against militant Islamists in Benghazi and attempts to seize the Parliament building.

May 30: Abdelfattah al Sisi is elected Egypt's president.

June 10: ISIS captures the Iraqi city of Mosul and much of the country's northwest, as Iraqi military forces collapse.

June 25: Libyan elections are marked by low turnout, and are followed by clashes between followers of outgoing and incoming parliaments. Islamists carry out a coup in Tripoli.

June 29: The leader of ISIS, Abu Bakr al Baghdadi, declares himself leader of an Islamic caliphate stretching from eastern Syria to western Iraq. Recruitment of foreign fighters surges.

July: As civil war intensifies in Libya, United Nations staff pull out and foreign embassies close. Tripoli airport is largely destroyed by fighting. The ISIS branch in Libya grows, eventually gaining base in the coastal city of Sirte.

August: The U.S. military launches air strikes against ISIS targets in Iraq and assembles a coalition. Strikes will later extend to Syria.

August: ISIS releases a videotape of the beheading of the American photojournalist James Foley. Other videos of hostage murders follow.

September: In Yemen, the Huthi rebels, now in league with the former Yemeni president Ali Abdullah Saleh, capture Sanaa, becoming the country's de facto rulers.

October 26: Tunisia's Islamist party, Ennahda, suffers losses in parliamentary elections. Victory goes to the secularist party led by Beji Caid Essebsi, who is later elected president and forms a coalition government with Ennahda.

December: The death toll in the Syrian civil war exceeds two hundred thousand.

2015

January: In Yemen, President Abdu Rabbu Mansour Hadi resigns and later flees to Saudi Arabia. The Huthis continue their push southward; Yemen fragments in their wake.

March 18: In Tunis, jihadi terrorists attack the Bardo Museum, leading to the deaths of twenty-two people, mostly foreigners.

March 26: Saudi Arabia and a coalition of allies begin a military campaign to oust the Huthis from power in Yemen, including large-scale air strikes. The conflict is widely viewed as a proxy war between Saudi Arabia and Iran, which provides limited support to the Huthis. Amid the fighting, Al Qaeda asserts control over the southern coastal city of Mukalla.

June 26: A lone terrorist at a Tunisian resort kills thirty-eight people, mostly foreign tourists. Tunisia's tourist industry is effectively destroyed.

June 29: Egypt's top prosecutor is killed in a car bombing in Cairo, amid signs that the jihadi insurgency in the Sinai Peninsula is spreading across the country.

September: Russia bolsters its military support to the Syrian regime, including air strikes against rebels (though its initial attacks on ISIS are limited). The expanded Russian role appears to galvanize many Islamists, who see a revival of the 1980s anti-Russian jihad in Afghanistan.

— A Note on Sources —

This book is derived almost entirely from interviews with its characters or with people close to them, including their relatives, colleagues, and friends. I have tried to attribute sources wherever possible, but in some cases I have omitted them for narrative purposes. The material on Soleyman of Adana in chapter 4 is drawn mainly from two sources: *Fifty-Three Years in Syria* by Henry H. Jessup (Reading, UK: Garnet, 2002 [1910]) and *Extremist Shiites: The Ghulat Sects* by Matti Moosa (Syracuse: Syracuse University Press, 1988). In chapter 6, my account of Islamic history is indebted to *God's Rule: Government and Islam* by Patricia Crone (New York: Columbia University Press, 2004) and *The Great Arab Conquests: How the Spread of Islam Changed the World We Live In* by Hugh Kennedy (Philadelphia: Da Capo, 2007). For the early years of Rached Ghannouchi and Beji Caid Essebsi in chapter 7, I drew on *Rachid Ghannouchi: A Democrat Within Islamism* by Azzam S. Tamimi (New York: Oxford University Press, 2001) and *Habib Bourguiba: Le Bon Grain et l'Ivraie* by Beji Caid Essebsi (Tunis: Sud, 2009).

In a broader sense, the book draws on a large number of sources on the history and culture of the Middle East, absorbed over many years. This is not an academic work, but I would like to acknowledge a debt to some of these authors. On Egypt, *The Society of the Muslim Brothers* by Richard P. Mitchell (New York: Oxford University

Press, 1993), *The Muslim Brotherhood: The Evolution of an Islamist Movement* by Carrie Rosefsky Wickham (Princeton: Princeton University Press, 2013), *Cairo: The City Victorious* by Max Rodenbeck (New York: Knopf, 1999), and *Egypt on the Brink: From Nasser to Mubarak* by Tarek Osman (New Haven: Yale University Press, 2010). On Libya, *A History of Modern Libya* by Dirk Vandewalle (New York: Cambridge University Press, 2006) and *Sandstorm: Libya from Gaddafi to Revolution* by Lindsey Hilsum (London: Faber & Faber, 2013). On Syria, *Asad of Syria: The Struggle for the Middle East* (Berkeley: University of California Press, 1989), *The Struggle for Syria: A Study of Post-War Arab Politics, 1945–1958* by Patrick Seale (New Haven: Yale University Press, 1987), and *The Asian Mystery Illustrated in the History, Religion, and Present State of the Ansaireeh or Nusairis of Syria* by Samuel Lyde (London: Longman, Green, Longman, and Roberts, 1860). On Yemen, *Tribes, Government, and History in Yemen* by Paul Dresch (New York: Oxford University Press, 1989), *Yemen Divided: The Story of a Failed State in South Arabia* by Noel Brehony (New York: I. B. Taurus, 2013), *The Last Refuge: Yemen, al-Qaeda, and America's War in Arabia* by Gregory D. Johnsen (New York: W. W. Norton, 2013), and *Yemen: The Unknown Arabia* by Tim Mackintosh-Smith (Woodstock, NY: Overlook, 2000). On Tunisia, *A History of Modern Tunisia* by Kenneth Perkins (New York: Cambridge University Press, 2004) and *Notre Histoire* by Habib Bourguiba Jr. (Tunis: Cérès, 2013). On Arab and Ottoman history in general, *From Deep State to Islamic State: An Arab Counter-Revolution and Its Jihadist Legacy* by Jean-Pierre Filiu (London: Hurst, 2015), *A Brief History of the Late Ottoman Empire* by M. Şükrü Hanioğlu (Princeton: Princeton University Press, 2008), *Justice Interrupted: The Struggle for Constitutional Government in the Middle East* by Elizabeth F. Thompson (Cambridge, MA: Harvard University Press, 2013), *A Peace to End All Peace: Creating the Middle East, 1914–1922* by David Fromkin (New York: Henry Holt, 1989), *The Arab Predicament: Arab Political Thought and Practice Since 1967* by Fouad Ajami (New York: Cambridge University Press, 1981), *Arab Awakening: The Story of the Arab National Movement* by George Antonius (Philadelphia: Lippincott, 1939), *The Fall of the Ottomans: The Great War in the Middle East* by Eugene Rogan (New York: Basic Books, 2015), *Self-Criticism after the Defeat* by Sadik al-Azm (London: Saqi Books, 2011), and *A History of the Arab Peoples* by Albert Hourani (Cambridge, MA: Harvard University Press, 2002).

— Acknowledgments —

My greatest debt is to the people whose stories are told in this book. They tolerated a journalist who hunched and hovered at the edges of their lives for years on end, frequently pestering them with queries as their world was collapsing around them. They did so with no reward apart from the prospect of a book whose outline changed again and again. I can only hope the finished product doesn't disappoint them.

I reported with the assistance of a number of fixers and translators, many of them also superb journalists in their own right, who deserve to be thanked here: Nagwa Hassan and Mandi Fahmy in Egypt; Nasser Arrabyee, Shuaib al Mosawa, and Kawkab al Thaibani in Yemen; Nawara Mahfoud and Batool Kazwini in Syria; in Libya, Safa al Ahmad and Sulaiman al Zway; in Tunisia, Hossam Saidi and Farah Samti; in Turkey, Karam Shoumali, Zaher Said, and Saad al Nassife; in Doha, Riham Shebl.

Hwaida Saad, *ukhti wa habibti* and my former assistant in Beirut, has helped out for years in more ways than I can count.

To Bernard Haykel I owe a special kind of acknowledgment. He has been a friend and generous mentor for many years, and his insights about the Middle East helped foster my interest in the region before I ever lived there. Any merit this book may have owes a great deal to him. A number of other scholars or observers of the Middle East have also shared their ideas over the years and helped to shape mine, among them Peter Harling, Renaud Detalle, Shadi Hamid, Jean-Pierre Filiu, Joshua Landis, David Cvach, Paul Salem, Nadim Houri, Muhammad al Mutawakel, Radhia al Mutawakel, Abdelrasheed al Faqih, Abdelghani al Iryani, Abdelkarim al Iryani, Muhammad al Basha, Gregory Johnsen, Khaled Fattah, Mohamed Okda, Hossam Bahgat, George Saghir, April Alley, Frederick Wehrey, Will McCants, Cole Bunzel, Khalil Anani, Emile Hokayem, and Samer Shehata.

My editor at Farrar, Straus and Giroux, Alex Star, was an extraordinarily clear-sighted and erudite guide throughout the process of writing this book. He is also a friend of long standing—and a former editor of mine at the *Times* magazine. I felt very lucky to have his eyes on the manuscript. His colleague Scott Borchert also provided valuable comments.

Sarah Chalfant, my agent at Wylie, deserves tremendous thanks for having pushed me to write this book in the first place, and providing encouragement throughout.

Parts of this book evolved from stories I wrote for *The New York Times Magazine*, and I'm grateful to the editors there for giving me the freedom to report and write on the uprisings and their aftermath for more than two years. Joel Lovell was a writer's dream: a font of encouragement, wise guidance, and deft line-editing skills. Hugo Lindgren, who ran the magazine, also deserves thanks, as do the copy editors and fact-checkers whose hard work saved me from many mistakes. A number of other colleagues and friends at *The New York Times* have shared insights and counsel about this book and its themes, including Anthony Shadid, Kareem Fahim, David Kirkpatrick, Sabrina Tavernise, Roger Cohen, Scott Shane, and Carlotta Gall.

I am grateful also to Robert Silvers of *The New York Review of Books*, for whom I wrote an essay exploring some of this book's themes in the summer of 2014. Bob Silvers is one of the great editors, and hearing his probing, courtly critiques is always instructive.

Many other friends have contributed advice and ideas that helped shape the book in ways large and small: Max Rodenbeck, George Packer, Adam Goodheart, Ghaith Abdul Ahad, Kate Seelye, Muhammad al Basha, Damian Quinn, Abdelaziz al Fahd, Tim Mackintosh-Smith, Adam Hochschild, and Jehad Nga. Anna Husarska read several chapters and gave me the benefit of her experience with many other wars and revolutions. My older brother, Alexi Worth, also read a chapter and gave detailed and helpful comments.

Borzou Daragahi and Delphine Minoui, old friends from Beirut, kindly put me up more than once in their Cairo apartment, and Helen Konstantopoulos hosted me in Dubai.

Joseph Sassoon, whom I met while working on the book at the Woodrow Wilson Center, has been an immensely generous colleague and friend, and provided all kinds of insight about the region. He also read two chapters and offered valuable criticisms.

The Woodrow Wilson International Center for Scholars, where I spent a year as a fellow while working on the book, was a perfect incubator, and I'm grateful to Robert Litwak and all the staff there for making it happen. I was very lucky to coincide with Joseph Sassoon, Roya Hakakian, and Max Rodenbeck, true friends and wonderful sparring partners on all subjects Middle Eastern. Many others at the center were great colleagues, including David and Marina Ottaway and Haleh Esfandiari. I was lucky to have the help of several interns while based at the center: Nicole Magney, Rami Yashruti, and Reina Sultan.

Hoda Gamal, a savvy and well-informed student of Arab politics, also provided research help in Washington, D.C., as did Marwan Ayad and Oula al Rifai.

Others have sustained the book in different ways. My wife, Alice Clapman, has lent her fine ear for language and her superb judgment on many occasions, and tolerated my long absences. My son Isaac predicted that this book would be finished "in a thousand years." He and his brother Felix keep my days full and happy and will someday, I hope, look inside these pages.

— Index —